BENJAMIN GRAHAM ON VALUE INVESTING

LESSONS FROM THE DEAN OF WALL STREET

JANET LOWE

Dearborn
Financial Publishing, Inc.

While a great deal of care has been taken to provide accurate and current information, the ideas, suggestions, general principles and conclusions presented in this text are subject to local, state and federal laws and regulations, court cases and any revisions of same. The reader is thus urged to consult legal counsel regarding any points of law—this publication should not be used as a substitute for competent legal advice.

Publisher: Kathleen A. Welton
Managing Editor: Jack L. Kiburz
Editorial Assistant: Stephanie Schmidt
Interior Design: Lucy Jenkins
Cover Design: Anthony C. Russo/The Complete Artworks

Published by Dearborn Financial Publishing, Inc.

Printed in the United States of America

95 96 10 9 8 7 6 5 4 3

Library of Congress Cataloging-in-Publication Data

Lowe, Janet.
    Benjamin Graham on value investing : lessons from the dean of Wall Street / Janet Lowe.
        p.   cm.
    Includes bibliographical references and index.
    ISBN 0-7931-0702-4 : $22.95
    1. Graham, Benjamin, 1894–1976. 2. Capitalists and financiers—United States—Biography. 3. Investment analysis. 4. Securities—United States. I. Title.
HG172.G68L69 1994
    332.6′092-dc20   94-26907
    [B]   CIP

DEDICATION

To those special friends who have inspired and supported my own quest for authenticity: Ann, Jolene, Lorena, Marilyn, Nancy and Sheila

ACKNOWLEDGMENTS

M any thanks to the following people for their help in researching, writing and editing this book.

The book is, in large part, based on interviews with Charles Brandes, Warren E. Buffet, Benjamin "Buzzy" Graham, Jr., George H. Heyman, Jr., William H. Heyman, Robert Heilbrunn, Elaine Graham Hunt, Marjorie Graham Janis, Irving Kahn, Thomas G. Kahn, Edythe and N. Morton Kenner, Rod Klein, Helaine Lerner, Howard E. "Mickey" Newman, James Rea, Sr., William J. Ruane, Rhoda and Dr. Bernard Sarnat, Walter Schloss, Geraldine Weiss and Sy Winter. Special thanks to Warren E. Buffett for his kindness and generosity.

Research assistance was given by Darwin Bayson, Arthur and Lorena Goeller, Jody Goulden, Hollee Haswell, John E. Heimerdinger, Elizabeth Husmann, Arthur Q. Johnson, Mary Lehman, H. Austin Lynas, Victoria Robbins, Myrna Roberts, Cathie Taylor and Elizabeth K. Warren. The cover photo was supplied by the Graduate School of Business at Columbia University. Other photographs were supplied by Benjamin Graham, Jr., MD, Walter J. Schloss and GEICO.

Selected material has been reprinted throughout, with permission, from *Benjamin Graham: The Father of Financial Analysis*.

Kathleen A. Welton, my editor and publisher at Dearborn, and Alice Fried Martell, my literary representative, have offered valuable insight and guidance in the preparation of the manuscript.

"Come, my friends, it is not too late to seek
A newer world. Push off, and sitting well in order to smite
The sounding furrows. For my purpose holds
To sail beyond the sunset and the baths
Of all the Western stars until I die.
It may be that the gulfs will wash us down;
It may be we shall touch the Harpy Isles
And see the great Achilles whom we knew.
Though much is taken, much abides, and though
We are not now that strength that in old days
Moved earth and heaven, that which we are, we are.
One equal temper of heroic hearts,
Made weak by Time and Fate, but strong in will
To strive, to seek, to find, and not to yield!"

 —Closing lines of Tennyson's *Ulysses*
  as quoted by Benjamin Graham on
  his 80th birthday,
  La Jolla, California, 1974

CONTENTS

PREFACE

I n many ways, Benjamin Graham's ghost resembles those of
Marilyn Monroe, JFK and Elvis. The longer he is gone, the
greater his luminescence, especially in the investment community. Like these other American legends, Graham has inspired
his followers by the authenticity of his thinking, living, working—of his being. We all long to be like these people—uniquely
ourselves, and in being so, achieve an extraordinary quality.

Graham's special contribution to the world was that he
brought the clarity of logic and reason to that elemental sector
of business, the investment community. At a very early age,
Graham realized that investments too often were made either
under the spell of salesmanship or under excessive optimism
or pessimism. Investors frequently were uninformed, misin-
formed or muddled in their thinking. These things could lead
only to abuse and exploitation. Graham did not completely
eliminate the uncertainty or the shadiness from the game, but
he did make sure that anyone who wanted to be a knowledgeable investor could be one. There has been an explosion of
information since Graham's time. All we have to do is seek it
out and ask the right questions. By studying Graham (and his
partner David Dodd) we can determine the questions to ask.

All that is needed to believe in Graham's legacy is to examine a list of his students and disciples. At the top of the "superinvestors" list is the person who coined the phrase, Warren Buffett. The chairman of Berkshire Hathaway, Inc., Buffett in 1993 surpassed Bill Gates as the wealthiest man in America. Adam Smith immortalized some of the others in his 1972 best-seller, *Supermoney.* Among the Graham stars are money managers William Ruane, Walter Schloss, Irving Kahn, Mario Gabelli and Charles Brandes. Both Irving Kahn and Warren Buffett admired Graham so earnestly that they named their sons after him.

The story of how Benjamin Graham formulated his theories regarding the investment markets and influenced generations of highly successful investment professionals is exciting, colorful and at times touching. It is difficult to pin down Graham's remarkable charisma, his ability to attract lifelong investors, followers and fans. Whatever his magnetism, Graham's teachings have served as a fixed point from which others could navigate in the world of investments, especially under stormy conditions. Perhaps Warren Buffett explained it best: "On a lot of people's compasses, Ben was true north."

As often is the case with legends, there are many apocryphal tales about Graham. He was a busy man and was generous in sharing credit, which means that it is difficult at times to know how much Jerome Newman contributed to the success of Graham-Newman Corporation or how much David Dodd was responsible for the success of Graham and Dodd's textbook, *Security Analysis.* In fact, all of Graham's collaborators were important and effective people, both in their work with him and in their own right. Graham chose to work with these men because they could help cast his many, many ideas into tangible forms. Yet most financial analysts and investors who study value investing realize immediately that Graham was the bright light behind *Security Analysis. The Intelligent Investor,* a solo effort and an enduring book if there ever was one, reinforces that perception.

Perhaps because I graduated from business school in 1968, during the "go-go years" of the stock market when growth stocks were everything and value investing was considered tedious, I was not exposed to Graham and his classic investment texts in school. My first contact with him was in the early 1980s when writing about a couple of con artists who swindled investors while at the same time claiming to be "Graham and Dodd" conservatives. As often is the case, they chose the description as a cloak of respectability to hide their methods. The pair ended up in jail. Since that murky introduction to Benjamin Graham, I have met dozens of honest, respectable and talented Graham-and-Dodd practitioners, a number of whom studied with Benjamin Graham when he taught at Columbia University.

I have wanted to write about Benjamin Graham, the father of "value investing," for some time, but when the chance finally came, there were several surprises. He had more followers and better friends than I ever imagined. It was exciting to learn that there is a passionate group of Graham fans out and about, many of them young enough to only have heard of him through the filter of several generations.

It is no wonder that Graham's experiences and writings still touch others. Benjamin Graham had everything in common with those who work in the investment field today—the possibility for great riches, the adrenalin rush of success, the responsibility of handling other people's money and fear of losing it and, finally, the intellectual challenge of the game. Graham's life can teach today's practitioners more than the mere mechanics of the stock and bond markets—though his lessons in those arenas remain valid. It teaches ethical standards and a dignified approach to the work.

Even after he had been deceased for years, Graham's friends and former associates were protective of his reputation. Many of those people had moved on to become part of Warren Buffett's crowd. Their allegiance to Buffett was as impressive as their loyalty to Graham. "Have you talked to Warren?" they asked, not thinking for a moment that it was necessary to use the Omaha investor's last name. Most would not talk to me unless Warren said OK. Fortunately, Warren Buffett was extremely kind and helpful.

The gathering of information on Graham's family was especially fascinating. On one research trip to New York, I took a ferry to Ellis Island, where many sagas of turn-of-the-century immigrants are so eloquently told. Though I could find no trace of the Grahams there, I came to understand that the story of the Graham family and his cousins, the Gerards, is part of the complex fabric of this nation. Immigration and success like theirs is the history of collective America. By coming, they made the United States of America an immeasurably better place.

Early in the writing project, I became worried about my attitude toward my subject. It was clear that Graham had certain personal characteristics that I did not admire. He was both a chauvinist and a womanizer. How can a writer spend more than a year in the presence of a person she does not necessarily like? Worse yet, how can she write fairly about such a person? Yet, over the several years spent on the project I gradually came to feel as if I were a silent, invisible member of Ben's family. In the end, my feelings for him were similar to those for my own father—I did not always understand him or like everything he did, but I cared deeply about him. The man was very human and inescapably likable.

Not all of my efforts were so successful as my interviews with Buffett and other Graham compatriots. I was not able to read the full text of an autobiography that Graham started but never finished or published. I was able to see the first chapter, however, though only with the understanding that I would not quote from it. The story was frank and descriptive, an obviously serious attempt at self-discovery. Benjamin Graham, Jr., MD, would have shared the biography, he said, because he believes in forthrightness in all dealings. Unfortunately, Dr. Graham's half sisters, who undoubtedly still feel the old pain, prefer to keep the accounts private of breakups of marriages, love affairs and other events within the family, "at any rate until all the principals are dead."

Even so, the story of this superinvestor was a pleasure to research because of the many intelligent, sensitive and interesting people I interviewed, especially the Graham children. Thanks to Marjorie Graham Janis, Elaine Graham Hunt and Dr. Graham, as well as Rhoda and Dr. Bernard Sarnat. From the investment community, Robert Heilbrunn, Walter Schloss, Irving Kahn and many others were generous with their time. The staff and faculty of Columbia's Graduate School of Business helped in many ways, as did the public-relations department at GEICO.

Although this never was intended to be a book about Warren Buffett, it is as impossible to write about Ben Graham and omit Buffett as it would be to leave out one of the Graham children. None of Graham's sons or daughters became their father's heir in terms of career or interest in finance. Buffett, who claimed Graham as a mentor when he was still a student, became the primary intellectual progeny of Ben Graham. More than that, even though Buffett sometimes disagreed with Graham, he holds deep affection, admiration and respect for his former teacher. Ben and his wife Estelle clearly felt the same way about Buffett.

Readers will find Benjamin Graham's life fascinating, offering many lessons on how to join the ranks of superinvestors.

—Janet Celesta Lowe

CHAPTER 1

The Dean of Wall Street

*"There is only one Dean in our profession, if security analysis can be
said to be a profession. The reason that Benjamin Graham is
undisputed Dean is that before him, there was no profession and
after him they began to call it that."*

—Adam Smith, *Supermoney*[1]

In 1968, the stock market was floundering badly and Omaha
investor Warren Buffett, who managed nearly $105 million
in his Buffett Partnership, was baffled and worried because he
could not find worthy securities to buy. Over the 12 years that
it operated, Buffett's Partnership had compounded funds at an
average annual rate of 29.5 percent and he wanted to maintain
the returns that his investors had come to expect.

"The market wasn't very good," said Walter Schloss, a New
York money manager and a longtime friend of Buffett's, "and
Warren said let's go out and see Ben and ask him what he would
do."

The "Ben" was Benjamin Graham, who for decades had
managed the respected Graham-Newman investment fund,
taught finance classes at Columbia and authored the most
successful books on investing that have ever been published.
Graham was the most influential investment thinker and philosopher of the twentieth century. He served as mentor to
Buffett and to dozens of other American money meisters. Graham had retired and was dividing his time between homes in
France and California.

"I found out Ben was back in the country," Buffett explained. "I called and said, 'If I get a few students together would you meet with us?' He said, 'Sure.' I called 10 or 11 people and every single one of them said "yes.""" The date was set for January 26, 1968.

THE QUEST

Those who made the pilgrimage to the coast already had earned reputations as investment superstars. They included Schloss, founder of Walter and Edwin Schloss Associates; Tom Knapp and Ed Anderson of Tweedy-Browne; William Ruane, chief of Ruane, Cunniff & Company and later founder of the Sequoia Fund; David "Sandy" Gottesman, head of the First Manhattan investment firm; Marshall Weinberg, stockbroker with the New York firm Gruntal & Company; Charles T. Munger, a Los Angeles attorney and at the time an informal partner with Buffett; Roy Tolles, Munger's Los Angeles law partner; Henry Brandt, senior vice president at Shearson Lehman Hutton; New York investors Jack Alexander, Buddy Fox and one of Buffett's associates, William Scott.

Members of the crowd "were moderately well-to-do then," Buffett said. Most are in their sixties or older today. "They're all rich now. They haven't invented Federal Express or anything like that. They just set one foot in front of the other. Ben put it all down. It's just so simple."[2]

LISTENING TO THE MASTER

Buffett wrote an admonition to those who would attend. ". . . we will engage in a little cross-fertilization. Knowing the propensity of some of you for speech making (and I feel a few fingers pointing toward me), I hasten to explain that he is the bee and we are the flowers! As I look at the addressees on this memo, I feel there is some danger of a degeneration of the meeting into a Turkish rug auction unless we discipline ourselves to see what we can learn from Ben, rather than take the opportunity to post him on how many of our great ideas he has missed."

The pilgrims converged from several cities, some of them meeting first in Las Vegas where they spent a few days at the glitzy new Caesar's Palace Hotel and Casino. They then traveled on to the Hotel Del Coronado across the bay from San Diego, the elegant Victorian hotel where the Marilyn Monroe–Tony Curtis–Jack Lemmon movie, *Some Like it Hot* was filmed.

Ben reserved a guest room for himself and a meeting room for the group. Each morning, the men gathered to discuss securities and the market and afterward, they relaxed at the beach.

AN INVESTOR BETS ON SOMEONE ELSE'S GAME

"He gave us a quiz," Buffett said, "A true-false quiz. And there were all these guys who were very smart. He told us ahead of time that half were true and half were false. There were 20 questions. Most of us got less than 10 right. If we'd marked every one true or every one false, we would have gotten 10 right."

Graham made up the deceptively simple historical puzzler himself, Buffett explained. "It was to illustrate a point, that the smart fellow kind of rigs the game. It was 1968, when all this phony accounting was going on. You'd think you could profit from it by riding along on the coattails, but (the quiz) was to illustrate that if you tried to play the other guy's game, it was not easy to do.

"Roy Tolles got the highest score, I remember that," Buffett chuckled. "We had a great time. We decided to keep doing it."

A TRADITION IS BORN

It was the first of a famous series of outings by the longtime Wall Street pals.

The group that called on Ben Graham—today informally known as Buffett Inc.—at first met annually. Eventually, Buffett's circle decided to convene every other year in luxurious resorts such as Laurel Point Inn in Victoria, British Columbia, Bishop's Lodge in Santa Fe, New Mexico, and the Williamsburg Inn in Virginia. The club has grown to include up to 60 other close friends Buffett accumulated over the years, including

Washington Post publisher Katharine Graham, former president of Coca-Cola Company Donald R. Keough, CBS head Laurence Tisch, Microsoft founder and second richest man in the United States, William Gates.

"In 1983, we took the top two decks of the *Queen Elizabeth II*," Schloss said. "It rained the entire time. We didn't get out on the deck."

The year after the trek to consult with Ben, Buffett disbanded the Buffett Partnership to await the stock market's decline and another cyclical low that would allow the acquisition of a new portfolio. Three years later, Wall Street suffered the collapse of 1973–1974.

Buffett and his friends had gone to California to consult with Ben Graham for two simple reasons: Graham knew more about the subject of stocks and bonds than anyone they knew and they trusted his insight.

THE WISDOM OF VALUE INVESTING

It was under the tutelage of Graham that this remarkable group of money managers came to understand the fundamentals of value investing—that is, to select securities by focusing on facts regarding a company's financial condition and its future earnings potential. Value investors fairly well ignore the price cycles of individual stocks or movements of the market as a whole. Market gyrations are of little consequence to them, except that upswings make bargain stocks harder to find and downturns make them plentiful. Graham was a pioneer in the development of hedging techniques and in the discovery of arbitrage opportunities, but even his activities in these sophisticated areas were based on knowing at what price a share should be bought or sold.

THE "SUPERINVESTORS"

In a now celebrated speech at Columbia University in 1984, "The Superinvestors of Graham and Doddsville," Warren Buffett described the spectacular success of the Graham disciples. In the speech, Buffett refuted the so-called "efficient-market" or "random-walk" theory, the notion that every bit of knowledge on the market is so thoroughly known that no single investor has an advantage over another. He argued that the track record of Graham's students proved that the market is still dysfunctional enough to allow a skilled and enterprising investor to outperform the crowd. Buffett's proof, the "super-investors," consistently provided 20-percent-plus annual returns on the money that they managed. "In this group of successful investors that I want to consider, there has been a common intellectual patriarch, Ben Graham," Buffet said.

Most students of investments know Graham for his preference for stocks that were selling below their net current asset values. While Graham's method of evaluation seemed to weigh heavily the assets, liabilities and other quantitative factors of a company to determine its appropriate share price and potential earning power (as opposed to cycles, management skills, industry outlook or other qualitative factors), his thinking was not so narrow or so methodical as some followers perceive it to be, claims Sequoia Fund founder Bill Ruane. Graham did not simply produce a formula and doggedly follow it.

"Graham developed a framework for making people think through what those numbers really mean," explained Ruane. Ruane, incidentally, began the Sequoia Fund in 1970 at Buffett's request to take care of his clients when the Buffett Partnership terminated. It started with $10 million. Ruane closed off the fund to new investors in 1982 when its value reached $350.7 million. "The money was coming in faster than I had ideas," Ruane explained.[3] Ruane still accepts no new investors. In 1992, the fund was worth $1.4 billion and its ten-year average total return was 17.3 percent.

GRAHAM AND DODDSVILLE

It was examples like that of Ruane on which Buffett built his argument against the random-walk theory. But more than just a handful of professional money managers, Buffett notes that as a result of Ben Graham's 40-year career, a community of prosperous investors has been spawned. "There really is a Graham and Doddsville," Buffett later mused. "It is an intellectual village." It is indeed a vibrant community extending beyond those who learned to invest by studying with Graham at Columbia. Graham and Doddsville is home to Ben's investor clientele, his colleagues, friends, and even people who know Graham only through his writing. These kindred spirits live in far-flung regions of the world.

Besides the first-generation of followers that Buffett talked about in "The Superinvestors of Graham and Doddsville," there are dozens of second- and third-generation professional disciples—investment managers and advisers around the globe who consider themselves adherents to Graham's investment principles. Many of these people, following the lead of Graham students such as Buffett and Ruane, have modified his basic theories in some way.

Robert W. Bruce III, formerly chief investment officer for the Fireman's Fund Corporation and managing partner of the Steamboat Group, claims to use Graham and Dodd in his daily work. Charles Brandes, who operates a $1 billion investment fund in Del Mar, California, for example, emphasizes the importance of cash flow when he applies the theories of value investing. Geraldine Weiss, publisher of the *Investment Quality Trends* newsletter, has built on Graham's devotion to dividends. John Neff of the Windsor Fund adheres to the basic principles, but looks for dividend yield plus strong growth. In the fall of 1993, John Bogle, maverick chairman of The Vanguard Group, paid homage to Graham in his book, *Bogle on Mutual Funds: New Perspectives for the Intelligent Investor. The Intelligent Investor,* of course, is the well-known title of one of Graham's books. The list is long.

After the *Financial Analysts Journal* published a remembrance that Warren Buffett wrote of Ben after his death, Buffett received letters from individuals in Canada, Arizona and many other distant places who had written to Ben for direction and guidance and had received both.

THE GURU

The slightly-built 74-year-old man with the large head, sparkling blue eyes and broad smile who met with Buffett's group that week in 1968 was showing his age. Yet, he exhibited a gentle dignity more commonly found in his generation than it is today. His was a rare charisma, lighted by an extraordinary intelligence and a richness of life experience.

While it is true that genius crops up at unexpected times and in unexpected places, Graham's family history, his early life and education prepared him for the times in which he lived and the role that he would play. His family's devotion to knowledge and his own education gave Graham the ability to apply scholarly precision to the field of finance. His early years set the stage for how Graham engaged mathematics and logic in his study of securities—of how he used his intellect to make so many of his clients wealthy and his students smarter. The story of how he came to be so revered on Wall Street took seed just before the dawn of the twentieth century.

A DAWNING AGE

In the first month of the first year of the twentieth century, Queen Victoria lay in state in London, marking the end of the second longest reign of the British monarchy. Thousands of silent mourners gathered to pay their final respects as the beloved "Mother" was drawn home in a carriage for burial. London streets were draped with purple cashmere tied with white satin bows—the Queen found black at funerals to be depressing. This sad but momentous changing of the guard, from one century to the next, from the Victorian era to the Edwardian, was one of the earliest memories of young Benjamin Grossbaum. Though Ben's family was living in New York when Queen Victoria died, England was their homeland, and like the whole world, they were absorbed by this solemn beginning of the new century.

Born in London on May 8, 1894, Benjamin spent the first year of his long life in cool, foggy Britain. The British formality, emotional reserve and wry sense of humor lingered with him for life, however.

AN IMMIGRANT LAD

Benjamin was just one year old when the Grossbaums decided that the household, which included three active little boys, should move to New York to expand the family business there. The Grossbaums, who had not yet changed their name to Graham, imported china, pottery and bric-a-brac from Austria and Germany.

Some nine million immigrants joined the Grossbaums in knocking at America's "golden door" at the turn of the century. It is almost certain that in their quest, the Grossbaums passed through that tiny and teeming patch of real estate in New York harbor—Ellis Island. The island was intimidating, with its swarm of confused refugees and their bundles of belongings. But the buildings were spacious and beautiful, and for the most part, the immigration officials were efficient and kind. No matter what else it was, Ellis Island was the gateway to a world of possibilities. The Grossbaums, thankfully, had an advantage over many of the other immigrants. At least they were coming from an English-speaking land, and by all accounts, they arrived with enough money to sustain themselves with dignity and at the same time to launch a new business enterprise.

The family must have felt sympathy for the hordes of Eastern Europeans with whom they rubbed shoulders at Ellis Island. They themselves were only a few years removed from the poverty-racked Old World from which most of the immigrants sought escape. Dora Gesundheit Grossbaum, Ben's mother, was the fourth of the 11 children of the Grand Rabbi of Varsovie (Warsaw), Poland.

AN INTELLECTUAL LINEAGE

Dora's father was a scholar and an intellectual. "He was the chief Rabbi of Warsaw," explained Rhoda Sarnat, Ben Graham's first cousin. "My father and Aunt Dora were born in Poland. The whole family was born there. But it was terrible there. There was no opportunity for a Jew."

Because of its early liberal attitudes toward religion, Poland over the centuries had become home to a large Jewish community. In Warsaw, Jews made up 40 percent of the population. When Europe experienced a population surge, Russia and Germany pushed and shoved, both partitioning and oppressing Poland. The country suffered excruciating political turmoil. Poverty swept through all of Europe and many Europeans, especially the scorned Jews, fled.

Dora, her older brother Maurice and several other Gesund-heit children left Poland to resettle in England. Other siblings sought hope and opportunity in countries on practically every continent. Maurice Gesundheit, who eventually changed his name to Maurice Gerard, in his early years yielded to the family expectation that the first son would pursue rabbinical studies. Not far into his training, Maurice decided that he was an agnostic and abandoned a religious vocation. He chose a career that, to his way of thinking, offered greater challenge. Maurice studied mathematics and became a professor at Manchester University.

But soon, hearing tales of a more vital and vigorous land across the Atlantic, Maurice followed his sister Dora and her family to New York and took up a totally new line of work. In the United States, where manufacturing and construction were prospering, he became a mechanical and civil engineer.

Maurice Gerard's resettlement proved to be a salvation for Dora and her three young sons. Ben's father died only a few years after the family arrived in New York, the first of a series of untimely deaths that tormented the Graham family. Without antibiotics or other modern medicines, diphtheria, typhoid and malaria were common diseases. Even a cold could develop into a fatal case of pneumonia, and such was the case with Isaac Grossbaum. The young father, only 35 years old, left sons Victor, age 11; Leon, 10; and 9-year-old Benjamin.

A WIDOW'S STRUGGLE

Dora and the children strove to keep the fledgling china-im-porting business going, but it finally failed. Dora Grossbaum then tried for several years to run a boardinghouse, and though she was strong-willed and energetic, that enterprise also fal-tered.

Her efforts to better the family fortune gave young Benjamin his first brush with the stock market when he was 13 years old. That year, his mother opened a margin account to buy an odd lot of U.S. Steel shares. The stock market, stimulated by exces-sive speculation and then squeezed by tight money, went into seizure. It lost 49 percent of its value in 22 months. The legen-dary panic of 1907 wiped out Dora's small account, draining even more of the widow's meager reserves. Hers was a classic case of an investor entering the investment arena at an over-valued stage and losing everything. The market was fully recovered by 1909, but that did not help small investors like Dora Grossbaum who had no staying power.

The Grossbaums were forced into a hand-to-mouth exist-ence, the poor relatives in a successful, affluent clan. For many of those early years, Dora and the children lived with Maurice Gerard and his family. Gerard, now a civil engineer and effi-ciency consultant to major corporations, was both a scientific thinker and a fatherly disciplinarian. He had a profound influ-ence on young Benjamin's intellectual development.

FAMILY SOLIDARITY

"My father knew art, literature, current events, theology, astronomy," explained Rhoda Gerard Sarnat, who was not born until 1915 after the Gerards had moved to Chicago. "Taking a walk with him was an education. He would describe the stars. He would take out his knife and describe the micah in the rock. It didn't matter what it was."

Even so, raising his own family plus a trio of nephews must have presented a challenge. Maurice, in fact, was only 23 years Ben's senior. Victor, the middle child of the Grossbaum boys, was a rambunctious child; Leon, the oldest child, was more settled; and Ben, the youngest, came to be known as the "brains" of the family. Clearly his mother's darling, Ben grew up with the self-confidence of a favorite son.

The children attended Public School Number 10 at 117th Street and Nicholas Avenue, which was then a very pleasant neighborhood. "Victor was in the fifth grade and he was always getting in trouble," Rhoda recalls hearing. "Ben was only in the third grade, but he had to bail Victor out. Ben was always recognized as very bright."

Life was arduous in many ways for immigrants and orphans like the Grossbaum boys, but America after the turn of the century was also a land of extravagant optimism. Food, land, new ideas and inventions to excite the imagination were plen-tiful. The typewriter, the sewing machine, the self-binding harvester and especially the automobile surely would make life glorious for everyone.

The Grossbaum youngsters grew up in New York during an era when the comics were created for kids and dime novels such as Booth Tarkington's Penrod and Sam described rambunctious escapades. Most youngsters pored over McGuffey's *Readers* at school. Little girls wore sailor dresses and both boys and girls laced their boots with buttonhooks. Children's lives were intended to be wholesome and for the most part were viewed with benevolence and good humor by adults.

A PERSONALITY IS FORGED

Ben learned moral lessons along with his reading, writing and arithmetic. He drew on one of those in a speech many years later. "When I was in elementary school in this city, more than 70 years ago," he said, "we had to write various maxims in our copybooks. The first on the list was 'honesty is the best policy.' It is still the best policy . . ."[4]

Like many intelligent children, Ben was emotionally sensitive and easily hurt and he struggled with ways to live with his sensitivity. Ben began choosing personal heros and role models from his literature and history books. Ulysses, Marcus Aurelius, Isaac Newton and his own namesake, Benjamin Franklin, were his favorites.

"In a way it is strange that the *Odyssey* has meant so much to me, since Ulysses's character is as different as possible from my own," Ben told his family at his 80th birthday celebration. "He was a great fighter and plunderer, while I have never fought with anyone or plundered anything in my life. He was crafty and devious, while I pride myself on being straightforward and direct." Yet, Ben admitted, wayward, wandering Ulysses had a continuous attraction for him.

Benjamin Franklin, a flesh-and-blood American hero whose autobiography included guidance on how to choose a mistress, also was among his favorite authors. "He had all the good characteristics I wanted to have," Ben explained to his family. "—high intelligence, application, inventiveness, also humor, kindness and tolerance of others' faults, and many more. Perhaps too—without trying, I shared some of his weaknesses . . ."

In the absence of a father and with a voracious appetite for knowledge, Ben adopted many of his ideas from books.

EMOTIONAL ARMOR

To guard his tender spirit from various wounds, Ben embraced stoicism as his personal philosophy. Slights, oversights, criticism and intentional wounds to his soul were to be endured without complaint, and certainly never were to be returned in kind.

School was a pleasure for him, but Ben also was learning from the practical world. He and his brothers took whatever jobs they could during those school years to help their struggling mother make ends meet.

The Graham brothers later admitted that they were terrified of the imposing Uncle Maurice, but, nevertheless, a family bond was knit. Whether the talent was inherited genetically, or whether it was nurtured by his uncle, Benjamin, like Uncle Maurice, became a skilled mathematician. Ben developed his memory and took handily to the classics, which he read in Greek, Latin and French.

"There was a parallel between Ben and my Dad," said Rhoda Sarnat. She explained that from each of the 11 Polish-born Gesundheit children, there was born one extraordinarily bright child. "It was sort of a good seed."

Rhoda's brother, Ralph Waldo Gerard, became an internationally known neurophysiologist. A cousin in Liverpool is said to have become one of the first women elected to the British House of Commons. Apparently, formidable Uncle Maurice realized that Benjamin was Dora's stellar one. He nurtured Ben's talents and valued them. Maurice Gerard later became one of Ben's earliest business partners and investors.

Following grammar school, Ben progressed to Boys High School in Brooklyn. Despite the fact that he was not very tall and was hindered by an inborn awkwardness, Ben enjoyed sports and was active. Among the lifelong friends he made were young Douglass Newman and his brother Jerome. The young men took home medals for their performance on the 90-pound relay team. Even though the Grossbaum family's money problems persisted, Ben finished up near the top of his class.[5]

FATE, THAT TRICKSTER

Expectations were high for the talented graduate, but Ben's dreams were not to be fulfilled without a few setbacks.

Warren Buffett recounts the story of when Ben graduated from high school and took a national scholarship examination. Everyone was surprised and baffled when they were told that Ben had scored poorly. It seemed unbelievable. Graham's long-time friend Irving Kahn described Ben as having a speed of thought so astounding that he could answer the most complicated question immediately after hearing it. His memory was so phenomenal that he learned to read in six languages.

Ben's disappointment was magnified by the fact that a relative with the same last name earned the second highest score ever given and was awarded a scholarship to Columbia. Resigned to his fate, Ben went out and got a job. After several months, scholarship officials discovered that the tests had been mixed up. The relative was not doing well and officials at Columbia offered the scholarship to Ben instead. Flying in the face of his friends who said if he gave up his job he would never again get one that paid so well, Ben enrolled at Columbia College, the oldest venue of Columbia University.

THE BATTLE TO PAY COLLEGE EXPENSES

Even with the righted wrong, money was tight. Though Ben's brothers pitched in to help carry his college expenses, he did not have enough. Ben finally was compelled to drop out of day classes and take a full-time job with U.S. Express.

That job became an education in itself. At U.S. Express, Ben was given responsibility for an intriguing research project. "We set out to find the effect on revenues of a proposed revolutionary new system of computing express rates. For this purpose, we used the so-called Hollerith machines, leased out by the then Calculating-Tabulating-Recording Company," Ben explained. "They comprised card-punches, card-sorters and tabulators—tools almost unknown to businessmen then, and having their chief application in the Census Bureau." The experience with the C-T-R equipment not only introduced Ben to principles of accounting, it left him with the sense that he was in touch with the very smartest technology. Some time later, of course, C-T-R changed its initials to IBM.[6]

INTOLERANCE AND RUMBLINGS OF WAR

By the time Ben had enrolled in college, the exuberant national mood of the earlier decade had worn itself out. World War I was simmering in Europe. Though the United States did not enter the conflict until 1917, anti-German and antisemitic sentiment was rampant in the United States and the Grossbaums, along with many thousands of recent immigrants, felt the strain. Robert Heilbrunn, a good friend of Ben's and an early Graham investor, also grew up in New York. He remembers those dangerous years.

"When I was about six years old, I was living with my parents and grandparents in one big house," Heilbrunn said. "My grandparents spoke German all the time. When I went to the first grade, my English wasn't very good. The other children called me 'Heilbrunn the hun.'

"When the war started, everything German, even the streets in Brooklyn, changed. Hamburg Street became Liberty Street, sauerkraut was called liberty cabbage," Heilbrunn recalled. Hamburgers became liberty steaks, dachshunds became liberty pups and in Cincinnati, pretzels were banned from lunch counters.

ESCAPE FROM A NAME

The Grossbaums, their relatives and friends changed their names as well. It was customary, Rhoda Sarnat explained, for people to take the first one or two letters of their original names, then find a British or some other non-Teutonic derivation. Grossbaum thus became the Scottish Graham and Gesundheit transformed into Gerard. Another part of the family became the Grevilles.

Despite the troubled era of his youth and the antisemitism he experienced at other times, Ben "never made a big deal of it," recalls daughter Elaine.

A TRIUMPHANT GRADUATION

Ben threw his energies into mastering mathematics, philosophy, English, Greek, Latin and music and is said to have graduated Phi Beta Kappa, the second in his class at Columbia College.

Despite his academic prowess, Ben's graduation fell into uncertainty at the last minute. There was a requirement at the time that every Columbia graduate must pass a swimming test, and Ben had never learned how to swim. He hurriedly took a lesson, managed to pass the test and enjoyed swimming the rest of his life.

A JOB FINDS BEN

As the final months of schooling drew to a close, Ben found that he had made an excellent impression on his professors at Columbia. The deans of three departments—English, mathematics and philosophy—stepped forward with offers of teaching positions. Despite the humble starting salary and unhurried rate of advancement for college teachers, each of the department heads pointed out the satisfaction and prestige of an academic career.

Ben Graham may not have yet realized that he had a gift for teaching and an affinity for young minds. Nevertheless, he had grown up and earned his degree under painful financial conditions and the prospect of a good job was foremost on his mind.

In his uncertainty over which post to accept, Ben sought the advice of Columbia's Dean Frederick Keppel, who as it turned out, now and then liked to steer a bright graduate into a business career.

As fate would have it, a member of the New York Stock Exchange came to campus to talk to Dean Keppel about his son's woeful grades. While he was there, the father asked the dean to recommend one of his best students for a position with his firm.

Even though Ben had dropped out of his only economics course a few weeks after enrollment, Keppel urged the 20-year-old to accept the offer to join the Wall Street firm of Newburger, Henderson & Loeb.[7]

THE GRACIOUS GOOD-BYE

Graduation was a gala affair. After several days of games and banquets, on June 3, 1914, Ben and 160 other students, including 23 who had come from China to study at Columbia, marched in a dignified procession across the green lawns of the campus. The men were dressed in dark blazers, white pants and straw hats and the women wore breezy white dresses.

Though Ben's days as a student at Columbia had come to an end, the leaning toward university life stayed with the young graduate. Ben accepted the job recommended by Dean Keppel and looked forward to his career on Wall Street with relish. He got the hang of some of the most obscure notions about finance almost instantly, but he eventually would return to Columbia to refine his ideas and make orderly sense of his knowledge.

Columbia had been a center of lofty ideals and a temporary home to handsome young people with stylish clothes and a sense of fun. Most expected distinguished careers in law, medicine or academia. The securities industry at the time was not a glamorous place to work. In fact, Wall Street wafted a slightly tainted cologne. At Columbia, a preoccupation with money was considered tasteless.

GOING DOWNTOWN

Nevertheless, as Ben shifted his attention to the opposite end of Manhattan—to the mysterious world of finance—he was armed with the excellent ammunition of a serious education. Even if he had dropped out of his economics course, Ben remembered virtually having to memorize a quotation by the British economist Walter Bagehot about the South Sea Bubble of 1711.

"Much has been written on panics and manias. But one thing is certain: That at particular times a great many stupid people have a great deal of stupid money. Several economists have plans for preventing improvident speculation—our scheme is not to allow any man to have a hundred pounds who cannot prove to the satisfaction of the Lord Chancellor that he knows what to do with a hundred pounds . . . At intervals . . . the money of these people—the blind capital (as we call it) of the country—is particularly large and craving; it seeks someone to devour it and there is plethora; it finds someone and there is speculation; it is devoured and there is panic."[8]

But along with the wise and echoing voices of Bagehot and his Columbia professors, Graham also seemed to be listening to the admonitions of his mother as he transferred his time and attention to Wall Street.

According to Rhoda Sarnat, spirited Dora Graham, who stood about five feet tall in three-inch high-heeled shoes, "gave her boys some advice: she told them all to have a lot of affairs, and I might say, they all followed her instructions."

AN EDUCATION ON THE STREET

When Ben went down to Wall Street in 1914, he took the first step in building a life as a legendary investor, an original thinker on economic issues and a leader in the establishment of professional standards for financial analysts. He also earned a parallel reputation as a resolute lady's man.

BEN GRAHAM'S LEGACY

The legacy of the Rockefellers had to do with big business. Baruch left a mass of money. Graham's contribution to American enterprise was a body of knowledge, a framework for thought, the drive for positive change and inspiration for generations of future security analysts and individual investors. While Graham was capable of deep and complex thinking, the appeal of his method is its simplicity. That legacy was passed through his teaching, his writing and his generosity to virtually anyone who sought his counsel.

Like most of us, Graham's life evolved as a series of what seemed like happenstances—some of them lucky, some of them desolating. Yet anyone who met him recognized Graham almost immediately as a person of extraordinarily high intellect, even as a genius. The "happenstance" was shaped by who Graham was, his inherent abilities and his lifelong yearning to be a good person.

The story of his life followed what mythologists describe as the hero's journey. He encountered moral dilemmas and behaved ethically; he faced failure but battled his way back; he led a full life that was far from perfect, but as his friends and children remember it, he continued to grow as a human being until the very end of his days.

"When some people get old, their worst characteristics emerge," observed his daughter Marjorie Graham Janis. Ben, on the other hand, conquered his youthful demons and became increasingly peaceful, warm and human.

Though his personal life was tainted by scandal, Graham profoundly affected almost everyone who met him.

CHAPTER 2

Graham's Early Years on Wall Street

"There are no sure and easy paths to riches in
Wall Street or anywhere else."

—Benjamin Graham[1]

Perhaps there is "no sure and easy path" to riches on Wall Street, but there *is* a path, and Graham found it.

The first years following Graham's graduation from Columbia included all of the uncertainties of a young man at the beginning of his career. With no preparation and little warning, he was tossed into the arcane machinery of capitalism. Additionally, Graham was caught up in the commotion of a nation facing its first war outside its own hemisphere.

Ben reported to work on Wall Street in 1914 earning, as a special favor from his employer, $12 per week. For the first month, he worked as a runner, delivering securities and checks, but he quickly showed he was capable of more. In the second month, he advanced to assistant in a two-man bond department. Ben's new assignment was to frame short, concise descriptions of every bond that was listed on Newburger, Henderson & Loeb's daily list of recommendations. Within six weeks, Ben was handed the additional duty of writing the daily market letter for the firm's Philadelphia office.

CONSEQUENCES OF WAR

This was heady progress for a young man on his first job, but the rumbling of war grew louder from Europe and soon echoed through the securities industry. Within months after Ben reported for work, Archduke Ferdinand of Austria was assassinated in Sarajevo and war exploded in Europe. European investors, in a rush to liquidate their American stocks and bonds, sparked a panic in New York. As a result, the New York Stock Exchange was forced to shut down for five months. Ben found his salary accordingly had been cut back to $10 per week, but at least he had a job.

Trading soon resumed on a limited basis and to the surprise of many, investor confidence was stimulated by the war.

"It looked as if the end of the world had happened, but after a year and a half, we were in the midst of a raging bull market," Ben observed.[2]

Caught short-staffed, Newburger put Ben's talents to work in a multitude of ways that gave him a thorough indoctrination in the operations of a trading firm. He lent a hand in the back office, operated the telephone switchboard, delivered an occasional security and helped the boardboy post stock quotations on a big board in the anteroom, which for more reasons than technology was far different than it is today. Prior to 1916, stocks were quoted on the exchanges not in dollars but as a percentage of their par value. "Westinghouse and Pennsylvania (Railroad) would sell, say, at 150, which meant they were selling at $75 a share—because their par value was 50," Ben explained to his students in the 1940s.[3]

WAR CHANGES EVERYTHING

Prior to the Great War, Wall Street had been a fairly predictable place. "When I came down to the Street in 1914," Ben said, "an investment issue was not regarded as speculative, and it wasn't speculative. Its price was based primarily upon an established dividend. It fluctuated relatively little in ordinary years. And even in years of considerable market and business changes, the price of the investment issues did not go through very wide fluctuations. It was quite possible for the investor, if he wished, to disregard price changes completely, considering only the soundness and dependability of his dividend return, and let it go at that—perhaps every now and then subjecting his issue to a prudent scrutiny."[4] This principle held true for both bonds and for certain stocks, but it did not last.

ANOTHER PROMOTION

When his experience in such matters had built up sufficiently, Ben was handed another advancement—he was sent out to call on customers. "This was then a pleasant occupation, because in those days the average businessman was flattered to be called upon by a bond salesman and even his 'no' was invariably polite."[5]

In this vocation, however, Ben's efforts did not pay off. Too often he was turned away without an order. "I was too shy," Ben recalled. "I didn't have the quality they describe today as chutzpa."[6]

Nevertheless, the experience showed Ben how little the customers knew about the bonds they were asked to buy. In fact, he himself felt the need for greater knowledge.

Ben studied the most reliable textbook then available, *The Principles of Bond Investment* by Lawrence Chamberlain. He then applied Chamberlain's doctrines to the industry that in the first half of the century issued the most important bonds—railroads. Though he had no formal training in accounting, Ben began to learn the dark secrets of the ledger, which he continued to probe until he could see right through the conjurings of the accounting sorcerers.

His examination of the June, 1914, reports of the then-popular Missouri Pacific Railroad convinced Ben that the company was in precarious physical and financial condition. He felt that the bonds should be neither purchased nor held by an investor. Such detailed analysis and strong sell recommendations were unusual even for statisticians, as analysts then were called. Ben shared a copy of his appraisal with a friend who was a floor broker at the New York Stock Exchange. The friend, in turn, showed the report to a partner at Bache & Company. The simplicity and clarity that became a hallmark of Graham's writing must have been evident in that first attempt, because

Ben was swiftly offered a job there as a statistician. Bache & Company's proposition of $18 per week meant a 50-percent salary hike.

DEMISE OF A SALESMAN

Because he had not yet brought in bond commissions to offset his salary, Ben assumed that his boss, Samuel Newburger, would willingly let him go. Instead, Newburger was outraged.

"But I'm not cut out for a bond salesman," Ben protested. "I'd do better at statistical work."

"That's fine," Newburger replied. "It's time we had a statistical department. You can be it."[7]

CONCEALED ASSETS

For the most part, Ben's promotion to the role of statistician would mean more analysis of debt issues. Investor interest focused primarily on bonds because income from incumbered debt issues was both substantial and sound. Common stocks, except for railroad and utility issues, were approached with greater trepidation. And for good reason: Only sketchy financial information was published by the corporations and that was used either to lure investors or to satisfy the stock exchange. Additionally, bonds, which are secured by assets in the event of a bankruptcy, take precedence over stocks, which by the nature of their ownership position have a secondary status. Bondholders get in line with the creditors, while shareholders split the remains once all creditors have been paid. Despite these disadvantages, Ben saw the potential in greater stock ownership.

In contrast to today, when figures are likely to be overstated to make a company look stronger than it is, management at that time tried to conceal assets. With less information afloat, management had greater control over the company. Ben's goals were to spot hidden assets and anticipate greater corporate value than was reflected in the share price. His was detective work, for annual reports often were nothing more than a four-page, folded-over pamphlet, with the names of the officers and directors taking up most of the space.

THE THREE Ms

Privileged intelligence—insider information—was the key to big profits. Manipulation of the market, as is clear in the autobiographies of Bernard Baruch and other Wall Street barons of the time, was an everyday occurrence. In fact, there were few regulations and no Securities and Exchange Commission (SEC) and the "three Ms," as Ben called them—mystery, manipulation and (thin) margins—were virtually guiding principles.

Nevertheless, information from companies themselves and from government regulatory agencies such as the Interstate Commerce Commission (ICC) sometimes could be flushed out by a diligent sleuth. Ben made his mark early by ferreting out and interpreting this data in resourceful ways.

In 1915, the Guggenheim Exploration Company, which held large interests in several copper-mining companies, announced it would dissolve. It would sell its assets and return the money to investors. Guggenheim was actively traded on the New York Stock Exchange and on September 1 of that year sold for $68.88 per share.

FACTUAL ANALYSIS

Ben figured that the value of each share of Guggenheim would be equal to the market price of the shares it held in various companies, plus Guggenheim's other assets.

One share of Guggenheim Exploration, therefore, would equal:

.7277 share Kennecott Copper @ $52.50	=	$38.20
.1172 share Chino Copper @ $46.00	=	5.39
.0833 share American Smelting @ $81.75	=	6.81
.185 share Ray Consolidated Copper @ $22.88	=	4.23
Other assets	=	21.60
Total:		$76.23

In terms simple enough for anyone to understand, his numbers indicated that Guggenheim was trading at a price ($68.88) below its asset value ($76.23), virtually ensuring an arbitrage profit of $7.35 per share when the company distributed its capital to shareholders. As with any other arbitrage, there were risks involved. For example, the shareholders might fail to approve the dissolution. Lawsuits could interfere, or the value of the underlying stocks might decline before the shares could be liquidated.

In the case of Guggenheim, the risks seemed relatively insignificant compared to the potential profit. On Ben's advice, Newburger arbitraged a large number of shares. Ben managed the venture in Guggenheim in return for a 20-percent share of the profits. On January 17, 1916, the dissolution took place and Ben's reputation, not to mention his net worth, soared.[8]

TECHNOLOGY IS NOT ENOUGH

Not all of Ben's suggestions were well received, however. Ben had never forgotten what he had seen during his work with the Calculating-Tabulating-Recording Company's Hollerith machines when he was forced to take a full-time job while in college. To him, it seemed like the future rested with such inventions.

"I entered Wall Street in 1914 and the next year the bonds and common stock of C-T-R Company were listed on the New York Stock Exchange," Ben said. "Well, I had a kind of sentimental interest in that enterprise, and besides, I considered myself a sort of technological expert on their products, being one of the few financial people who had seen and used them. So early in 1916, I went to the head of my firm, known as Mr. A. N., and pointed out to him that C-T-R stock was selling in the middle 40s (for 105,000 shares); that it had earned $6.50 in 1915; that its book value—including, to be sure, some non-segregated intangibles—was $130; that it had started a $3 dividend; and that I thought rather highly of the company's products and prospects."

Mr. A. N. looked pityingly at Ben and curtly instructed him to never mention that stock again. The bonds were selling at 6 percent and were no good, Mr. A. N. snapped, because the company was mostly "water," a term for goodwill and other ephemeral assets.

"So much was I impressed by his sweeping condemnation of Calculating-Tabulating-Recording that I never bought a share of it in my life, not even after its name was changed to IBM in 1926," Ben laughed.[9]

RISK ANALYSIS

While Ben regretted not having bought into IBM at an early stage, he understood full well the principle under which his employer operated. It was basic: In most cases, a company with too few assets and sales too uncertain to back up its debt is a poor investment. There is a one-in-a-million chance that a company of questionable leverage will turn into an IBM and the common investor could go broke fishing for the right strike. In lectures to his students in later years, Ben compared Mr. A. N.'s philosophy to that of a bridge player. "I recall . . . the emphasis that the bridge experts place on playing a hand right rather than playing it successfully. Because, as you know, if you play it right you are going to make money and if you play it wrong you lose money—in the long run."[10]

THE WAR BOOM

Ben's early years on Wall Street were packed with many important lessons. The World War I bull market pushed on through 1915 and 1916. Because the war was not on U.S. soil, American companies were in an ideal position to profit. Between 1910 and 1920, the U.S. gross national product (GNP) grew from $30.4 billion to $71.6 billion.[11] American companies made enormous amounts of money from orders for munitions and equipment from England and France. The profits were amplified by the fact that U.S. corporations at that time were lightly taxed. Ben, his firm and all of Wall Street were riding high.

BRANCHING OUT

Ben continued his work for Newburger, but managed some investments and handled a few business deals of his own, mostly for friends and relatives. Among Ben's clients was Algernon Tassin, a professor of English at Columbia. Tassin set Ben up with $10,000 of capital, with the agreement that the profits and losses would be split equally between them. In the first year, the fund performed extremely well and each of them took out several thousands dollars of profit.

Ben had a keen interest in music, and together with his oldest brother Leon, Ben invested $7,000 in The Broadway Phonograph Shop. The store was located on Manhattan at Broadway and 98th Street.

Ben also conducted a consulting business with his Uncle Maurice Gerard, though the exact nature of their company is somewhat fuzzy. This company may have been a New York branch of a management-consulting firm Uncle Maurice now ran out of Chicago. A sheet of "Gerard, Graham & Co." letterhead survives, describing the company as "industrial engineers, developers of latent earnings." A modern-day comparison might be a consulting firm that helps in corporate restructuring, finding assets that can be sold at a sizable profit or services that are better provided from outside sources.

"My dad was president, though it was more in name," explained Rhoda Sarnat, "and my brother, Ralph Waldo Gerard, a neurophysiologist, was the secretary." Ralph Gerard's role was titular as well. Apparently, Ben did most of the work.

A MENACING MOOD IN THE NATION

The World War I spirit was simmering ever hotter in the United States, destabilizing the stock market and fanning the smoldering coals of bigotry.

In the fall of 1916, a "peace scare" brought the bull market to an end, and prices continued to drop for a year after the United States entered the fray. The decline meant Ben's private investment account—the Tassin account—took a drubbing. Though the Tassin account was invested in rather obscure secondary stocks that were worth more than their market value, their prices fell dramatically. There was a margin call on the account, and Ben had to sell shares at a significant loss. Because his money was tied up in The Broadway Phonograph Shop, Ben was unable to settle his share of the Tassin losses.

Later, Ben would tell his readers and teach his students that a true investor seldom is forced to sell his shares. He sells in his own time, when the investment has matured and suitable earnings have been realized. At this early stage in his life, however, Ben still had not come to terms with the trap of unmanageable debt.

The trusting Professor Tassin was shocked at what had happened, but his faith in Ben was unshaken. He allowed the deficiency to be repaid at $60 per month. Within two years, the market had recovered enough to allow Ben to make up the loss. In time, Ben was able to rebuild Professor Tassin's account to an exceedingly healthy level. Along the way, Ben and his brother got out of the phonograph business.

WAR IS DECLARED

In April, 1917, the United States entered the war, and Americans were warned that spies were everywhere. Indeed, there were a few bombings and several outrageous conspirators were uncovered. Yet, most of the hysteria was government-inspired—in the name of patriotism.

The *Old Humor Magazine* printed an editorial about the Kansas City trial of antiwar activist Mrs. Rose Pastor Stokes on charges that she violated the Espionage Act. "Mrs. Stokes is a Jewess, born in Russia. The Russian Jews of her sort—the intellectual sort—have no national feeling." Mrs. Stokes was sentenced to ten years in prison for penning a letter to a newspaper that read, "I am for the people, and the government is for the profiteers." Later, her conviction was set aside.[12] Tragically, before the frenzy subsided, several American Jews, including a young boy, were murdered by mobs.

THE MARCHING BRIGADE

It was in this atmosphere that Ben applied for the Officer Candidate Training Camp. He was summarily rejected on the basis that he was still a British citizen. He was permitted to join Company M of the New York State Guard, where Ben spent his time marching with the band. The band's leader was Victor Herbert, classical cellist, conductor and composer of light operas such as *Babes in Toyland* and *Naughty Marietta*. Herbert, too, was an immigrant—from Ireland.

Despite the social and political strife, Ben was developing traits that helped him make lasting friends. At the same time, these characteristics kept him distant from others. "He had a wonderful personality and could make friends with anybody," explained his friend and former student Irving Kahn. "But he was such a workaholic he didn't have much of a social life." Even so, Ben enjoyed outdoor activities and was a founder of the first Wall Street ski club.

Never a person to need much sleep, Ben turned out a prodigious amount of work. Though Graham toiled diligently and appreciated the salary he was earning, it was intellectual energy, rather than the need for an enormous amount of money, that motivated him even in those early days. "What kept Ben up at night was trying to find out a better way of doing things," said his cousin Rhoda Sarnat. "He'd lie there trying to figure out how to notate music better, and how to improve the teaching of the Morse code." This same curiosity and inventiveness also was applied to his investments.

TAXES TAKE HOLD

Though taxes had been relatively simple during the prewar years, this gradually changed. Taxes increased and they became more complicated. Ben soon realized that it was important to understand both the tax law and corporate tax returns to determine their influence on corporate earnings. Surprisingly, the study of tax consequences led to the solution of another exasperating mystery.

As mentioned earlier, the financial statements of public companies at that time typically carried a large amount of goodwill, which was lumped together on the balance sheet with tangible assets. The exact portion of assets that actually were intangible was a carefully guarded secret.

A MYSTERY REVEALED

The Excess Profits Tax of 1917 allowed a credit for a certain percentage of tangible invested capital, but excluded such intangibles as goodwill, patents and so forth. Working backwards from three balance-sheet items—taxes, pretax income and the property account—Ben devised a method for determining the exact value of goodwill.

He explained the method in an article for *The Magazine of Wall Street*. The editor complained that no one in the magazine's offices understood what Ben was talking about. "It looks as if you've done the whole thing with mirrors," the editor groused, but he agreed to print the piece anyway. [13]

Fortunately, Ben's computations proved correct, though it was years before disclosure rules were changed and anyone could be absolutely certain. By then, many corporations were writing off excess goodwill, for earning power had replaced assets as the most impressive and appealing characteristic of a publicly traded company.

FROM FRICTION, A NEW FRIEND

Ben continued to plow new ground in corporate analysis. In 1919, he wrote a report comparing the Chicago, Milwaukee & St. Paul Railroad with the St. Louis & Southwestern Railroad. Ben decided to show the analysis to the management of the Milwaukee Railroad in advance, because the report made the company look rather fragile. Ben went to see the railroad's financial vice president, Robert J. Marony. The executive briefly glanced at the material. "I don't quarrel with your facts or your conclusions," Marony said. "I wish our showing was a better one, but it isn't and that's that."[14] Afterward, the two men became friends and, eventually, colleagues in business.

A TIRESOME MATTER

Not everyone that Ben dealt with was so direct and honest, especially one colleague who was touting new issues on the over-the-counter (OTC) market. An acquaintance of Ben's had earned a lavish profit by participating in a syndicate that bought privately held Ertel Oil common stock at $3 per share and then offered the stock over the counter, where it opened trading at $8 per share. The friend offered to let Ben in on his next OTC syndicate.

The next opening turned out to be Savold Tire, created in April of 1919, to take advantage of a newly patented process for retreading automobile tires. Automobiles now were really taking hold as a popular mode of transportation, but the technology for tires was woefully backward. Tires did not last long, and as luck would have it, neither did some tire ventures.

Ben invested $2,500 for 250 shares of Savold at $10 share. Shortly afterward, the shares started trading at $24 and in a flurry of excitement rose to $37. The syndicate sold their shares and Ben's quick profit was nearly 270 percent of his investment.

Soon the company decided to license its process to companies in other states, where these companies would be taken public in the same manner. Four weeks after Ben's first profitable venture, another syndication was organized. Just after his 25th birthday, Ben received a check for his original investment plus 150 percent of the take. No accounting of the proceedings was supplied with the check, and based on his confidence in his friend and associates, Ben did not ask for a reconciliation.

The second round of syndication sold so fast that Ben was unable to get in, but soon a larger deal was structured. The Pennsylvania Savold would include rights to market the process in all the remaining 46 states. Any more than four corporations, the organizers explained, would be cumbersome. Ben did not quite understand the reasoning behind the plan to restrict growth, but he did not question the organizers' ability to make money. Taking the bait, Ben's various associates and friends pooled $60,000 for the venture. By now, it was late summer and the original Savold, riding a bull market, reached a peak price of $77.75. In the week ahead, the investors waited for Pennsylvania Savold to start trading. Instead, the original Savold tumbled by 30 percent. The new offering was delayed, and the decline continued until Savold disappeared entirely, as did investors' cash.

PENNY STOCK FRAUD

Ben accompanied the friend to a meeting of Savold "investors," where the promotor finally was pressured into coughing back some of their funds—a sum amounting to 30 percent of their investment. Then, as now, such swindles were common. The difference was that back then, fewer victims complained to the district attorney. There were no SEC or National Association of Securities Dealers (NASD) to turn to.

Ben's black adventure with Savold Tire brought him in closer contact with the manipulative element of Wall Street that he already disliked and ultimately came to abhor. Later, Ben told the story of "Same Old Tires" as an example of how even an insider's tip can turn out to be a fake. The bungle must have been additionally exasperating, for the concept actually had potential. Retreading tires later became a common and profitable practice and companies like Bandag were successful in the industry.

A WRITER OF NOTE

During these war years, Ben increased his writing for financial publications. Several more of his articles, including, "Bargains in Bonds," were published in *The Magazine of Wall Street*. His thorough study of debt issues illustrated discrepancies in prices among bonds that in other ways were comparable. He became a frequent contributor to the magazine and soon was asked to join the staff. Ben turned down the opportunity to become its editor, though the salary was attractive. Newburger again squelched any idea of leaving the company by countering with a promise of a junior partnership in the investment house.

Ben's outgoing older brother Victor did become an advertising salesman for *The Magazine of Wall Street*, however, and later advanced to vice president in charge of the department. Victor was perfect for the sales job. He may not have had Ben's investment acumen, but he had the chutzpa. Victor was suave, good-looking, an excellent dancer and could tell more jokes than anyone in his crowd.

ROMANCE

Ben's financial success was becoming more important to him because despite his heavy work load, he wanted to get married. He met the vivacious, strong-willed Hazel Mazur through his brother shortly after Ben went to work on Wall Street. "My mother's family lived in Bensonhurst and my father lived in the Bronx, so when they were courting that was quite a ride for him," explained their daughter Elaine. A teacher of dance and elocution at the time they were married, Hazel earned more money than Ben did. Perhaps because both of them were such independent thinkers, they could have strong differences of opinion. Yet in many ways, Ben and Hazel were similar, says their daughter Marjorie. "Whatever they did, they went about it energetically."

A WAR ENDS, A BABY IS BORN

In 1919, two important events took place. World War I ended and Ben and Hazel's first child was born. Named Isaac Newton after his own father and the scientist that Graham so greatly admired, the baby would be the young couple's greatest source of joy.

A FULL PARTNER

The end of World War I meant a new phase for Wall Street in general and for Ben in particular. In 1920, Ben took his place as a partner in Newburger, Henderson & Loeb, having proved that though he was only 26, he could manage unusual and complex investment strategies. As a partner, Ben kept his salary and gained a 2.5-percent interest in the profits without liability for losses.

Considering that the postwar bull market of 1919–1921 was both chaotic and dangerous, his promotion was all the more significant an achievement. All the least attractive stock market motivating factors—fear, greed, imprudence, gullibility—were at work. The Dow Jones Industrial Average (DJIA) made its fourth stab at breaking 100 since the beginning of the century, then scampered back to prewar levels. Yet Ben already was well on his way to the philosophy ascribed to him by Warren Buffett in the introduction to *The Intelligent Investor.* "The sillier the market's behavior, the greater the opportunity for the business-like investor." Buffett told readers that if they followed Graham's suggestions, they would "profit from folly rather than participate in it."[15]

Perhaps it was the recollection of his earlier misjudgments, including the uncomfortable memory of Professor Tassin's account, that guided Ben through that troubled postwar stretch. He was, after all, successful in exploring where no one else cared or dared to go.

Long before their business was hotly pursued and Japanese investment operations loomed alongside major U.S. investment houses in New York, Ben made his mark in Japanese bonds.

THE JAPANESE BOND CAPER

One of Ben's friends who worked for the public utility bond dealer Bonbright & Company introduced him to Junkichi Miki of the Fujimoto Bill Broker Bank of Osaka. Miki had tried to interest Bonbright & Company in acting as agent for the Osaka bank in acquiring Japanese government bonds that had been sold in the United States and in Europe during the Russo-Japanese War of 1906. The bonds were payable either in a European currency or in yen, whichever the holder chose. Because of currency problems in Europe and Japan's parallel prosperity, the bonds had become extremely attractive to Japanese investors. Bonbright was too busy to get involved, but Ben was happy to take on the new business.

Through Newburger's correspondents in London, Paris and Amsterdam, Ben arranged for massive amounts of the bonds to be purchased. The bonds then were sent to Japan with the draft attached. For two years, Ben's firm served as exclusive agent for the bonds, a task that provided more than $100,000 in commissions for the company (in 1920 dollars!).

A PAPER MOUNTAIN

Newburger's back office appreciated the commissions, but disliked the Japanese bonds themselves. Many of the bonds had been sold in $100 denominations, or the equivalent in pounds or francs. These small denominations were a real nuisance by Western standards and sold at substantial discounts. The conscientious Japanese saver, however, loved these "small pieces." Newburger's back office was swamped with paperwork, because $100,000 in bonds represented 1,000 separate documents. A special safe-deposit box was designated for the bonds and called, with grudging affection, the "Ben Graham" box.

Eventually, the Fujimoto Bank established its own operations in New York, but two other Japanese firms engaged Newburger's services and more than made up for the loss of business. However, Ben was well-liked by members of the Japanese financial community. Years later, his books were reprinted in Japan and his Japanese friends visited him bearing gifts of appreciation from their homeland, even after Ben had retired.

During the early 1920s, Ben continued to search for understated earnings and hidden assets that might foretell the unexpected rise in a stock price.

THINGS CHANGE SLOWLY

Despite his other adventures, Ben remained a statistical expert. Along with his assistant, Leo Stern, he handled all questions about security lists and individual issues. This was not particularly time-consuming work, for Wall Street during that era was a fairly simple place. The narrow list of public companies still was dominated by railroad and industrial stocks. Investors, for the most part, continued to cling to permanent, reliable investments that were free from change or worry. On behalf of his own clients, however, Ben insisted on looking beneath the surface for better earning opportunities and trying out new tactics that occasionally startled those who were content with the status quo.

Often, the issues that he studied and his experiences emerged in later writings. For example, Consolidated Textile, a conglomeration of cotton mills, was a popular speculative stock of the time and one of Newburger's senior partners bought large quantities of the common stock for his clients. Ben pointed out to the partner that Consolidated Textile's convertible seven-percent bonds appeared to carry less risk than the common shares and at the same time yielded an uncommonly high return. The partner dismissed Ben's observations, saying that his clients liked to be in an active stock. As Ben suspected might happen, Consolidated Textile's stock price soon tumbled from $70 to $20 per share.[16] The bonds, on the other hand, were refinanced and redeemed at a premium above par value. The story of Consolidated Textiles later cropped up in an appendix to *Security Analysis,* in a lesson explaining the mechanics of conversion privileges.

CHALLENGES DISTURB THE OLD GUARD

From time to time, Ben and Leo issued a circular with more detailed analysis of a security and occasionally their bold moves alarmed the New York investment community. In May of 1921, for example, they recommended the sale of U.S. Victory 4¼ bonds, which were selling at 97¾ and due in 1923. They suggested reinvesting in U.S. Victory 4¼s, which were selling at 87½ and were due in 1938. The recommendation was based on the belief that interest rates would fall and that longer-term bonds had better possibilities for appreciation. The recommendation was advertised in newspapers under the banner "Memorandum to Holders of Victory Bonds."

The New York Stock Exchange immediately demanded a copy of the leaflet because by unwritten code, stock exchange members were forbidden to encourage switches from government bonds to corporate securities. Naturally the circular made no such unpatriotic suggestion—it said only that buyers should switch from one government bond to another. As it happened, the young analyst again was right and those who followed his recommendations prospered.

A FRESH LOOK AT SPECULATION

One of Ben's pamphlets was entitled *Lessons for Investors.* "Of course, it took a brash analyst in his middle twenties like myself to hit on so smug and presumptuous a title," Ben observed years later. In the pamphlet, Ben made a statement that surprised and puzzled his colleagues and clients alike. "If a common stock is a good investment, it is also a good specu-lation," Ben wrote. He reasoned that if a company was so sound that its stock carried little risk of loss, the company also must present excellent chances for future gains. It is easier for a company to build a profitable empire on a solid foundation than on a shaky one.

Ben also turned around his own statement. A speculation, he taught, cannot be a good investment, because speculation is based on anecdote rather than actuality. The absence of verifi-cation pushes the risk far too high.

The first part of Ben's philosophy was easier to live by in the early 1920s when a bull market was in its infancy. At the top of a rising market, it becomes difficult to find any stock—even that of a first-rate company—that does not involve some sig-nificant element of price risk. But again, at the top of a bull market, potential future gains are limited, so Ben's philosophy endures even today.[17]

OOPS!

Yet another one of Ben's early circulars offered a detailed statistical comparison of all the exchange-listed tire and rubber stocks. Ajax Tire and Rubber Company, according to Ben, ap-peared to be the best buy among them. The president of Ajax, within a few days, called on Ben at his office and Ben immedi-ately wished that he had met him before distributing the report. The president's message was not a positive one. Not long afterward, Ajax Tire filed for bankruptcy.

Even though he could occasionally make a miscall, Ben's reputation as a money manager, and especially that of an innovator and a pioneer in the use of arbitrage and hedging, flourished.

DEFENDING THE FLANKS

Ben devised several sophisticated maneuvers to hedge his investments against market risks, techniques that have since become commonplace. For example, if Ben needed to protect an account against declining bond prices and rising stock prices, he might purchase a convertible bond near par value, with the simultaneous sale of calls (a call is the right to buy a specific number of shares at a specific price by a specific date) on an equivalent amount of common stock. If the greater risk was in rising bond prices and falling stock prices, then the bonds would be bought, the stock sold short (a short sale is the sale of a stock not yet owned by the seller, but which he expects to buy at a lower cost at a later date) and a put (the right to sell a specific number of shares at a specific price by a certain date) would be sold. Because the premium prices received for puts and calls were substantial, these procedures could guarantee a good profit regardless of whether the stock increased, decreased or remained constant in value. These hedging moves have since become a major part of the option or futures exchanges.

Ben's reputation spread and a growing number of clients opened private accounts for which Ben charged 25 percent of the share of the cumulative net profits after deducting any losses.

A PROUD UNCLE RETURNS

Among the private investors was his uncle, Maurice Gerard. Gerard had relocated in Chicago where he made a comfortable fortune as a management consultant. Still in his early 50s, Gerard decided to retire and return to New York in 1922.

"Chicago was our home. I was born there, was content with my school and playmates," recalls Rhoda Sarnat. "Nevertheless, my Dad decided we had to move to New York City. Apparently, he felt he needed to be near the action and near Ben." Her father had placed all of his investment money with his prodigy nephew.

A DAUGHTER ARRIVES

In the midst of all this investment activity, Ben took the time to become a naturalized U.S. citizen and in 1921 to welcome a second child, Marjorie. Marjorie showed all the intelligence and spark of her older brother Newton, and though she was graced with her father's affection she was, after all, a girl. In her father's eyes, females were emotional in nature and therefore had limited potential. Newton, a boy, was destined to be a rational thinker.

Nevertheless, Ben was a loving parent to Marjorie, and she believes that she was fortunate to have been a child when he was at his best as a father. Marjorie recalls strolling around the reservoirs in Central Park with her father. "He was very dapper and carried a cane," she remembers. She was proud of Ben and felt secure that he was an important man, not only to her, but to the whole world.

Rhoda Sarnat also recalls happy years as part of a close-knit family. A little on the uncoordinated side, Ben nonetheless was very energetic and took the children on adventurous outdoor excursions. Rhoda, who was closer to the age of Ben's children than to her cousin, enjoyed those outings.

"One summer, when I was a little girl, the two families went to Hewlett, Long Island," Rhoda said. Hazel Graham yearned for their own cottage where the family could spend summers and weekends, but Ben refused. He preferred to rent. It was among the topics they often argued about.

Certainly money was not the issue. From his straight investments and from his hedge operations, Ben continued to do well.

DANCING DOWN WALL STREET

New York was feeling the pressures of Prohibition and while young people everywhere were cynical and rebellious, these were golden years for the Grahams. For the third time, Ben was tempted away from Newburger, Henderson & Loeb, with whom he had now served for nine years. In 1923, a group of clients and friends, impressed with Ben's acumen, proposed the formation of a $250,000 account. More money would be added later if the fund performed well. The initial investors included several members of the Julius Rosenwald family, an early partner in Sears, Roebuck and Company. Under the agreement, Ben could bring in other accounts as part of the original capital. Ben's salary was set at $10,000 per year. The investors would receive at least a 6-percent return, and above that, Ben would be entitled to 20 percent of the profits.

ON HIS OWN

The New York Stock Exchange recently had tightened its rules on the amount of underlying capital required by its member firms, and because Ben's arbitrage operations had brought in so much additional investment money to Newburger, the firm could not accommodate the new operation. Furthermore, Ben's operation had moved beyond the traditional scope of his employer, a firm that still earned most of its money from commissions on securities transactions and from interest charged on loans to its margin accounts. Ben was allowed to leave the company to go out on his own, but Newburger agreed to let him use an office there, in turn for doing his securities transactions through them.

CHAPTER 3

Pushing a Poker Hand
for All It's Worth

"Ben didn't need any gilding. He had a lot of gold in him."

—Irving Kahn[1]

The 1920s were born on a razzmatazz note when Woodrow Wilson, disheartened by his attempts to create a permanent peace, passed the presidency to happy-natured but ineffectual Warren G. Harding. Sick of war and world social problems, Americans turned their thoughts to all things fresh and fearless. Sigmund Freud and Albert Einstein exploded intellectual thinking with astounding new ideas. Women bobbed their locks and raised their hemlines. Handsome and daring Charles Lindbergh redefined distance by flying nonstop from New York to Paris. Prohibition handed the country over to mobsters such as Scarface Al Capone and George "Bugs" Moran. In New York, Eugene O'Neill's intense psychological dramas drew crowds, and dandies motored about in Niagara Blue roadsters and Arabian Sand phaetons.

These were exhilarating times for the U.S. economy and for anyone connected with the stock market. Following a slump in 1920 and 1921, the gross national product (GNP) soared from $74 billion to $104.4 billion by 1929. Corporate profits also skyrocketed and, thanks to the ingenuity of the assembly line, manufacturing production also spiraled. U.S. Steel became so efficient it was able to reduce its workday from 12 to 8 hours, hire 17,000 additional workers and still stockpile money. The securities markets, powered by these heady events, took wing.

BUILDING ON A FIRM FOUNDATION

Graham, the man who eventually would be venerated as "the father of security analysis" and the mastermind of "value investing," was 25 years old at the dawn of the decade. Already a six-year veteran of Wall Street, Graham had dazzled colleagues and clients with his hard work, acumen and integrity. He took another step forward when he left Newburger and began his own company.

THE GRAHAR FUND

The Dow Jones Industrial Average was at a tender 95 when Grahar Corporation, Ben's first stab at independence, kicked off operations on June 1, 1923. The company was named for Graham, its 29-year-old money manager, and Louis Harris, a luggage store owner, and the major investor. Grahar was a private fund, or one in which investors were gathered from among friends and other contacts, but no offering was made to the general public. Ben was able to draw about $500,000 in this way. He, as a result, was not the dominant shareholder.

"My own participation was very small," Ben explained. "I had very little money."[2] While some shareholders held large blocks of Ben's companies, no individual had such a large block that he controlled investment policy. That remained in Ben's hands.

Ben concentrated on finding either deeply undervalued securities, overvalued stocks that he might sell short or promising arbitrage opportunities.

DU PONT–GM ARBITRAGE

One of Ben's first trades was based on the close ownership relationship between the Du Pont Corporation and General Motors (GM). Pierre du Pont, (the du Pont family spells its name differently from the company), under his presidency, used surplus cash to buy a large block of GM stock for his explosives and chemical company. Subsequently, du Pont became chairman of GM in 1920. Du Pont's company history dates back to the American revolution, and even in the 1920s, the company held massive assets and dominated several industries, both in military and industrial manufacturing. Despite this, Du Pont was selling on the stock exchange for no more than the value of its GM shares. Basically, the market either overvalued the GM shares or did not recognize the worth of Du Pont's own operations.

When Ben spotted this imbalance, he bought Du Pont and simultaneously sold short seven times as many shares of General Motors. As Ben expected it would, the market soon corrected the misconception and Du Pont's price rose. Grahar sold the Du Pont shares and took its profit and then closed out the short position in GM. There was no risk in this arrangement, because if the imbalance was corrected by a decline in the price of GM, Ben would have made his profit by exercising the short position. Eventually, Du Pont and General Motors were forced into an arm's-length relationship by antitrust actions.

Ben's best investments were based on finding inconsistencies such as the price of Du Pont stock. He bet on the likelihood that the market eventually would see the error of its ways. Yet he always recognized the possibility that either the market would continue to be blind for a long time or that some other unexpected event would intervene. These are the inherent risks in all stock market investments.

SHORTING SCHRAFFT'S

Ben's calculations did not play out favorably every time, perhaps leading to his preference later on to be diversified into an extraordinary number of shareholdings.

At one point, Ben decided that Shattuck Corporation, the owner of the popular Schrafft's restaurant chain, was overly popular with shareholders. He sold short several hundred shares of Shattuck. Grahar's shareholder group had been holding a weekly lunch meeting at the restaurant, but after the short sale, felt it no longer was proper to do so. Time passed, but the stock market's passion for Shattuck did not. In fact, the share price continued to climb. Finally, the group closed out the short position, took a $10,000 loss and went back to lunching at Schrafft's. Ultimately, the company went downhill and sold out to a private investor.

A GROWING FAMILY

If things were going well with his career, they seemed equally comfortable at home. Ben pampered his widowed mother, providing her with a limousine to get around the city. In 1925, a second daughter, Elaine, was born, joining brother Newton and sister Marjorie. Marjorie remembers that the cozy nursery partners did not actually care much for their Central Park duplex at the Beresford, though, as cousin Rhoda Sarnat explained, it was very "hotsy-totsy." The posh two-story duplex had a sweeping staircase and a lovely terrace with a view of the park. Because a terrace was such a treat, the children were expected to want to play there. The callow young Grahams disagreed, Marjorie recalled, and badgered their parents to let them frolic in the park itself.

Even if they felt put upon by not being able to play in Central Park, unlike their father had done, the Graham children were growing up in a world of stability, security and comfort. There was no reason to believe it would ever be different.

ATTEMPT AT RESTRUCTURING

The bull market continued its stampede, and everyone seemed to be making money. It was common for brokers, then called customers' men or registered representatives, to run discretionary investment accounts of their own on the side. The profits would be evenly split, but the losses accrued to the client. His colleagues convinced Ben that he was foolish to manage his fund for such a paltry percentage of the earnings. Though no investor was in a position to guide investment policy, compensation was another matter. Accordingly, he proposed a new arrangement to the predominant investor, Louis Harris, in which Ben would give up his salary. After the first 6 percent of profits, however, he would earn 20 percent on the first 20 percent, 30 percent on the next 30 percent and 50 percent on the balance.

The profits then would be divided in the following way:

Return on Investment	Investor's Portion	Graham's Portion
6%	6%	0%
26	22	4
56	43	13
100	65	35[3]

As the chart shows, Grahar investors would receive a higher percentage of the profits than previously when returns were low and a gradually smaller percentage as profits rose. The incentive for Ben to turn in a top performance was built into the split. Even at the maximum, however, Ben's share was less than the customers' man was typically receiving.

GRAHAR REPLACED BY THE JOINT ACCOUNT

Despite the obvious advantages, Harris rejected the proposal and the two agreed to dissolve the corporation. When Grahar wrapped up at the end of 1925, the Dow had burst through the 100 barrier and rose 79 percent in just 18 months. Grahar investors collected a sizable profit on their funds.

Exact returns on the Grahar fund are not known, but they were good enough that a number of Ben's friends willingly contributed $450,000 to launch the Benjamin Graham Joint Account. Ben's compensation was basically the same as he had proposed to Harris. The new venture began on January 1, 1926. Between 1925 and 1928, the Joint Account delivered an average annual return of 25.7 percent, compared with 20.2 percent for the Dow Jones Industrials. Three years after the Benjamin Graham Joint Account was established—by the start of 1929—the fund had grown to $2,500,000. Much of that gain represented capital appreciation rather than additional contributions. These excellent returns were achieved with limited risk.

NEWMAN BECOMES A PARTNER

In the meantime, however, Ben's business was expanding in other ways. He added a partner, who took the burden of management from his shoulders and allowed him to do what he did best—figuring out new and better ways to reap investment returns. Ben originally asked Douglass Newman to join him at his small investment firm. His boyhood chum turned him down, recommending his brother Jerome for the job instead. The Newman brothers also had attended Columbia, where Jerry had gone on to law school. After graduation, Jerry Newman went to work for his wife's father in the textile industry for several years. He soon grew impatient with running the family business while his father-in-law, Elias Reiss, spent six months in Europe, only to become an office boy again when Reiss returned.

"He quit in a huff," says Howard "Mickey" Newman, Jerry's son. Jerry, who was two years younger than his new boss, took the job with Ben for the salary of $5,000 per year. Ben quickly recognized Jerry's knack for business management and suggested a change. "He came to my Dad and said, 'You shouldn't be working for me. We should be 50-50 partners,'" Mickey Newman explained. Thus, the bond between the original "Ben and Jerry" was cemented. Despite the fact that Ben often became so tired of Jerry's relentless bargaining techniques that he had to leave the room, the match proved to be brilliant. Ben was the president and Newman was vice president and treasurer in a partnership that sustained and prospered for 30 years.

A NETWORK STRENGTHENS

The remarkable loyalty of both Graham's business contacts and his investors was becoming apparent. Many of the Joint Account clients had been investors in Ben's earlier pools, but he also attracted new investors in unexpected ways. Robert J. Marony, who Ben first met in 1919 when he published the pessimistic report on the Chicago, Milwaukee & St. Paul Railroad where Marony was financial vice president, became a substantial investor and finally a director of Graham-Newman.

THE VICHY REUNION

Business was going so well that Ben was too busy to join in when his mother's family scheduled a family reunion in the ancient spa town of Vichy, France. The 11 Gesundheit children never had been reunited since their scattering many years earlier. Dora Graham, her brother Maurice Gerard and young Rhoda Gerard were among those who made the trip abroad to see brothers, sisters, aunts, uncles and cousins, most of them for the first time.

Rhoda recalls that several of the family members were very well off, while others were not. Money to pay for the reunion was collected and placed in a central fund, with each family contributing as much as they felt they were able. Gerard and other wealthy family members made up any shortfall. The cousins all stayed in a modest hotel so that nobody would feel out of place—all except Aunt Dora. Financed by her son Ben, the flamboyant Dora lodged at the city's finest resort.

Money was not the only problem encountered at the reunion. The children had been split up at very young ages and now were raising their families on every continent except South America. They spoke many different languages, and in some cases, brothers and sisters could not converse with one another. Uncle Maurice made up a chart in which the languages each spoke was listed. Translators were matched to help those who could not converse with one another. A person who spoke both English and Polish could interpret for someone who spoke only one language or the other. Translations were made between Spanish, German, French, Yiddish and other tongues. It was a happy gathering, which was fortunate, because it was one that never would be repeated.

Back in New York, Ben continued to work hard for himself, for Uncle Maurice and for his other investors. All through the 1920s, financial data continued to be scarce and Ben searched many different sources for more detailed information, including government documents from numerous agencies.

SUNSHINE IS NOT WELCOME

A favorite "mystique" stock of the day was Consolidated Gas of New York, which owned the profitable New York Edison Company. While Consolidated reported dividends from Edison, it did not divulge the utility company's earnings. The Edison earnings were the hidden element underlying Consolidated's genuine value.

"To my surprise, I discovered that these hush-hush figures were actually on file each year with the Public Service Commission of the state," Ben said. "It was a simple matter to consult the records and to present the true earnings of Consolidated Gas in a magazine article." *The Magazine of Wall Street* published the piece.

Not everyone saw the point in what Ben was trying to do. "Ben," said one of his older friends, "you may think you are a great guy to supply those missing figures, but Wall Street is going to thank you for nothing. Consolidated Gas with the mystery is both more interesting and more valuable than ex-mystery. You youngsters who want to stick your noses into everything are going to ruin Wall Street."[4]

STRIKING OIL

Ben was not to be deterred. In 1926, when examining the annual report of the ICC for information about railroads, he came upon an interesting batch of statistics about competing carriers, oil pipeline companies. A footnote indicated the figures had been gleaned from one company's annual report to the ICC. His curiosity tweaked, Ben wrote to the commission to request a blank copy of the report so that he could see what data the pipeline companies were required to submit. As soon as he saw the 50-page document, Ben knew he had struck gold. The report contained key financial information that he had never been able to find before. Ben hopped a train and headed for Washington, D.C. (Life was indeed cumbersome before copy machines and faxes.)

All eight of the pipeline companies that carried oil to refineries at the time were spin-off companies from John D. Rockefeller's Standard Oil Trust after 1913. Rockefeller's original

Standard Oil had been split up into 31 different companies by the U.S. Supreme Court and the Justice Department in 1911 in response to the Sherman Antitrust Act. The Standard Oil breakup was a publicly rancorous and prolonged case, provoked by a widely acclaimed muckraking book, *History of the Standard Oil Company,* by Ida Tarbell.

THE ROCKEFELLER GRIP

The eight oil pipeline companies were fairly small and published only the barest-bones income statement and balance sheet, perhaps because the largest shareholder in the companies was the Rockefeller Trust. The two Wall Street firms that specialized in trading the former Standard Oil subsidiaries refused to supply additional data.

At the ICC, Ben discovered that each of the pipeline companies was sitting on substantial amounts of investment-grade railroad bonds. The value of the bonds sometimes exceeded the total market value of the pipeline company itself. Because each of the companies had comparatively small gross revenues and healthy profit margins, there seemed to be no reason to hold the bonds in reserve. This anomaly provided the ideal special value Ben became famous for locating, a company that was trading at a price well below its actual asset value. The margin of safety for investments such as the pipeline companies was expansive, to say the least.

HOARDING ASSETS

The gem among the pipeline companies was Northern Pipe Line. Its shares traded at $65. The company paid a $6 dividend, a payout amply covered by earnings, for a dividend yield of 9 percent. The company's hidden asset was a cache of high-grade bonds equivalent to $95 per share.

The public was under the false impression that the pipeline companies were on a downtrend because of the advent of large railroad oil tank cars that were cutting into their business. The companies had reduced their dividends in recent years, an action that contributed to the erroneous perception.

THE BLACK KNIGHT

What followed was a battle between a perceptive young investment manager—Ben—and an entrenched corporate establishment—a spin-off of Standard Oil. It was the old guard versus the new. What Ben did next was considered less than gentlemanly by traditionalists in the investment arena.

Cautiously and doggedly, Ben began buying shares of Northern Pipe Line. Soon he had acquired 2,000 of the company's 40,000 shares. Next to the Rockefeller Trust's 23-percent interest, this small amount made his the largest shareholding.

PERSUASION

When he owned enough shares to fortify his claim, Ben arranged to meet with the president of the pipeline company at the Standard Oil Building. Ben laid out his point of view. It was unnecessary, he said, for Northern Pipe Line to hold $3.6 million in bond investments when the company's gross revenues were only $300,000. Ben explained that he believed that surplus cash of $90 per share should be distributed to the shareholders. The president responded with several road-weary arguments: The railroad bonds were necessary to cover the company's $100 par value of stock; the funds might be required in case the pipeline needed replacement sometime in the future; and the present pipeline might need to be extended.

The president's parting shot was a rejoinder exactly like one shareholder advocates have heard the decades over. "The pipeline business," the president said, "is a complex and specialized business about which you know very little, but in which we have spent a lifetime. We know better than you what is best for the company and for the stockholders." And he closed with the classic assertion, "If you don't approve of our policies, you should sell your shares."[5]

KNOCKED FROM HIS HORSE

Ben was not ready to give up so easily. He asked that he be able to present his proposition at the January, 1927, Northern Pipe Line annual meeting. He traveled to Oil City, Pennsylvania, for the meeting, but because he was a novice at the game, he overlooked an essential detail. Ben did not bring another shareholder to second his motion. After a brief, perfunctory session, the meeting was dismissed.

A SECOND ASSAULT

Again, Ben would not be spurned. With the partnership's capital, he began buying additional shares of Northern Pipe Line. He then hired a knowledgeable and respected attorney. The new strategy had two parts. He would solicit proxies in favor of his resolution to reduce corporate capitalization and to return the surplus to shareholders in cash. Additionally, he would try to capture two seats on the company's board of directors. Pennsylvania's corporation regulations allowed mandatory cumulative voting, which was to the advantage of minority shareholders. Cumulative voting lets a shareholder cast all of his votes for a single board candidate, rather than to spread total voting rights among all possible seats. It was necessary, therefore, to recruit the vote of only one-sixth of the shares outstanding to elect one director to the five-person board.

Northern Pipe Line, to Ben's surprise, supplied a list of shareholders without a lawsuit—perhaps because they did not yet take Ben seriously. Each side sent letters to shareholders outlining their positions—the chairman's being exactly the one presented to Ben at their first meeting.

To promote their cause, Ben and his associates paid personal calls on the Northern Pipe Line's major shareholders, among them the financial adviser for the Rockefeller Foundation. The adviser told the rebels that the foundation did not interfere in the operations of the companies in which it held investments.

THE SMOKE OF BATTLE

When the 1928 annual meeting came around, Ben attended with proxies for 38 percent of the shares, which readily guaranteed the election of two directors. Northern Pipe Line's president proposed that the slate include any two members of Ben's group, except for Ben himself. That suggestion did not fly, and Ben and one of the attorneys won seats on the board, becoming the first people not directly associated with Standard Oil and Rockefeller family interests to be named as directors to one of the company's former subsidiaries.

Within a few weeks, Ben achieved nearly complete victory. Northern Pipe Line's president invited him to a meeting, where he explained that he had never actually objected to Ben's proposal, that he had merely felt the timing was wrong. He acquiesced to a special distribution of $70 per share to stockholders. Ben later learned that when the Rockefeller Foundation had returned its proxies, it had notified management that it would like to see a distribution of as much capital as the company felt it could release.

TRIUMPH

Taking the distribution of $70 per share and the price of Northern's shares afterward, Ben's profit exceeded $100 per share, a return on investment of nearly 54 percent. Standard Oil's affiliates, however, had not seen the end of Graham-Newman.

Ben began buying shares in another Standard Oil spin-off company, National Transit Company. In addition to running an oil pipeline, National Transit manufactured pumps. Again, the company held a chunk of unproductive assets that Ben believed should be used either to enhance the share price of the company or returned to investors. Again resisting the idea, management proposed its own unproductive plan to utilize the bonds. With the help of other interested investors and the Rockefeller Foundation, a consequential distribution of cash was made to the shareholders. In time, the other pipeline companies followed suit with their own distributions.

A LIQUIDATOR

Though Ben may not have been comfortable with the characterization, Sy Winters of Lehman Brothers, one of Ben's early students and business associates, described Ben as "one of the earliest liquidators. When a corporation is sitting on a lot of assets and earning nothing, it becomes a target. The value is not being used in the business," Winters explained. "You have to flush them out, one way or another."

Because of the growth of the Benjamin Graham Joint Account, Ben had been forced to move from the rented space at Newburger, Henderson & Loeb. His larger quarters were in a building at 60 Beaver Street that also housed the offices of H. Hentz & Company. Dr. Herman Baruch, younger brother of the great speculator and midcentury sage Bernard Baruch, was a partner of H. Hentz.

THE BARUCH ALLIANCE

Ben and Baruch soon became acquainted, and as a result Baruch and his clients had joined with Ben in buying National Transit shares. Baruch realized a sizable profit from the deal, and in appreciation, Herman Baruch gave Ben the use of his fully manned yacht for a week.

Ben organized a luxurious sailing party, which Ben's daughter Marjorie remembers with great pleasure. "I was about eight and I was so excited," she recalled, "I still have the visual memory of the sailing and of the yacht itself. It was thrilling!"

Marjorie had another reason to be grateful for a vacation. The cruise was a happier time for a family that still was buried in mourning. Her older brother Newton, a bright, healthy and happy boy—a child of shining promise—the year earlier, 1927, had developed an earache. Very quickly, the minor illness developed into meningitis, and without the benefit of antibiotics, Newton suddenly died.

DESPAIR AT HOME

The entire family was sunk in grief for years afterward. Always a reserved person, Ben seemed to withdraw from his family, and to shy away from future emotional entanglement.

Marjorie, who had just started school, was frightened and dismayed by her nine-year-old brother's death. Her parents, themselves so overwhelmed with anguish, were of little comfort. "I would wake up at night and go to my grandmother," she recalled. Her mother's mother, "who slept in the attic room at our summer place would let me come to bed with her and comfort me."

The little girl had night terrors and wanted to sleep with all the doors open and the lights on in her room for such a long time that Hazel Graham finally took her to a psychological counselor. A practical man, the counselor simply said, "Why not let her?" The immediate effects passed, but Marjorie says the rest of her life she felt "death could happen to anyone at anytime. He died in April, 1927."

Elaine Graham believes that Ben never actually recovered from the loss of his first son. "He used to say children were hostages to fortune," she recalled, and after that, he was kind and thoughtful, but kept a prudent distance from his children and even later his grandchildren.

His desolation over the death of the boy he adored was apparent even to Ben's clients; he seemed to seek escape from the pain by burying himself more deeply in his work. Ben's reputation for business acumen spread swiftly and his dealings became increasingly sophisticated. Again, however, Ben was drawn into activities that tested his integrity and helped define his ethical base.

FIREWORKS AT UNEXCELLED

One of these episodes occurred when a trader from a large over-the-counter firm approached Ben with an elaborate strategy to seize control of Unexcelled Manufacturing Company. Unexcelled was the country's premier fireworks company. The company's shares were selling at $9, which was less than its working capital and only six times its earnings. Under the plan of the aggressors, the president of the company, an older gentleman, would be replaced by a younger vice president and Ben would become financial vice president of Unexcelled, on a part-time basis. Ben's partnership agreed to 10,000 shares and sought to find appropriate investors for the remainder. Bernard Baruch, who after Ben's experience with Herman had taken increasing interest in Ben's activities, bought the balance of the block of shares.

CRUEL REALITY

It was not until Unexcelled's annual meeting, where the voting and the coup would take place, that Ben first met Unexcelled's president. Ben suddenly felt troubled at his role in a plot to unseat an innocent man who had run a company for 25 years. It did not sit well with him. Because of changes in the law regarding fireworks and other business contingencies, the Unexcelled investment was not unexcelled. In fact, it worked out very poorly.

While Ben did serve on corporate boards later, he was reluctant to do so unless he felt welcome. Walter Schloss recounts the story of Ben and Bernard Baruch buying shares in Northern Pacific (Railroad) until they became the company's largest shareholder. Ben visited the company and asked to be placed on the board of directors. The company made it clear it was not interested and Ben withdrew. Not long afterward, industrialist Norton Simon demanded a seat on the board with only a small percentage of shares and the company conceded.

Seat or no board seat, the Northern Pacific investment worked out well. The company struck oil in the Williston Basin of North Dakota and the price shot up.

"Ben didn't buy it because they were going to find oil in the Williston Basin," Walter Schloss mused. "He bought it because it was a cheap stock."[6]

A DREAM OF AUTHORSHIP

Ben had accumulated nearly a dozen years of experience on Wall Street and his career was moving exceedingly well when he had a new idea. Ben's magazine writing had met with success, so he began thinking about a more demanding project. Ben believed that there was a need for a book laying down the fundamental principles of investing and he felt that he had something worthwhile to say about the subject.

Ben figured that if he could teach a class on investment principles, the classroom would provide an ideal framework for organizing his material and testing his presentation. It was both customary and convenient for Wall Street practitioners to study and to instruct at the nearby New York University's

Graduate School of Finance. Ben chose another way. Never mind that it would mean a long afternoon subway ride from the Graham-Newman office on Beaver Street to Morningside Heights, Ben applied for a position at his alma mater instead. Columbia accepted his proposal and Ben began teaching in 1928.

BACK TO COLUMBIA

A notice regarding Ben's class survives in the December 8, 1928, Columbia College class bulletin. The sessions began February 6 and ran through May 25, 1929. "Advanced Security Analysis" met from 7:40 to 9:30 PM, Mondays, in room 305 of Schermerhorn Hall. Leo Stern, who was Ben's assistant at Newburger, Henderson & Loeb, would assist in the classroom. Students could earn three credits for the course.

The class was announced without fanfare. The Wall Street investment manager, according to the catalog description, would teach "Investment theories subjected to practical market tests. Origin and detection of discrepancies between price and value."

The following semester an entry-level class was taught. Even that class presupposed "a general knowledge of investments."

IF YOU TEACH, THEY WILL COME

Though the class was offered for the benefit of undergraduate and graduate students at Columbia, those who worked on Wall Street also were permitted to enroll. Many of them did so because of Ben's reputation for formulating theories that worked well in practical application. Even Columbia faculty members registered for the course with the goal of gaining practical insight into the markets. As usual, these conclusions were based primarily on information gleaned from financial statements.

Ben taught his students to scrutinize bonds and other debt issues for their likelihood to pay their semiannual coupon with full interest and to return the principal at maturity. But he also gave great attention to the more complex subject of stocks, a practice that no doubt appealed to his ambitious young audience. There was little doubt that without rigorous study, stocks could be a highly speculative animal, as events repeatedly proved. But stocks also could be more profitable than bonds. Graham clad his students in the full protective armor of practical knowledge before they made such perilous choices. There was much to learn, he explained, for "The true measure of common stock values, of course, is not found by reference to price movements alone, but by price in relation to earnings, dividends, future prospects and, to a small extent, asset values."[7]

DODD TAKES NOTES

Among the Columbia faculty members in the first class was David L. Dodd, who was asked to record class discussions and transcribe them each week. Dodd had graduated from The Wharton School at the University of Pennsylvania in 1920 and then enrolled at Columbia for his master's degree in economics. After graduation, he worked for three years in the research department at the National Bank of Commerce. Dodd then returned to Columbia to teach.

"Dodd said he wasn't sure if he got to be Ben's assistant because of his request [to get practical experience] or because he had recently married the former secretary of Dean Roswell McCrea," Walter Schloss said. Whatever the reason for being assigned to the recorder's job, Dodd threw himself into the task with precision and vigor.

The classes caught on very quickly. By early 1929, the majority of the working statisticians had heard of Ben's class at Columbia and enrollment jumped to 150 pupils. Some of the students would take the course over and over, primarily because Ben drew examples from the current market pages and many students routinely used the information in their work. Ben required that all his theories meet the test of examples.

A CLASSIC METHOD OF INSTRUCTION

"He used the Harvard case system," explained former student Irving Kahn. "Ben never asked you to believe what he said unless there were concrete examples to support what he said."

ACCOUNTANCY FOR THE INVESTOR

In his book *The Interpretation of Financial Statements,* which was published in 1937, Graham gave a quick sketch of accounting principles, how they apply to the balance sheet and income statement and what investors should glean from corporate books. Ben's lectures at Columbia were built on principles like these:

Working Capital

Working capital, the excess of current assets over current liabilities, is a key measure of a company's strength. Not only is it what a company uses to finance its daily operations, but by examining working capital and its fluctuation over a period of time, an investor can get an idea of management's ability to grow its assets and cope with changing economic conditions.

Cash

This term includes cash proper, marketable securities or any asset that may be used to park money temporarily. A company should not keep any more cash than is needed to transact its usual business, plus a reasonable margin for emergencies—though often it does. "Where the cash holdings are exceptionally large in relation to the market price of the securities, this factor usually deserves favorable investment attention," Graham wrote. "In such a case, the stock may be worth more than the earning record indicates, because a good part of the value is represented by cash holdings which contribute little to the income account. Eventually, the stockholders are likely to get the benefit of these cash assets, either through their distribution or their more productive use in the business."[8]

Corporate raiders have learned this lesson well. Increasingly in recent years, raiders have targeted cash-rich companies so that they can loot them and run. In fact, Ben took advantage of such cases himself. An individual investor who spots the cash cow early enough, however, can profit even from takeover warfare.

Fixed Assets

This includes land, buildings, equipment and office furnishings. Because some assets appreciate over time and others depreciate, the true value of fixed assets is easily confusing. Graham suggested that the insured value of the assets be included in the annual report in a footnote. Though the insured value (likely to be based on replacement costs) is no guarantee of actual market value, it casts further light on the issue.

Intangibles

Even though analysts, including Graham, tend to look askance at intangible assets, he noted that intangibles can have real value. Brands, leaseholds, trademarks and the like are genuine assets and should at least be acknowledged. The "quant," or analyst who concentrates on quantitative factors, always will be uncomfortable with intangibles because their specific worth is impossible to pin down.

Net Current Asset Value

While book value often is thought of as the value of a company if all its assets were sold and the business were liquidated, Graham considered the net current asset value to be a better rough measure of liquidating value. This is because, he said, current assets usually suffer a much smaller loss in liquidation than do the fixed assets. While any company selling below its net current asset value caught Graham's attention, that factor alone was not conclusive evidence that the stock was undervalued. Net current assets are calculated by subtracting current liabilities from current assets.

Thoughts on Par Value

Though the word *par* still is used in relation to stocks, its meaning has become so obscure that it only confuses the individual who happens upon it in a prospectus. It once meant the original price at which a stock sold and therefore was a measure of the shareholder's initial investment and, later, an indication of the growth of the investment over the years. Corporations now assign random par values to shares for bookkeeping purposes only. This seems like a change for the worse from the shareholder's point of view, for par value at one time was an informative number.

An adherent of the Socratic philosophy of instruction, Ben stimulated discussion and guided his students to the correct answer by intense questioning, not only by the professor himself, but by fellow students as well. When a student reached the right conclusion and saw the point Ben was making, the result in many cases was a kind of epiphany.

In 1929, for example, a student who expressed great enthusiasm for the warrants of American and Foreign Power Company was asked to go to the blackboard (all chalkboards were black in those days) to calculate the total market value for the outstanding warrants. American and Foreign Power was a holding company that had been formed to leverage a public-utility empire. The practice of forming utility holding companies had just gained popularity and there was much puzzlement regarding the solidity of the various related offerings. Warrants are tricky to analyze, because they give the right to buy shares of the company at a future date, at a price higher than the current price. The student's computation soon showed that the price of the utility warrants was greater than the stock market value for the entire Pennsylvania Railroad, a genuine blue-chip company in the late 1920s. The degree of speculative excess surrounding American and Foreign Power became immediately apparent to the class.[9]

A NATURAL

The role of teacher seemed to be a natural part of Ben's personality. Marjorie Graham Janis says that her father's ability to debate a point with a young person was unique. She always went away from their discussions with a sense of satisfaction. Even when her notions were the opposite of his, "he took my ideas for what they were worth. He was receptive to hearing about them, and treated me with acceptance and respect."

Nevertheless, she laughed, "as much as I thought I'd learned and as convincing as I thought my arguments were, I never left one of these arguments thinking I'd won. He'd come out ahead. It was marvelous to put myself up against this man!"

Victor Graham's son Richard recalled that while it was always illuminating to talk to Ben, his uncle had little tolerance for small talk.

"You were always trotting with him," Richard Graham said. "He didn't speak especially fast, but either you caught what he said or you missed it. He'd give the conversation all his attention—very sharp and intense, but for a limited time. He had a habit of looking at his watch—politely, of course—and saying, 'I think we've spent enough time on this.'"[10]

ASK MR. WEBSTER

While at home with his children, in the office and in the classroom, Ben took the school marm's view that young people should look up answers for themselves. Jerome Newman's son Mickey recalls that when he was confirmed on his 15th birthday, Ben gave him a large library edition of Webster's dictionary. He inscribed it, "May you never be at a loss for words . . . Uncle Ben."

Irving Kahn never forgot the time that Ben sent him—an adult—to the dictionary. "This ad shows a $10 million tranche of a French government issue being offered," Kahn had said to Graham. "What does tranche mean?" Graham pointed to the dictionary, where Kahn discovered that a tranche was a slice, such as a portion of cake. In the advertisement, it referred to a slice or a portion of the underwriting. "If I had told you the answer," Ben said to Kahn, "you might have soon forgotten it. Now you will remember."[11]

THE PAYOFF

Ben's long hours of work were paying off handsomely. "My father really was quite wealthy before the crash," remembers Ben Graham's daughter, Elaine Graham Hunt.

The 1920s had been the snappy years, the sophisticated years, the triumphant years for Ben. But they were drawing to an end. Before they were over, they would become the sobering years for the Wall Street wunderkind—and one day its most scholarly citizen—Benjamin Graham.

CHAPTER 4

The Crash—1929 and the Great Depression

"Sooner or later a crash is coming and it may be terrific."

—Roger Babson, economist, early 1929

B en's relationship with the Baruch brothers was growing stronger. He made a number of recommendations that pleased the most esteemed and successful member of this first family of finance, Bernard. Though the market scrambled higher and higher, many out-of-favor and fledgling companies still presented enticing investment opportunities. Pepperell Manufacturing Company, Plymouth Cordage and a leading baby carriage manufacturer, Heywood & Wakefield, were among them. Though Baruch invested profitably in the stocks recommended by Graham, Baruch seemed to think that for the younger man to be associated with such a respected name was payment enough.

Then, early in 1929, Baruch invited Ben to his office for a conference. The 57-year-old financier explained to Ben that he wanted to take a partner. At his age, he said, he thought it was wise to share his burdens and his profits with a younger man. Obviously, Baruch had no idea that he would live vigorously until age 95, continually increasing his personal wealth and achieving fame as the "park-bench statesman," respected adviser to several presidents. A millionaire by the time he was 30,

Bernard Baruch multiplied his wealth 30-fold by the end of his long life.

What kept clients in Graham's funds, drew students to his classes and attracted Baruch's attention was Graham's then unique view of security analysis. Until the Securities and Exchange Act of 1934, insider trading was not illegal. It was customary for the great investors to build their wealth by private knowledge, stock tips or other privileged information. Baruch was well connected on the street and got his share of tips. Less well-connected investors followed the leaders like lemmings, hoping they were behind the right animal. Graham was not the slightest prone to follow the crowd. He unflinchingly treated investing as a science. Companies—and the stocks and bonds that they use to raise money—he proved, had some intrinsic value. The great trick was to find out what that value was. Such a deduction could be based only on facts and the unprejudiced analysis of the facts.

A POLITE "NO"

Ben was flattered by Baruch's offer, of course, but it held little appeal. He had just finished a year with a 60-percent return for the Joint Account, compared to a 51-percent return for the DJIA. Ben's personal net profit was more than $600,000. The seasoned 35-year-old Graham saw no reason to become a junior partner in any firm, even that of the esteemed Bernard M. Baruch.

Baruch may have been startled and somewhat dismayed by Graham's rebuff, but before the year was over, he surely realized how fortunate he was to be turned away. Experience and age would show their advantage over youth and enthusiasm.

A DIRE PREDICTION

In their discussions about securities market behavior, Baruch and Graham agreed that stock prices had reached a rarified altitude and that a crash was likely. Between 1921 and 1929, the market had surged by 450 percent, driven in large part by easy margin rules. Stocks could be purchased with as small a down payment as 10 percent of the price, with the rest financed by brokers' loans. In 1928, the last full year of the bull market, the return on the Dow Jones Industrial Average was 51 percent. Baruch pointed out that it made no sense for short-term interest rates to be at 8 percent at a time when the DJIA offered only a 2 percent dividend yield.

"By the law of compensation," Ben agreed, "someday, the reverse should happen."[1]

A SURGING TIDE

When he reflected on events some years later, Ben found it strange that though he sensed danger, he did not completely sell out of the market. Apparently, the young investor did not yet realize that a rising tide floats all boats, including his own. Nonetheless, Ben took most of his usual precautions to protect the Joint Account by selecting undervalued stocks and hedging his investments.

And though he demurred when asked to affiliate with Bernard Baruch in a partnership, there were other prospects on the horizon that challenged and excited Ben.

MAKING PLANS

Investment trusts were gaining in popularity, and the H. Hentz partners thought they should have such an operation and they wanted Graham to run it. The earliest investment trusts were set trusts, with a fixed portfolio of predetermined common stocks. Much like today's index funds, the shareholders held a pro rata portion of this unchanging group. H. Hentz had in mind the English version of the trust, which was a managed list of stocks. H. Hentz and Ben would direct the $25 million fund for a fee, plus commission on the sale of shares and the other business of the trust.

The prospects were superb for the account, considering the mood of the late 1920s. The soaring market had attracted experienced as well as novice investors. Tales circulated of a modestly paid nurse gaining $30,000 on her stock investment and a broker's valet pocketing a quarter of a million dollars. The catchword of the day was a "New Era," an expression based on the belief that the United States had entered an epoch of permanent growth and prosperity.

BLUSTERY WEATHER

The organization of the Hentz-Graham trust took more time than expected, however, and by September of 1929, when the fund was ready to go, cracks were spidering across the stock market. The fissures widened and spread so swiftly that Ben soon found himself too busy to even think about the new fund.

THE SUDDEN STORM

As usual, the closer to a top, the more unpredictable stock prices become. There was market turbulence in late summer and early autumn, but the precipitous fall came on Black Tuesday, October 29, 1929. That single day of horror cost the stock market $14 billion. The Dow Jones Industrials, which began its ascent in 1921 at around 75, peaked in 1929 at 381 and within weeks, plummeted to below 200. By 1932, it scraped bottom at 41.[2]

While Ben's principles of value investing cushioned the fall, they were not keenly honed enough so that he was able to avoid trouble altogether. In the $2.5 million Joint Account, Ben carried a large number of arbitrage and hedging operations. These involved about $2.5 million in long positions and an equal amount in short sales. Additionally, there were about $4.5 million in securities, of which $2 million was bought on margin. In keeping with his usual practices, Ben had purchased stocks that were bargain-priced, but out-of-favor issues.

MANY ERR, BUT NOT BARUCH

It was the vulnerability of the smaller stocks and the margin calls that ambushed Ben, along with thousands of other investors. Bernard Baruch, according to various accounts, was virtually out of the securities market by October when the deluge came.

Ben's problems with the Joint Account were intensified by modifications that he had made to his hedging operation.

Generally, to protect an investment, he would purchase a convertible preferred stock and sell short the same amount of common stock. If the market rose, Ben would have a long-term gain and a short-term loss. In cases where the market went down, the common declined faster than the preferred, and the hedge could be undone at a nice profit. When the market would recover, however, as it always had, Ben bought the convertible preferred again to reestablish the hedge. Often, the preferred had to be bought at a higher price than it had been sold earlier. Lulled by a long bull market, the practice seemed to unnecessarily cut into profits. Ben began exercising only half of the hedge, covering the short position but holding on to the preferred shares, or at other times, covering the short by only half as much common stock as was necessary to undo the hedge. The adaptations worked well for a long time, despite the elevated risk. Even as the market collapsed, Ben did not sell the convertible preferred shares that he had bought for a hedge, because their prices seemed abnormally low. The short cut was almost his undoing.

DANGER

Ben had plenty of company in this menacing situation. Everyone in the business struggled to understand and cope with the extreme conditions of 1929. Ben was among many shareholders who received a letter from R. H. Scott, President of Reo Motor Car Company, regarding the cause of the company's plunging share price.

"The real answer," Scott wrote, "is that the stock market quotations have ceased, for the time being at least, to have any meaning or value whatever in measuring the worth of a corporate stock."

BEDLAM

The chaos on Wall Street was unbelievable, recalls Lehman Brothers' Sy Winter, who had taken his first job on the Street in 1927. "People who thought they were wealthy discovered they were bankrupt," Winter said. "We didn't go home for six weeks. We stayed in the office, slept there. The bosses paid for our food, and we got $10 for sleeping overnight. We went across the street to a hotel to clean up. They even bought our clothes when we needed something."

A BREATHER

Because the market calmed, then rallied slightly at the end of 1929, many investors believed that they had seen the worst. Ben's Joint Account finished the year with a loss of 20 percent, compared to a 15 percent decline in the Dow Jones Industrials. He apparently was among the optimists, since following the October debacle, Ben was given—and disregarded—a second warning.

AN ANCIENT SAGE

Ben traveled to Florida in early 1930, where he met with a 93-year-old, but keen of mind, retired businessman, John Dix. Dix bombarded Ben with perceptive questions about the New York markets.

"Mr. Graham," Dix said when he heard Ben's answers, "I want you to do something of the greatest importance. Get on the train to New York tomorrow. Sell out your securities. Pay off your debts and return the capital to the partners in the Joint Account. I wouldn't be able to sleep at night if I were in your position."[3] In his polite way, Ben thanked Dix and left, thinking that the old man must be somewhat in his dotage. If he had listened to the elderly gentleman, Ben would have remained a "near millionaire" and both he and his clients would have been spared enormous pain.

A SECOND PLUNGE

The next year, 1930, turned out to be the worst in Ben's entire career. It is to his credit that he survived. Despite the fact that Ben had managed to cover almost all of the short positions, his substantial long positions in stocks with crumbling market prices was accentuated by the $2 million in margin debt. Though the market rally stretched through April, it did not hold. By the end of the year, the Joint Account suffered a 50 percent skid, compared to a 29 percent tumble for the Dow and a 25 percent decline for the S&P 500.

Ben and Jerry struggled along, continuing to pay a distribution of ¼ percent of capital quarterly. However, many strapped or terrified investors withdrew all or part of their funds, which made it even more difficult for Ben to make up his losses. Jerry Newman's son Mickey says that Ben was so discouraged that he was ready to throw in the towel, but his partner insisted that they keep going.

UNCLE MAURICE LEAVES TOWN

Faithful Uncle Maurice Gerard was one of the victims when the Graham-Newman account went down the drain. "We lost $100,000 at that time with Ben," said Rhoda Gerard Sarnat. "As a matter of fact, that's why we moved to California. After 1929, my parents had very little left and we couldn't continue to live in New York City.

"My Dad looked over the world and said to my Mother, 'we can either go to southern California—which was still an infant and things were very, very cheap—or we can go to Belgium.' "

Rhoda's mother chose California, where the family rented a Hollywood bungalow for $40 per month. Rhoda, still a school-aged youngster, loved California. A decade later, when Hitler marched across Europe, the Gerards were desperately glad that they had not returned to the continent.

A FORGIVING FATHER-IN-LAW

Fortunately for Ben and Jerry, Newman's father-in-law Elias Reiss did not hold grudges. Even though Jerry had marched off his job with Reiss in a temper, Reiss was the only person to make a new investment in the Joint Account during the difficult early 1930s. Reiss's $75,000 contribution held Graham-Newman together until permanent relief came.

Though the account continued to lose money, Ben was able to correct his mistakes faster than the market as a whole. Within two years, Ben was narrowing the margin of loss. For the three-year period between 1929 and 1932, the Joint Account lost 70 percent of its value. But in 1931, the Joint Account was down only 16 percent, compared to 48 percent for the DJIA and 44 percent of the S&P 500. In 1932, the Joint Account declined only 3 percent, versus 17 percent of the DJIA and 8 percent of the S&P. The fact that Ben and Jerry were able to keep the account going during those treacherous years set them apart from other small Wall Street firms, most of which collapsed and vanished.

BAD DREAMS OF DEBT

Ben never forgot the punishment he had suffered for carrying a 44 percent margin debt in the Joint Account. Graham said that he realized that prices were too high in the late 1920s. He felt, however, that he had good investments. He had purposely stayed away from speculative issues, but he owed money, which was a mistake. "I didn't repeat that error after that," Ben said.[4]

Additionally, though Ben felt that any analyst worth his salt could have seen the market crash coming, the massive economic collapse that followed surprised and ravaged everyone.

THE ECONOMY BREAKS

At the Great Depression's peak, one-third of the United States labor force was unemployed. Between 1929 and 1933, the gross national product plunged from $103 billion to $55 billion. Graham struggled to contain the losses of his investment fund, which he and his partner Jerome Newman eventually succeeded in doing. For five years while they worked out the problems, Graham and Newman managed their investment operation without pay.[5]

The distress Ben felt at what had happened deeply affected the family. "He felt the difficulty very strongly," said his daughter Marjorie. "So many family members and close friends had invested with Ben. It was a big responsibility for him. How terrible it was!"

UNGILDING THE LIFESTYLE

He no longer could pay for the limousine to squire his mother around Manhattan. He moved his wife and children to a smaller and darker flat at a less impressive address.

Though she was barely four years old when the stock market crash of 1929 struck, Elaine Graham Hunt recalls her first luxurious home, then her little-girl confusion as the family moved to less-imposing quarters in a different neighborhood. Their new home at the Eldorado at 91st Street and Central Park West was a comfortable apartment by any standard but lacked the grace the family had grown accustomed to. The Grahams got a bargain on the rent because the owner, a friend of the family, could find no tenant who was able to pay the full price. To the children, the new apartment had certain joyous aspects. Their new home did not have a veranda, so they were obliged to play in the park itself. That made them very happy.

Marjorie remembers depression-era stories about brokers jumping from windows and recollects strolls through Central Park where she saw the cabins of homeless people. The most important aspects of her life did not change, however. "To me," Marjorie said, "school mattered the most. I went to the Lincoln School of Teacher's College. I had close friends there and good teachers. I was able to continue." Hazel Mazur Graham made certain that the children were well educated by returning to work. Both of Marjorie's parents valued their children's achievements in school.

"Grades were very important to me," Marjorie noted. "I remember once I came home with a good report and showed it to Ben. He called me his 'Blue Ribbon mayonnaise' girl. Blue Ribbon mayonnaise was a popular product at the time."

A RAY OF HAPPINESS

There came another small blessing during these difficult times—the birth of "little" Newton in 1929. This second son was named for the beloved child whose death two years earlier still haunted the family.

"My father wrote a poem at his birth," Marjorie said. It was entitled, "He has returned from the cold, cold ground."

Little Newton, Marjorie noted, definitely was a "replacement child. But this was a different child. This was a child with a lower threshold of tolerance." Little Newton's life would be very different from his older brother's, but it, too, carried a dark destiny.

"I don't think it was very helpful for my younger brother to be named after an older brother," said Elaine Graham Hunt, who grew up to become a psychologist and teacher at Cambridge University in England.

The Graham governess, who was kept on despite the family's reduced circumstances, did not make the children's life any pleasanter. "We had this horrifying German governess," Marjorie recalled. "We called her Fraulein. She divided the children into Grahams and Mazurs. The first Newton, Elaine and I were Grahams and that was good. The second Newton and Winnie (who was born in 1934) were Mazurs, and that was bad." To Fraulein, the Graham children were rational, but the Mazurs were emotional. Somewhat like Ben, she encouraged the displacement of feelings by logic.

CASTING BREAD UPON THE WATER

Trying times often draw people closer than they ever would become during easier days, and that was the case in Ben's professional life. Robert Heilbrunn, a young man who lost his father a week before the crash of 1929, sought Ben's help in saving his inheritance. In doing so, Heilbrunn initiated a gratifying, lifelong relationship.

"In 1926, I was a student at the New York Military Academy," Heilbrunn said. "When I came home from school, I remember my father telling me he had just met a new young stockbroker by the name of Benjamin Graham. He was going into kinds of investments my father had never heard of. My father said, 'that young man will be a millionaire some day.'"

Young Heilbrunn graduated from prep school and continued on to the University of Pennsylvania Wharton School. He had been there only briefly when his father suddenly died. Heilbrunn was obliged to abandon college and take over his father's leather business. Because of the cataclysmic events around him, however, Heilbrunn's stock portfolio tumbled and the leather business suffered a serious setback as well.

"I was wracking my brain to see what I could do to help myself," Heilbrunn continued. "I recalled my father's conversation about Ben Graham. Easily enough, I found his name in the telephone book and called him.

BUT WHAT DO YOU WANT?

"He remembered my father very well, but he sounded unfriendly and rather cold on the telephone," Heilbrunn recalled. "My suspicion was that things were very bad at the time. I think he was afraid I was going to ask him to lend me some money.

"He had a small office downtown, and I went there. I told him about the investments my father had and he studied them for a while, and he said he thought he could be of help. He asked if $25 per month would be all right."

He agreed to the terms and Ben "immediately got to work on the list," Heilbrunn said.

"First, sell the bonds," Ben advised him.

"Why? They're safe!" Heilbrunn replied.

"Yes," Ben said, "But you can't make any money on them."

A MILLIONAIRE AGAIN

By 1932, when the market revived, Heilbrunn was in an ideal position to take advantage of the rising market. He had by then realized he could make more money in investments than in any other way, and he began the tedious process of liquidating the leather business. Once the business was converted to cash, Heilbrunn spent the rest of his life as a full-time investor, managing his own money, participating in Graham's accounts and then moving on to become a client of Warren Buffett in the late 1950s.

Heilbrunn enrolled in Graham's class at Columbia and eventually became a personal friend. When Heilbrunn was married in 1934, Ben attended the wedding. The young investor also became an occasional independent researcher for Ben.

LEARNING BY DOING

"He would send me out to various parts of the country to interview management," Heilbrunn said. "I went to Colt Patent Fire Arms Company in Hartford, Connecticut. I gave Ben a whole report on Gray Telephone Pay Station Company, a manufacturer of patent telephones."

Heilbrunn found plenty of unusual investments to investigate. "In the depression years, there were a great many bankruptcies," he said. "Stocks were being given away at that time. In those cases, protective committees were formed to protect various classes of shareholders. Over time, some of the securities became quite valuable. Railroad bonds were selling at 5 cents and 10 cents on the dollar. Some paid off later in full with accrued interest.

"One of the things that brought on the crash was overbuilding of real estate in New York City. Outstanding mortgage certificates were selling at 25 cents on the dollar," Heilbrunn explained, and this is one area where Graham-Newman was able to make an investment without tying up any capital. "National City Bank offered anyone who owned these bonds to come in, and it would lend you 25 percent on the face value. Because you could buy the bonds for 25 cents, they didn't cost you a nickel. Eventually, the bonds paid off."

"I didn't get paid for the work," Heilbrunn said. "I did it to learn about the business."

STEADY AS SHE GOES

In Heilbrunn's search for sanity in troubled times, Ben's intellect and his unruffled mind gave the young man confidence. "Ben was the first person I met who made sense."

In much the same way that he befriended Heilbrunn and acquired a faithful client, Graham retained the lifelong loyalty of most of his earlier investors. True, some desperate people did withdraw their money, which made it even more strenuous to manage the account. But the majority of Ben's clients stuck it out. When the Benjamin Graham Joint Account finally did recover, all of the Graham-Newman investors saw their capital restored and profits resume.

WE'VE BEEN SAVED

"Ben saw that everyone got everything back," Rhoda Sarnat explained. "He had integrity that wouldn't quit."

Because Newman's father-in-law invested near the market's low, Elias Reiss profited handsomely in the remainder of the 1930s.

In the meantime, Ben and Jerry worked for five years without taking income from the Joint Account. They made ends meet in various ways. Ben still taught at Columbia. He increased his writing, managed some private accounts and together, the pair generated income by living with the circumstances.

NEWMAN'S SINGULAR SKILLS

Survival was due, in large part, to Jerry Newman's talent for liquidations. Heilbrunn, in his dealing with Ben, came to know Jerry Newman rather well.

"Jerry Newman—he wasn't so much a security analyst as he was a shrewd and successful businessman," Heilbrunn explained. Newman was especially in his element during the depression. He was quick to recognize chances to make money by buying troubled companies and liquidating them. Many investors could not stomach liquidations, which required closing plants, firing people and selling assets. It took quick decisions and a ruthless bent of mind. But Newman "was tough, very hard. Ben was more easy going," Heilbrunn said.

SCRAMBLING FOR WORK

Yet their survival also rested on Ben's well-developed ability to ferret out special circumstances, his aptitude for arbitrage and his diverse range of activities. When Warren Buffett became a junior employee at Graham-Newman in the 1950s, he made a detailed study of arbitrage earnings from 1926 to 1956—the entire life span of the company. He discovered that unleveraged returns from arbitrage averaged 20 percent per year. Buffett soaked up the tricks of arbitrage used at Graham-Newman and has used and improved on them ever since. He has not done a detailed calculation of his own arbitrage earnings, but Buffett knows that they have been higher than 20 percent. "Of course," Buffett wrote in his 1988 annual report, "I've operated in an environment far more favorable than Ben's: He had 1929 to 1932 to contend with."[6]

STANDING UP IN COURT

Ben put in long days during the depression utilizing his experience and knowledge in new ways. Some of the extra duties were as fascinating as they were lucrative.

He often served as an expert court witness, testifying in more than 40 cases. Many of these suits came to him through his colleagues at Columbia. On one occasion, the U.S. Treasury contacted the School of Business at Columbia seeking an expert to help resolve a case involving inheritance tax. The executors of the estate claimed that the stock market price of Whitney Manufacturing Company, a maker of chains, was the correct basis for determining the value of the estate. Ben testified that because the shares represented a controlling interest in Whitney, the shares should be treated as a private business. Ben figured that the actual liquidation value of the business was its working capital with no adjustment for plant or equipment. Considering the depressed state of the stock market, the value of the estate thus had a higher value than the heirs would have liked. Using Ben's platform, the Treasury won the case.

Ben sometimes served as a corroborating witness in court for Professor James Bonbright, a Columbia professor who wrote the most authoritative text of the day on property valuation. These often were complex and time-consuming suits involving railroad assets, a subject that Ben had studied since his first days at Newburger. He understood railroads exceedingly well.

Because expert witnesses were paid $100 a day for preparation time plus $250 for each day in court, the testimony became an important source of depression income. Ben's writing also provided additional income.

BEN'S WRITING LEADS THE WAY

Regular readers of *The Magazine of Wall Street* knew Ben's name well and through his writing there, it is possible to trace the path of his progression through the 1920s and early 1930s. In articles written in the run up to the crash, it was clear that he had been thinking seriously about the subjects that would come to distinguish his work throughout his life—how to figure out what a company was truly worth, its future value to a stock market investor and the shareholder's place in the greater scheme of things. His ideas shook readers out of their habitual ways of thinking, and they laid the groundwork for Ben's work in the third decade of the century.

In 1926, Ben wrote about an esteemed company that he always enjoyed badgering about its cryptic accounting practices. "The Riddle of U.S. Steel's Book Value" took on the very company in which Ben's mother had lost her investment in the panic of 1907. In another, "Shareholders—Do You Know When Periodic Dividends Help and When They Hurt You?", Ben presented a detailed discussion of regular cash returns, a subject that he often thought required a barrister's defense.

In 1927, Ben wrote a prophetic piece for *The Magazine of Wall Street* pointing out the "Severe Unsettlement in Stock Prices." The article proves that Ben comprehended the overheated direction of the market, even if he was himself only partially prepared when the "unsettlement" reached catastrophic proportions.

THE FORBES SERIES

To his credit, Ben was quick to announce to the world that the market crash had converted Wall Street into a discount bargain basement. Ben caught the attention of a vastly wider readership in 1932, when he wrote a three-part series for *Forbes* magazine that posed the question: Are American businesses "worth more dead than alive?" It talked about something with which he and Jerry Newman were very familiar—breaking up major companies to retrieve cash.

When the first *Forbes* article ran, the magazine included a box with a note from the editor. "*Forbes* takes pleasure in offering this exposé of injustice and maladjustment in the stock and corporation world, presented in a fearless, frank and interesting series, of which this is the first article."[7]

A CALL TO ARMS

The initial article appeared June 1 and was bannered, "Inflated Treasuries and Deflated Stockholders." In it, Ben pointed out that for the most part, publicly traded corporations were seriously undervalued by investors. More than 30 percent of the companies listed on the New York Stock Exchange were selling at less than their net quick assets, or the cash in the company's treasury after debts were resolved. In other words, if an investor bought all the shares, then liquidated the company, he would reap a substantial profit.

"Corporation treasurers sleep soundly while stockholders walk the floor," Ben proclaimed. His conclusion was, of course, that while stocks had been overpriced in 1929, the pendulum now had swung to the opposite extreme and stock prices were preposterously low.

Ben's education in classic languages and literature lent itself naturally to clear and expressive writing. He addressed his topics with vigor, he wrote without frills and Ben was unafraid of controversy. Neither powerful companies nor contentious topics deterred him.

The crash of 1929 and the following depression had terrorized both professional and individual investors and scared them away from the stock market; to both groups, Ben's article was a startling revelation. The *Forbes* articles showed that no matter how debilitating the past four years had been, Ben was unafraid of the future. The time had come to move forward. Because the author himself had been bloodied by market forces, the essays not only illustrated personal courage, they offered a ray of hope to others.

CALCULATED COURAGE

"Even Graham used to say," Walter Schloss explained, "that you can't run your investments as if a repeat of 1932 is around the corner. We can have a recession and things can get bad. But you can't plan on that happening." Timidity prompted by past failures causes investors to miss the most important bull markets, Schloss added.[8]

The last article in the series, "Should Rich but Losing Corporations Be Liquidated?", was an impassioned discourse urging stockholders to stand up for their rights as owners of a company. This series of articles and the enthusiastic public reaction to them stimulated Ben to move forward with his next big project—the book.

By the time the *Forbes* series appeared and Ben had the Joint Account under control, he had been teaching at Columbia for nearly half a decade. During that time, he had survived the most calamitous event in U.S. stock market history. He was seasoned timber and he was ready, he believed, to tackle the book that he had been planning for so long.

THE REWARDS OF SURVIVAL

Despite their disastrous end, the 1920s gave Graham the deep well of experience from which he later would draw. Graham, who had a profound sense of responsibility, had to face clients who had placed their trust and their fortunes in his hands. In the end, he and his partner Jerome Newman pulled them all through by patiently sifting through what was left of the U.S. stock and bond markets, looking for the main chance to recoup.

THE WINDS SUBSIDE

The worst was over for Graham-Newman by 1932, though because of the unusual profit-sharing method they used, Ben and Jerry seemed a long way from earning an income from the Joint Account. Because of the severe decline in prices of the securities held in the portfolio, the value of the account would need to triple before the managing partners were eligible to share in the income. One partner in the fund suggested that management compensation for the fund be changed, and after reviewing the idea with major investors, it was agreed that Ben and Jerry would receive a straight 20 percent of profits earned after January 1, 1934. The pair was once again earning an income and by 1935, all investor losses for the account were made good.

Many of the Wall Streeters with Graham's experience were forced out of the business in the crash and Great Depression that followed. Most of those who battled it through were Graham's colleagues and friends. They became the nucleus of the close-knit investment clique that survives today, several generations down the line.

THE END OF A SOBERING EXPERIENCE

Graham always had been a prudent man, basing his decisions on actualities rather than optimism. But before the crash, he had taken a few shortcuts and he made some mistakes. Though Graham was able to stumble back and regain his footing in the market rather quickly, after Black Tuesday, Ben's high-risk days were over. Afterward, he struggled to squeeze the best possible return from his investments, while at the same time seeking that wide margin of safety. He avoided aggressive deals in which someone would be hurt, perhaps because he had seen such extreme suffering. The average returns on Ben's portfolio descended from the heights of the predepression years, but he continued to consistently deliver substantial and reliable profits, and in the case of Government Employees Insurance Company, he lit a firecracker under the investors' total return.

The stock market rallied marvelously between 1932 and 1937. Investors gained hope and spirit, though in truth the Dow merely worked its way back into the 200 range. For decades, the DJIA fell far short of the 380 high at the time of the crash. Nevertheless, Graham-Newman rode the recovery like champions and during the 1930s Ben's standing in the investment community flourished.

CHAPTER 5

The Gospel According to Ben: *Security Analysis*

"When Benj. Graham was not communicating in Latin or Greek, he depended on two other languages: English and numbers."

—Adam Smith[1]

Though Ben's primary motive for teaching was not to earn more money, the salary must have been helpful during the deep, long depression. Both the ranks on Wall Street and that of college students thinned out during that time, and enrollment at Ben's Columbia class withered. The course, however, survived those slow years and Ben stuck with it. He even took additional teaching assignments that came along.

Ben accepted a position instructing at the New York Stock Exchange's in-house school, the New York Institute of Finance. Birl Shultz, father of former Secretary of State George Shultz, was the school's director and all of the students worked in the investment trade.

In the process of teaching at the Institute and at Columbia, Ben organized his thoughts and was able to test and retest some of the theories he had developed. David Dodd continued to take and transcribe the proceedings of the classes at Columbia. These notes would become the basis for Ben and Professor Dodd's classic text, *Security Analysis*.

DEMANDING WORK

Irving Kahn, who became an investment manager at Lehman Brothers and later started his own investment firm, in 1931 replaced Stern as Ben's teaching assistant. Kahn remembers well the rigor of the classroom exercises. He worked on Wall Street from 10 AM to 3 PM each class day, then caught the train to Columbia. Kahn went directly to the library to begin preparing for class, which started at 5 PM. In the classroom, Ben routinely talked about companies in groups of two, three or more—sometimes in related industries and sometimes not—so that he could accentuate his point by comparison. Because Ben refused to accept management's performance numbers at face value, Kahn was required to produce a lot of verification. For more than 20 years, Kahn worked up statistical analyses for classroom use. He also guided and graded student exercises and examinations.

When a student posed a challenging question, Ben often directed Kahn to organize a small team of students to study the question and prepare an evaluation to present before the entire class. The presentation then was open to spirited attack and debate. Like Kahn, many of Ben's students got their early analytical practice in preparing analyses for class. His students, who became the "superinvestors" who dominated Wall Street for six decades, obviously benefited from the teaching technique.

THE LIGHT SIDE

While Ben's courses seem to satisfy the voracious, probing minds of his younger and his already accomplished students, the class sessions were far from stuffy. Known for quick puns and a puckish sense of humor, Ben reinforced important points by making his students laugh. The eccentric but obliging Mr. Market, a character whom Warren Buffett has immortalized in his annual reports, originated in Graham's classroom.

Ben's mind could take off on inspired flights without a moment's notice, but his conversation also could be scattered with embarrassingly silly puns. Walter Schloss recalls once when an acquaintance badgered Ben to take a look at the stock

MR. MARKET

Ben Graham, my friend and teacher, long ago described the mental attitude toward market fluctuations that I believe to be most conducive to investment success. He said that you should imagine market quotations as coming from a remarkably accommodating fellow named Mr. Market who is your partner in a private business. Without fail, Mr. Market appears daily and names a price at which he will either buy your interest or sell you his.

Even though the business that the two of you own may have economic characteristics that are stable, Mr. Market's quotations will be anything but. For, sad to say, the poor fellow has incurable emotional problems. At times he falls euphoric and can see only the favorable factors affecting the business. When in that mood, he names a very high buy-sell price because he fears that you will snap up his interest and rob him of imminent gains. At other times he is depressed and can see nothing but trouble ahead for both the business and the world. On these occasions he will name a very low price, since he is terrified that you will unload your interest on him.

Mr. Market has another endearing characteristic: He doesn't mind being ignored. If his quotation is uninteresting to you today, he will be back with a new one tomorrow. Transactions are strictly at your option. Under these conditions, the more manic-depressive his behavior, the better for you.

But, like Cinderella at the ball, you must heed one warning or everything will turn into pumpkins and mice: Mr. Market is there to serve you, not to guide you. It is his pocketbook, not his wisdom, that you will find useful. If he shows up someday in a particularly foolish mood, you are free to either ignore him or to take advantage of him,

---

but it will be disastrous if you fall under his influence. Indeed, if you aren't certain that you understand and can value your business far better than Mr. Market, you don't belong in the game. As they say in poker, "If you've been in the game 30 minutes and you don't know who the patsy is, *you're* the patsy."[2]

---

of the Buda Company, Ben threatened the man that he was about to become a "Budapest."

WRITTEN BY THE SMITTEN

Ben's students also got a chuckle, not from their professor's jokes, but from his other caprices. A former student tells of the afternoon that Ben hurried into the classroom and on his way dropped a sheet of paper. The student glanced at the page to see whom to return it to and was astonished to find a love poem. It was ludicrously purple prose addressed to a blond model whom Ben had fallen for. His colleagues and students knew Ben took an avid interest in the ladies. Whether women chased Ben or Ben chased women, however, often depends on whether you ask a man or a woman.

"Today, he would be called a male chauvinist," claims Edythe Kenner, who was Ben's neighbor in New York and often protested to her husband about Ben's advances. Apparently, not every woman felt as offended.

"On the other side," according to Dr. Bernard Sarnat, who married Ben's cousin Rhoda and later lived across the street from the Grahams in Los Angeles, "I think women enjoyed Ben."

Ben's daughter Marjorie holds yet another view. She believes that relationships with women were important to her father for many reasons, not the least of which was that he savored the fun of spirited flirtation that takes place between men and women. Such flirtation perhaps provided relief from the seriousness of Ben's work and the difficulty he was having maintaining deeper relationships.

Whatever his friends, colleagues and students thought of Ben's personal life, they liked him and respected him for his accomplishments. George Heyman, who began working for Ben's friend Otto Abraham at Abraham & Company in 1936, says he used the analytical skills he learned in Ben's class throughout his career. Some of the messages, such as the concept of buying a stock as if you are buying the whole company, have become universally accepted. Others require a reasonably good head for numbers. Heyman adds that analysts and investors with an accounting background have found that their training has made it easier for them to grasp and apply Ben's value investing principles.

THE BOOK PROPOSAL

Ben had been teaching at Columbia for more than five years and finally it was time to write the book. Professor Dodd, with his mountain of carefully transcribed notes would collaborate. The book would be written in Ben's style, based on his lectures and his writings. Dodd, who later became a director of Graham-Newman and an accomplished investor on his own, would make suggestions, check facts and references and prepare charts and graphs. Dodd, who stood out in a crowd because he was well over six feet tall, was the ideal partner in such an undertaking. He was known for precision in everything he did.

The two men prepared an outline and sample chapter, which were then submitted to McGraw-Hill Publishing Company. The publisher contacted a professor of finance at Harvard and asked him to review the proposal and report back on its merit. The book proposal made such an impression that the professor recommended a contract that called for the authors to receive a straight 15 percent royalty on the domestic retail sales and 7.5 percent on foreign sales, rather than the publisher's customary 8 percent on domestic sales and 4 percent on sales abroad.

A CONTRACT IS SIGNED

The simple one-page book contract was signed at the beginning of 1934, with Ben receiving 60 percent of the royalties and

Dodd earning 40 percent. Irving Kahn also contributed to the research and many classroom examples were incorporated into the text. The book was published later in 1934.

Professor Dodd, in a letter to Warren Buffett following Ben's death, addressed a question that readers invariably ask. How much of the 850-page text was Graham and how much was Dodd?

GRAHAM VERSUS DODD

"I have said publicly on at least three occasions that Ben's invitation that I join him in producing THE BOOK was a characteristic act of grace on his part, was a great boon for me, and reflected his generosity of spirit. The product was his and my role was to glow in his reflected glory."

Dodd added, "I treasure his comment when the job was done that we had made a good team."

Buffett, who admired both Dodd's teaching and his investment skills, believes that Dodd is overly modest about the significance of his contribution. Buffett agrees, however, that the concepts and examples in the book strolled straight off the page of Graham's Columbia syllabus.

A LASTING MESSAGE

The theme of *Security Analysis* echoed both what Ben had been teaching in the lecture hall and practicing daily on Wall Street: The stock market is a highly illogical place where sheep-like participants follow the flock and buy when prices rise and just as mindlessly sell as prices fall.

"In other words," wrote Graham and Dodd, "the market is not a 'weighing machine,' on which the value of each issue is recorded by an exact and impersonal mechanism, in accordance with its specific qualities. Rather, it should be said that the market is a voting machine, whereon countless individuals register choices which are the product partly of reason and partly of emotion."[3]

The disciplined, rational investor neither follows popular choice nor plays market swings; rather he searches for stocks selling at a price below their intrinsic value and waits for the market to recognize and correct its errors. It invariably does and share price climbs. When the price has risen to the actual value of the company, it is time to take profits, which then are reinvested in a new undervalued security.

A MOVING TARGET

To Ben, the intrinsic value—the genuine worth—of any security would be revealed by the numbers. "Price," said Professor Roger F. Murray, who helped write the fifth edition of the book, "will tend to fluctuate around value. The price of a security is like a stopped clock—it will be right twice a day, and will be wrong all the rest of the time. The main principle in what we are saying is that securities are chronically mispriced in relation to their intrinsic value."[4]

THE BOOK TAKES SHAPE

In the first edition of *Security Analysis: Principles and Techniques,* Ben introduced a format that he followed fairly closely in the three subsequent editions in which he participated. The book builds on one concept after another, until the reader has the knowledge that he needs to do his own analysis of stocks, bonds, debentures, treasury securities and other issues. Readers were taught how to critically appraise a company's income statement and balance sheet and, ultimately, spot discrepancies between price and value.

As he consistently did, Ben emphasized that stock selection should be based on the fullest, most objective and trustworthy information that can be found.

It is a mistake, Ben contended, to rely on the corporate version of the company's condition without scrutiny. Management can make mistakes or even lie; reported earnings can be manipulated; future earnings are unpredictable, as are market factors such as new products or market share. A skilled analyst picks through the numbers, removes the shine, corrects for any spin that has been put on the data and considers all possibilities.

EARNINGS AS AN INDICATOR

At the core of it, readers are urged to investigate a stock as if it were an exercise in buying the entire business. To a large extent, the intrinsic value is revealed in the company's book value, discounted by goodwill and accounts receivable. This is the asset side of the picture. A company's "normal earning power," however, which may be considerably more or less than reported earnings, also is key. Earning power is evaluated in light of past earnings and long-term earning trends. While assets protect an investment, earning power—good or bad—defines a company's future prospects. If the share price advances, it is because most investors expect earnings to grow.

Yet both asset strength and earning power can be overburdened by debt, which makes it essential to understand capital structure and encumbrances.

THE SECRET OF DIVIDENDS

One of the most engrossing discussions in the book involves the debate over whether it is wiser for management to pay earnings out to shareholders in terms of dividends or to plow the money back into the company. The answer to the question, wrote Graham and Dodd, lies in the response to a second question—how are the retained earnings to be used? If they are misused, they benefit the shareholder in no way. On the other hand, if they are paid out in cash dividends, the investor can always use the profits as he sees fit, even to buy additional shares in the same company when management is competent. At the very least, reliable dividends provide a foundation for share price.

THE PROPER ROLE OF STOCK DIVIDENDS

In the book, Ben took on critics who dismiss stock dividends as nothing more than a mirage that results in the dilution of the value of the existing shares. While the practice of declaring stock dividends can be abused, Ben argues that when properly used, it is a justifiable practice. A stock dividend can capitalize retained capital by making stock available to the investor to keep, to collect dividends on or to trade as he or she sees fit. It is up to management to use restraint in limiting the use of stock dividends to no more than the amount of retained earnings and, conversely, to retire an appropriate amount of stock when capital no longer is needed in the business, Ben insisted.

BONDHOLDERS AND SHAREHOLDERS ARE IN IT TOGETHER

The early editions of *Security Analysis* placed special significance on bonds, especially those of heavy industrial companies. The emphasis was justified, according to Ben's way of thinking. Bondholders and stock purchasers should look for the same characteristics in a company, except that stockholders will sacrifice some safety (the safety of being a creditor rather than an owner in the event of bankruptcy) in return for potential share price appreciation.

A VALUABLE TIP

The many examples involving railroad stocks in the first edition of the book served readers of the late 1930s particularly well. Railroads were the single most important mode of transportation during that era, especially for commercial and industrial freight. When World War II engulfed the United States, railroads became even more significant as transportation for troops and war supplies to both coasts. Railroad stocks took off.

PUTTING IT IN PERSPECTIVE

While the era of railroad dominance may be gone, there is one advantage in reading *Security Analysis* in its earlier editions. The investor will be cleansed of any notion that there is much that is new on Wall Street. It soon becomes clear that scams, frauds, misrepresentations and clever approaches to salesmanship simply get dressed up in new clothes for subsequent generations of investors. The underlying ruses have not changed much.

Ben was especially perturbed by what he called "corporate pyramiding," or the creation of a capital structure by using holding companies or a series of holding companies. "Usually, the predominating purpose of such an arrangement is to enable the organizers to control a large business with the investment of little or no capital and also to secure to themselves the major part of its surplus profits and increased going-concern value."[5] Corporate pyramiding was popular several times during the first half of the twentieth century, once to suck the guts out of the youthful public utilities business and again to drain off profits from the networks of small railroads that honeycombed the nation.

In *Security Analysis*, Graham describes how pyramiding works, and with a fair amount of loathing and disgust. What he described is identical to many of the leading corporations of today, and perilously close to Warren Buffett's Berkshire Hathaway, Inc. Pyramiding, he explains, can be used to cleverly shuffle and distribute the deck in such a way that the bona fide value of a company's stock is distorted, and investors eventually are bilked.

About the time the reader is beginning to squirm with suspicion, Ben tosses in a caveat. "To avoid creating a false impression, we must point out that, although pyramiding is usually effected by means of holding companies, it does not follow that all holding companies are created for this purpose and are therefore reprehensible. The holding company is often utilized for entirely legitimate purposes . . . ."[6] The clues for recognizing the evil pyramid is when the principals finance the deal with notes, banks loans and other devices that require no actual cash infusion on their part, and when a barrage of new issues, warrants and other nearly incomprehensible securities suddenly appear.

A MEASURE OF THE MARKET

While it was a company's measurable performance, rather than crystal-ball gazing at the market as a whole, that interested Ben, he did teach a sophisticated, mathematical method for calculating the actual value of the entire market. His computation estimates the true value of the DJIA, rather than the public perception of the value, which is a clue as to where the market is in a cycle. If it is below Ben's computation, the market is undervalued; if it is above, it is overvalued.

"I have found it useful to estimate the central value of the Dow Jones Industrial Average by the simple method of capitalizing ten-year average earnings at twice the interest rate for high-grade bonds," Ben once explained to a congressional panel. "This technique presupposes that the average past earnings of a group of stocks presents a fair basis for estimating future earnings, but with a conservative bias on the low side. It also assumes that by doubling the capitalization rate presented by high-grade bonds, we allow properly for the differential in imputed risk between good bonds and good stocks. Although this method is open to serious theoretical objections, it has, in fact, given a reasonably accurate reflection of the central value of industrial common stock averages since 1881."[7]

The concepts introduced in *Security Analysis* were absolutely revolutionary and enlightening at the time they were first presented, and the book is still a valuable source for anyone with a serious interest in financial markets. But like so many other of Ben's ideas, some of the concepts have become so generally accepted that many investors no longer realize where they originated.

FIGURE IT OUT FOR YOURSELF

Some of Ben's advice is elemental and cannot be repeated too often. In *Security Analysis,* he gave his unusual forthright admonition to investors to think for themselves—"You are neither right or wrong because people agree with you."[8]

Security Analysis was dedicated to Roswell C. McCrea, the dean of the school of business at Columbia who hired both Graham and Dodd to teach. Mrs. Dodd served as McCrea's secretary before she was married.

READERS ARE READY FOR GRAHAM AND DODD

The timing for *Security Analysis* could not have been better. The Securities and Exchange Act of 1934 had just been passed, giving investors access to more information than they had had before and putting a lid on some of the market manipulation that characterized the first third of the century. Maybe now, the public reckoned, everyone had a chance against the pools and syndicates such as those used by Baruch, the Rockefellers, Joseph Kennedy and their compatriots before the crash.

The country and the investment community were looking for financial reform. The book quickly became the cardinal textbook for both practicing analysts and for students of investment principles.

The book, rather than reduce his motive for teaching, kept Ben in the classroom. His classes were more in demand and he continued to teach at Columbia and at the New York Institute of Finance.

WRITING AND TEACHING ARE SYNERGISTIC

"Back in 1935 while working at Loeb Rhoades," recalled Walter Schloss, "one of the partners, Armand Erpf, gave me a good piece of advice when I asked him how I could get into the 'statistical department.' Mr. Erpf told me that there was a new book called *Security Analysis* that had just been written by a man called Ben Graham. He said, 'Read the book and when you know everything in it, you won't have to read anything else.' "

Schloss worked at Loeb Rhoades for seven years, first as a runner, then in the cage. Soon after being introduced to *Security Analysis*, Schloss enrolled in Ben's course at the New York Institute of Finance. He studied there between 1935 and 1940. "I rushed to class, then back to work," he said.

GRADES PLUS PROFIT

Most of the other students did the same thing. Many, like their counterparts at Columbia, took Ben's lessons directly back to work with them. In one session, Ben walked through the numbers on the when-issued bonds of Baldwin Locomotive, which was in bankruptcy. When-issued bonds are a transitional transaction often used for relaunching companies undergoing reorganization. Ben's analysis showed that based on the assets that backed them up, the bonds were a sound buy.

Gus Levy, who was head of Goldman Sachs & Company's arbitrage department and later became chief executive of Goldman, purchased the bonds the very next day.

"He made a lot of money on them," laughed Walter Schloss.

Like most other students, Schloss took two courses at the Institute each semester. The $10 enrollment fee for the classes was covered by his company. "When the last course came, Loeb Rhoades didn't want to pay," Walter said. "We negotiated, and split the cost." His company's contribution was crucial to him, because at the time, Schloss said, salaries on Wall Street were low and the prestige was not much higher. During the depression more than ever, the public regarded Wall Street as a corrupt place, a notion that Ben fought hard to dispel, not only by example, but by working for better education and standards for all analysts.

For many years, Ben's course material was the essence of the classes offered by the New York Institute of Finance. Then, during a period when it was experiencing financial troubles, the New York Stock Exchange sold the Institute of Finance to private investors, but Irving Kahn, along with Walter Morris and Steve Jaquith, adapted Ben's lectures on security analysis into a correspondence course. In 1947, a student could buy a print copy of Ben's lectures and a set of ten audiotaped lectures for $5.

A TRADE-SCHOOL EDUCATION

To Schloss and many of his friends who grew up in the depression years and never got the chance to go to college, Ben's books and his classes at Columbia and the New York Stock Exchange's Institute gave them their only formal education. Even among those who had attended universities, the book became *the* doctrine.

THE BOOK CONFERS CACHE ON COLUMBIA

Columbia Graduate School of Business and *Security Analysis* often were uttered in the same breath, for generations of students there—and at other business schools—carried the textbook to class. Successful Columbia Business School alumni and money manager Mario Gabelli and Leon Cooperman, former partner in charge of investment research at Goldman, Sachs & Company, are among the countless financial experts who keep a copy of Graham and Dodd within easy reach. Cooperman now runs his own fund.

Muriel Siebert, a pioneering woman on Wall Street and president of the discount brokerage Muriel Siebert & Company, mentioned the book in 1986 when she was interviewed for *Sylvia Porter's Personal Finance.* "When I was a student," Siebert said, "*Security Analysis* was the first one that really made a dent. It said to buy values at discounts. If you look at some of these [recent] takeovers, they could have been Graham and Dodd stocks."[9] Siebert was not the only one who saw the light through *Security Analysis.*

Warren Buffett credits both his classroom work and his reading of Graham and Dodd as priceless. "In Berkshire's investments, Charlie and I have employed the principles taught by Dave [Dodd] and Ben Graham. Our prosperity is the fruit of their intellectual tree."[10]

THE INVESTORS' BIBLE

Graham and Dodd's "words are now considered gospel on Wall Street," wrote journalist Thomas Easton in 1990, "and *Security Analysis* is about as close as such a secular vocation gets to a Bible."[11]

Security Analysis survived, figures Buffett, because it was teachable and did not require deep business insight. But even more of the value of *Security Analysis* and Ben's other writings, Warren Buffett pointed out, is derived from their honesty. Unlike so much that is written by investment authorities, Ben's books lacked the hidden agenda of self-promotion. "He never was touting his own operation," Buffett said.

The book has continued to be popular because each subsequent edition used current examples, case studies that invariably captured the readers. The 1940 edition, for example, included two lists of special situations, or examples of unpopular stocks that had some veiled appeal. Those two stock lists advanced an average of 252 percent in the next eight years, contrasted to a 33 percent gain for the Standard & Poor's industrial average.

Although the examples hold up, it is the underlying principles that are the most durable. Schloss, a decade later, helped Ben prepare the third edition (1951) of *Security Analysis.* "In the appendix is an article on 'special situations' that first appeared in *The Analysts Journal* in 1946," Schloss said. "In the article, he had worked out an algebraic formula for risk-reward results that could be applied today, 30 years later."

A TEACHING TEAM

Eventually, Graham and Professor Dodd, united in people's minds because of the book they coauthored, evolved into a sort of teaching partnership. Ben delivered the investment seminar one day each week, and Dodd taught the other investment classes. Though they did not share a classroom, students often considered them a duo. Graham toiled in the street and knew the score firsthand. Dodd was on campus and readily accessible to students with whom he often forged strong bonds.

"From the moment I arrived at Columbia, Dave personally encouraged and educated me," wrote Warren Buffett when Dodd died. ". . . Everything he taught me, directly or through his book, made sense. Later, through dozens of letters, he continued my education right up until his death."[12]

Under various titles, Ben led investment courses at Columbia for 26 years. In 1951, his class moved to the Columbia Graduate School of Business and he became an adjunct professor, not to mention something of a fixture, at the school. Graham's stature as a teacher grew along with his reputation as an investor and writer.

Over the years at his various venues, Graham (and Dodd as well) taught many of the brightest young men either working on Wall Street or destined for a career elsewhere in the investment world. There, professors and students sometimes established relationships that lasted a lifetime.

THE LIFE CYCLE OF THEORY

When Ben first started teaching there, Columbia was neither known nor especially admired for its business program. Ben's classes and his writing helped elevate Columbia's business school from a rather ordinary program into a unique and esteemed course of study. Unfortunately, Ben Graham's theories are taught at few universities today. "The fact that [value investing is] so simple makes people reluctant to teach it," Buffett says. "If you've gone and gotten a Ph.D. and spent years learning how to do all kinds of tough things mathematically, to have it come back to this—it's like studying for the priesthood and finding out that the Ten Commandments were all you needed."[13]

The tradition of Benjamin Graham and his colleague and coauthor David Dodd had waned even at Columbia, but in the early 1990s, it has enjoyed a revival. In 1984, Professor Dodd's family contributed $1.3 million to the Graham and Dodd Asset Management Program, which sponsors faculty research, holds symposia and provides financial aid to students who might otherwise not be able to attend Columbia.

A POIGNANT ACKNOWLEDGMENT

As a gift for his 80th birthday, the family of Robert Heilbrunn, Ben's longtime client, student and friend, established a professorship in Heilbrunn's name at the Columbia Business School. At Heilbrunn's request, the $1.5 million chair was dedicated to the teaching of investments in the Graham and Dodd tradition. Then, in 1993, on his 85th birthday, Heilbrunn himself added another $1 million to the endowment.

When the first lecture under Heilbrunn's program was presented on Wall Street, Roger Murray, who took over Ben's classes when he moved to California and later collaborated on Graham and Dodd's textbook, *Security Analysis,* was the primary speaker. So many people from the investment world turned out for the lecture that there were not enough chairs. When Heilbrunn's series was offered as a course option at Columbia Graduate School of Business, the enrollment was so large that students had to compete for a spot by writing an essay on why they wanted to take the classes. Only 75 students were admitted to the seminars, but at the first session 90 students showed up anyway.

It was not only Graham's investment prowess, however, that Heilbrunn valued so dearly and wished to honor. "He certainly did add a lot to my life," Heilbrunn said of Ben. "I'm terribly indebted to my father for having mentioned him to me. I don't know where I would be if it hadn't been for Ben."

A HALF CENTURY OF SHELF LIFE

In 1984, McGraw-Hill threw a 50th anniversary party for *Security Analysis* at Columbia. Graham had died in 1976, but David Dodd, then 88 years old, attended, as did Graham's disciple, Warren Buffett. Dodd was awarded an honorary doctorate by Columbia, and Buffett delivered a speech that is still quoted in investment circles. That speech, "The Superinvestors of Graham and Doddsville," was reprinted in the Columbia Graduate School of Business magazine, *Hermes.* Reprints of the article are requested so often that the magazine staff keeps a stack on hand at all times.

The publishers can only estimate the number of copies of *Security Analysis* that have been printed, but believe it is well in excess of 800,000. In 1988, a fifth edition was published after Ben's death with the help of Stanford Professor Sidney Cottle, Frank E. Block, former member of the Financial Accounting Standards Board, and retired Columbia Professor Roger Murray. (Dodd still was living, but he was 92 by then.) That edition still is available in major bookstores, and according to Benjamin Graham, Jr., it and *The Intelligent Investor* continued to pay considerable royalties as recently as 1993. For the first half of 1992, according to the last royalty statement that Ben, Jr., received, *Security Analysis,* a book that dated back 58 years, sold 2,500 copies. The book invariably sells poorly during bull markets, but sales revive during bear markets. "It is a perennial best-seller" and a truly remarkable property for the publisher, says Philip Ruppell, editor in chief of business books at McGraw-Hill.

FROM CLASSROOM TO COLLECTOR'S ITEM

While investors who are looking for effortless ways to invest may view *Security Analysis* as ponderous and passé, purists laugh at that notion. Anyone who doubts how much readers value their copies of *Security Analysis* should try to check one out from a library or locate one in a used bookstore. A check of the public libraries in several cities shows that the book—usually in its latest edition—is almost always out on loan. If you find a used copy in a bookstore, you are lucky indeed. The Burlington, Vermont, book dealer, Books of Wall Street, will place your name on a waiting list to buy a first edition, which will cost upward of $1,000 when and if it shows up. Second and third editions are much cheaper—$125 and up—when they can be located. A new copy of the last edition, the fifth, sells for around $60. McGraw-Hill now is considering publishing a special collector's copy of the original edition of *Security Analysis*.

CASTING LIGHT ON THE LEDGER

In 1936, Ben wrote a second book that also enjoyed a long run of popularity, but is less known today, *The Interpretation of Financial Statements*. Spencer B. Meredith coauthored the first edition of the book. In 1955, Ben revised *Financial Statements* with the help of Charles McGolrick, a security analyst with Cosgrove, Miller & Whitehead, and a fellow instructor at the New York Institute of Finance. The publisher was Harper & Row. The purpose of the book was to help businesspeople, stockbrokers and individual investors decode financial statements. Though some accounting procedures and terminology have changed since the book's second printing in 1955, the fundamentals of accounting have not. *The Interpretation of Financial Statements* is still an uncomplicated guide to the study of corporate finance. The book is especially useful to readers who may be reading older editions of Ben's investment books, for it clarifies exactly what the author meant by such terms as *capitalization, working capital, net quick assets* (similar to working capital but more stringent) and *intrinsic value*. Intrinsic value is the "real value" of a company and may be far different from its market or book value. Intrinsic value is an indefinite concept, but it approximates the price the whole company would bring if it were sold to a private buyer.

Though it was not touted as such, *Financial Statements* could be called an absolutely bare-bones *Security Analysis*. In the book's conclusion, Ben summarized his belief in quantitative analysis. "The investor who buys securities only when the market price looks cheap on the basis of the company's statements, and sells them when they look high on the same bias, probably will not make spectacular profits. But, on the other hand, he will probably avoid equally spectacular and more frequent losses. He should have a better-than-average chance of obtaining satisfactory results. And this is the chief objective of intelligent investing."[14]

As usual, Ben was too conservative to blow his own whistle and insist that disciples of his teachings would enjoy marvelously high and remarkably reliable returns, though that is what they have done.

HOME FIRES

The year *Security Analysis* was published, 1934, life at home was brightened by another baby, Winifred. A little charmer, Winnie was the freest spirit of the Graham children. It was also a year in which Ben celebrated a midlife, round-numbered birthday. Robert Heilbrunn remembers bringing Ben a birthday present, a popular new book called *Life Begins at 40*. Ben thanked Heilbrunn very politely, but said that he already had received several copies of the book.

Even with the joyous events, 1934 was not a perfect year, and there were lengthening shadows of a midlife crisis.

BEN OFF-BROADWAY

In 1934, Ben tried his hand at play writing. His comedy, "True to the Marines," appeared off Broadway, and friends, family and most of Wall Street trooped to the Red Barn Theatre at Locust Valley on Long Island to see the summer-season production.

Elaine, Ben's second daughter, was left at home. "I remember that I was very insulted because I was considered too young to see it," she said. "It was mildly risque."

A SCATHING REVIEW

Marjorie, five-and-a-half years older than Elaine, was allowed to attend. When she had seen the production, Marjorie was both baffled and embarrassed that her father, whom she considered an extremely intelligent person, should write something so superficial. Apparently, the theater critic for the New York Times agreed. He printed the following review:

> If one of Mr. Graham's students at Columbia University were to turn in an essay on security analysis as trite and diffused in its substance as this little play of his about a nationally famous journalist whose editorial policies are influenced by a moronic chorus-girl mistress, then the student would undoubtedly receive a D-minus—and for a very good reason, too.
>
> As a well-known figure in the financial world, Mr. Graham should know that neither businessmen with millions of dollars invested in Nicaraguan bananas nor Undersecretaries of State act and talk like a cartoonist's caricature—not even when they're serious. Alas, the only humor in his comedy comes during those pathetic moments when the unfortunate actors—who are here spared the humiliation of identification—find themselves with nothing more to do than laugh at their own pitiful jokes.
>
> Mr. Graham had better stick to one thing or the other— or find himself a new hobby.[15]

The production folded after four performances. A revision of the same play, "Baby Pompadour," also failed. However, a movie made using a peculiarly similar plot—*Born Yesterday*— was filmed in the 1940s and remade in 1993 starring Melanie Griffith, John Goodman and Don Johnson.

Ben's ineptitude at play writing perhaps did not surprise those who knew him well. He had a quick mind, a well-developed intellect and an enormous respect for logic. When it came to matters where the natural or instinctive part of his brain was concerned, he could not always relax and let things happen. He read and wrote in six languages, for example, but his accent when speaking was dreadful. Though he enjoyed theater, poetry and music and often tried his hand at them, they depended too much on intuition and the expression of personal feelings for him to excel.

A STRUCTURAL CHANGE

As for Ben, it did not seem to bother him when these side interests were unpopular or unproductive. He had his work, which continued to present new challenges. In 1935, the Internal Revenue Service began to question the Joint Account's status as a partnership, suggesting that it was actually a quasi-corporation. During testimony before a U.S. Senate committee later on a different subject, Ben explained what happened:

Mr. Graham: We incorporated for a very peculiar reason. We had originally operated as a joint account, and the individual members reported [his earnings for tax purposes] on a partnership basis.

Chairman: Each participant in the fund?

Mr. Graham: That is correct, reported his share of the results. But before 1936, the Treasury claimed that we were an association taxable as a corporation, and we had considerable problems as to where we stood, whether we were or were not a corporation. So our counsel said, "You had better incorporate and settle this matter once and for all, because the Treasury will get you either way."

The Chairman: This was the original group of friends; is that right?

Mr. Graham: That is correct.

The Chairman: That is all there were in it in 1936?

Mr. Graham: There were accretions on a private basis. I had more friends in 1936 than I had in 1923.

The Chairman: When did you make them? During the depression?

Mr. Graham: Not so many as afterward.[16]

The upshot of the Treasury's demand was the creation of a follow-on fund, the Graham-Newman Corporation. On January 1, 1936, it replaced the Joint Account.

AN EASIER ERA AHEAD

As the depression began to fade, and Graham-Newman again gained a solid footing, Ben branched out into other realms of economics and put him in the same arena with the nation's most innovative thinkers. Though the economy followed an uneven path, Ben was able to conquer the uncertainties.

Though the downtrend that began in 1937 was the longest the stock market had yet seen, lasting five years, Graham-Newman coped with the setback. Graham made some bear-market adjustments to his practices and switched the emphasis of the accounts, and ultimately, the tail end of the depression years presented exceptional opportunities to buy undervalued assets. There was a bear market in the late 1940s, though this time the decline was neither deep nor long-lasting. The Korean War again stimulated the market and launched another sustained upward sweep. The rich crop of undervalued companies that were up for grabs set the stage at Graham-Newman for the prosperity of the 1940s and 1950s. Except for the reversal between 1946 and 1949, the general uptrend lasted until long after Ben's retirement in 1956.

CHAPTER 6

Graham's Economic Influence: A Cure for War and World Hunger

"The ability to do more than one thing well is often the difference between competence and excellence."

—Bell South advertisement, 1993

As often was the case in Ben's life, the 1930s and 1940s were a rough blend of personal adversity offset by impressive accomplishments. The trouble this time was far from his control. Ben's aunts, uncles and cousins in Europe were caught under Hitler's marching boots. Europe's largest Jewish community, including many of the Gesundheits, had resided in Poland, which took an especially cruel blow from the Third Reich. By 1945, nearly one-fifth of the prewar Polish population had perished either in sweeps of the ghettos or in death camps.[1]

As the depression faded, Ben's business began to return to normal. His personal life, however, turned to shambles.

FLEEING TO CALIFORNIA

Ben's demanding career—and his avid interest in women—finally took its toll at home. Marjorie began hearing her parents arguing in the night, then suddenly her mother whisked Marjorie and the other children away on an ocean voyage. They cruised through the Panama Canal to California.

Rhoda Sarnat was attending the University of California at Los Angeles at the time and remembers coming home from school one afternoon in 1936 and finding her mother consoling Hazel Graham in the living room.

"My mother and Hazel were good friends," Rhoda explained. "And I saw Hazel there weeping. She wasn't that sort. She was very upbeat, creative and dramatic, a bright gal. I was shocked.

"Later I found out Ben was having an affair. Hazel was absolutely devastated," Rhoda said. "Ben," she added, "was absolutely ethical and honest, but on the sexual side, he erred."

While she was in California, Hazel received a letter from Ben saying that he would file for divorce. Hazel was so distraught that she went off alone, leaving Marjorie with the other children. Finally, Marjorie wrote to her pleading with her to return. "We were out of money," Marjorie said.

Marjorie, as the oldest of the children, endured the most stress. "While they were separating, the quarrels were deeply disturbing. I was awakened at night to hear them. I wanted my parents to resolve their problems and stay married, but he was determined to have a divorce."

"When he was living at home, he was very busy," recalls daughter Elaine. "I was ten when he and my mother separated."

A SPLIT

Ben moved out of the house, obtained his divorce and took up residence at the Cardinal Hotel. In 1936, Ben flew to Reno for six weeks and obtained a divorce. He pleaded guilty to the customary charge—"extreme cruelty."

Even seven years after the tragedy of her brother's death, Elaine believes the death of their first son exacted a toll on her parents' relationship. But marriage and divorce seldom lend themselves to simple scenarios.

"I think it was a very complicated relationship," she said. "They were both strong characters in very different ways."

Marjorie agrees and does not entirely blame her father. Her mother, she said, was "talented, emotional and hard to grow up with in certain ways. I have a lot of admiration for her, but she was enormously bossy."

Elaine, the middle sister, seemed to take the split more in her stride, but she missed her father. As busy as Ben was, there had been time for tennis, for family excursions and for going to see the Columbia football team play.

"He had immense physical courage," Elaine recollected. "He took us skiing in New Hampshire. The 1936 Winter Olympics at Lake Placid had a bobsled run. Not only did he go down it, we went down it, too. It was terrifying.

"I regret that he didn't teach me very much in the formal sense," she said. But, "He was nice to us, and intellectually a great influence."

The children had called on his wide-ranging interest in mathematics, science, music and literature to help them with their schoolwork.

"He had a few blind spots," Elaine noted. "One was art. His visual side was not developed, to put it kindly."

AN INVENTIVE FATHER

"He was very interested in inventions. He was very clumsy with his hands—not a father who could knock things together or put up a shelf, but he had a Leonardo da Vinci approach. He loved inventing things," Elaine continued.

Ben spent hours at his avocation and kept notebooks in which there were sketches and scribbles and anagrams, she recalled.

Elaine says she does not know whether Ben ever took an intelligence-quotient test, but she believes he would have scored extremely high. "He had the kind of mind that IQ tests test."

Intelligence, as Dr. Ben Graham, Jr., pointed out many years later, is a great asset, but it does not always help people make wise personal decisions or deal well with their emotional lives and intimate relationships.

A GENEROUS STOCK MARKET

Always oblivious to personal pain, the stock market continued a steady climb that started in the 1930s, and except for periodic corrections, was generous to the long-term investor. Conditions were ideal for the application of value-investing principles. During the 1937–1938 dip, Ben and Jerry fine-tuned their investment procedure and in the 1940–1941 correction, the company earned money without any change to its strategy. At the end of the war, Graham-Newman took on a new employee, whose first project was to prepare a summary of the first decade of the company's operation. His report provides a detailed look at how an investment company operated during that interval.

Like most young men during World War II, Ben's former student Walter Schloss took a leave of absence from his career to serve in the army. Before he left New York, Schloss put the $1,000 he had accumulated in the care of Leon Graham, who was both a friend and a stockbroker, for investment.

When he returned, the $1,000 was worth $2,000. Better yet, Schloss received a note from Ben, his former professor, saying that there was an opening at Graham-Newman for an analyst.[2]

LOOKING BACK ON THE DECADE

Schloss was so anxious to work for Ben that he reported to work while he was still on leave. It mattered even less to Schloss that his first day on the job was New Year's Eve. He was offered the position on December 31 and Schloss reported to work at the offices at 52 Wall Street on December 31, 1946.

"Ben had a very good record, he was very honest," Schloss said. "He was a straightforward man, a soft-spoken gentleman. If he hadn't given me a job, I don't know what I would have done, not being a college graduate."

Graham-Newman was a small operation by contemporary standards, both in terms of number of employees and in terms of dollars managed. Right away, Schloss bought a few odd shares of Graham-Newman that nobody else wanted.

"In the beginning, it was just Ben and Jerry," Schloss noted. "Seymour Cohn was secretary. I was the security analyst. One thing about a small firm, it keeps the costs down.

"My first project was a report on the first ten years of Graham-Newman [corporation]," Schloss said, a job that renewed his familiarity with Ben's philosophy. "Ben's emphasis was on protecting his expectations of profit with minimum risk."

Schloss's findings were reported to shareholders and no doubt pleased them. "The annual percentage gain to stockholders, based on net asset value at the beginning of each year, averaged 17.6 percent. This compares with 10.1 percent in the same period shown by the Standard Statistic Poor's Index of 90 stocks and 10 percent shown by the Dow Jones Industrial Average, in both cases with allowance for dividends received.

"In the first six years of operation [calendar 1936–1941]—a period of generally declining prices—our overall gain averaged 11.8 percent per annum, against a loss of 0.6 percent for the 90-stock average. In the past four years (calendar 1942–1945 inclusive)—a period of steadily rising prices—we averaged 26.3 percent against 26.0 percent for the 90 stocks.

"In our last fiscal year, we showed, for the first time, a lower percentage gain than that of the general market. These comparative results follow directly from our investment policy, which grows more conservative as the market level rises."

SEEMINGLY SIMPLE OBJECTIVES

The uncomplicated objectives of the company were stated in its annual report. They were:

- To purchase securities at prices less than their intrinsic value as determined by careful analysis with particular emphasis on the purchase of securities at less than their liquidating value, and

- To engage in arbitrage and hedging operations in the securities field.

"This policy," the stockholders report read, "means that, in our operations, relatively little stress is laid upon forecasting the future course of the securities market or the future prospects of individual companies on a basis differing materially from their past performance. With regard to 'general portfolio operations'—it means that we tend to purchase securities when general sentiment is pessimistic and prices are generally low, and to sell them in periods of optimism and high prices."

CALLING THE CORRECTION

The sharp reduction in Graham-Newman's portfolio in 1946 "has not been based on an opinion that the rise in the market now has run its course, but on the fact that very few common stocks remain attractive holdings *judged by our technical standards.*" The 1946 annual report further noted that "as long as the present rising market continues, it is not likely that we shall be able to match the percentage gain shown by common stocks generally." The investment portfolio did, however, continue to show a profit.

When Schloss examined Graham-Newman's holdings, he discovered that there were relatively few stocks in the fund. In a total portfolio of $4.1 million, only $1.1 million was in common stocks. Many of the shares were in small, practically unknown manufacturing and industrial companies, but, said Schloss, "they were cheap on the numbers."

Apparently, the acquaintance who earlier had pestered Ben to consider buying shares in the Buda Company succeeded. The 1946 portfolio of Graham-Newman included 2,500 shares of the Buda Company.

Ben still hedged his investment in much the way he had done before the crash of 1929, except that these days he fully guarded his assets against the risks to margin debt and naked positions.

"I always thought related hedges tied up a lot of capital. But then you could borrow money very inexpensively, the preferred paid a dividend of 5 percent and the common (often) paid nothing," Schloss explained.[3]

The portfolio was light, as Ben's report explained, because he believed he spotted an all-too-familiar trend. The first time the DJIA sold at 100 was 1906 and the last time it sold at that level was 1942. After breaking through that historic number, the market made a steep climb. The Dow was trading at about

212 in 1946 and the secondary stocks, which had benefited greatly from the war, were even higher than the blue chips. Ben had sold many stocks to take profits and he could find few undervalued stocks to replace them.

"Graham was out of the market by then, waiting for the shoe to drop," Schloss said. "In September, 1946, the Dow took a big wallop. The secondaries were badly hit." The bear market lasted until mid-1949.

BUYING BACK INTO THE MARKET

A Graham-Newman annual report several years later, January 31, 1950, reflected the expansion. It showed that the fund held assets of $5.7 million. There were 75 common stocks in the portfolio, including nine public utilities. The Graham-Newman portfolio included American Hawaii Steamship Company, Inc.; Baldwin Locomotive Works; Douglas Aircraft Company; Fairchild Engine—Aircraft Corporation; Hercules Motor Corporation; Real Silk Hosiery Mills, Inc.; Todd Shipyards Corporation; White Motor Company and, of course, Buda.

Many of the companies have been taken over or have disappeared entirely. Douglas Aircraft, for example, is one half of McDonnell-Douglas, and Fairchild Engines—Aircraft Corporation is Fairchild Industries.

Not only did Ben anticipate market changes in his portfolio, in his lectures for his classes at the New York Institute of Finance, he prophesied the longer-term problems that awaited heavy industry, railroads and big steel in particular. By dissecting the earnings of U.S. Steel, he was able to point out to his students that the company's earnings were even more erratic than actually reported by the company, because U.S. Steel regularly set aside reserves in good years, which then were used to prop up earnings in bad years.

BROAD ECONOMIC CHANGES

"That fact," Ben said, "I think, points up the peculiar problem which the United States Steel Corporation has been facing for a great many years now—its inability to establish a sustained earning power commensurate with the size and position of the corporation."[4]

Ben also commented on the street's extreme pessimism over the ability of railroads to contain costs and manage rates in the post–World War II economy. "In the past, they have always been able to deal with their operating expenses one way or the other—by greater efficiency or higher rates. The thing they haven't been able to deal with was their debt. That point may have considerable significance for the future of our carriers."[5] Debt, management and union problems, as well as increased competition from truckers and airlines did, indeed, diminish the influence of railroads.

AN APPRENTICE LEARNS A TRADE

Schloss spent most his hours at Graham-Newman scouring the Standard & Poor's reports and other research data looking for stocks selling below their working capital. "Ben gave valuable power to the people who [worked] there," Schloss observed. Among those Schloss located were Diamond T Motors and Easy Washing Machine. Thanks to a rising standard of living and new consumerism, such investments performed as hoped. Schloss placed orders to buy these and other stocks.

Though Schloss admired Ben, he did not always agree with him, and in fact, even after 30 years in the business, Ben still made an occasional bad call.

"For example," Schloss said, "Graham decided that Illinois Central was a cheaper railroad at the price than Missouri Kansas Texas. So, employing a hedge 'by proxy,' he bought Illinois Central and sold Missouri Kansas Texas short.

"While [Ben's theory] may have been true statistically, it worked out very badly. It's very difficult to short one railroad and buy another over a short period of time. Maybe over a longer period of time it would work. Anyway, we stopped doing it."[6]

Nevertheless, Ben did best when he followed his personal train of logic. Some of Ben's shortcomings, Schloss says, stemmed from his willingness to consider other people's ideas and to compromise, even when he felt certain he was right. A prime example involved a company Ben had studied for years.

U.S. Steel had entered an agreement to buy Consolidated Steel at a premium and Ben acquired what seemed at the time like a large block of Consolidated for an arbitrage. The Graham-Newman board balked, worried that the U.S. Supreme Court would invalidate the U.S. Steel–Consolidated deal on the grounds of antitrust violations, leaving their investment in the lurch.

"So Graham said, 'Well, I think the Supreme Court is going to rule five to four in favor of the company,'" Schloss recalled. "And he named the justices who he believed would vote for it and the justices he believed would vote against it."

The board persevered and demanded that an antitrust lawyer be consulted. The lawyer decided that the court would uphold the antitrust charges five to four and disallow the merger.

Though Ben believed he was right, he did not push his opinion. He relented and sold half the shares.

"When the decision came down from the Supreme Court, sure enough, Graham was exactly correct and the authority was wrong," Schloss said.[7]

SPREADING THE WORD TOO LIBERALLY

It also bothered Schloss that people took advantage of Ben's generous nature, though it did not seem to disturb Ben himself.

A business friend came to the office to take Ben to lunch, Schloss recalled. "We'd just bought Lukens Steel. He went out and bought it when he heard that." Graham-Newman had been buying Lukens shares gradually between $19 and $20 per share. The stock was earning $6 per share. Ben's lunch partner acquired such a large block that he drove the price up, eliminating the buying advantage for Graham-Newman.

"One of the reasons I resented this was because I found the stock and was pleased that Ben was buying it for Graham-Newman," Schloss said. "I also resented it that he [the friend] didn't ask Ben's permission."

Another time, a complete stranger came to the office and asked to talk to Ben. Ben was out of town, but the caller left a message. He just wanted to thank Ben. Every six months, Graham-Newman published their holdings and the caller would go out and buy the same stocks. He expressed his appreciation for all the money he had made.[8]

Because it irritated Schloss that copycats could ride free or even interfere with investment strategy, he never published his own portfolio. "When it is known, it affects the stock."

Ben knew the risks of being too frank, but did not seem to worry about it. "I have been accused of telling all my secrets," he once joked at a U.S. Senate hearing. "I have written a number of books and reveal them all in these books."

Actually, Graham-Newman did take some action to mitigate the situation, which Ben described at the 1955 Senate hearings. When Graham-Newman was first incorporated, 50,000 shares were sold for $100 per share.

But, Ben explained to the committee, "We discovered—this may interest you, Senator [to Senator James William Fulbright]—that we were beginning to get a great many one-share stockholders, people we had never heard of who came in and invested a hundred-odd dollars and then got our reports and found out what we were doing and imitated it. So to deal with that situation, we perpetrated a reverse split-up in which we issued one share for ten, increased the unit value in the market to about $1,200 or $1,300 a share, and from that time on, we did not get quite so many one-share stockholders."[9]

ECONOMIC THEORIES TAKE WING

The trauma of the 1930s and the easier stock market of the 1940s allowed Ben to expand his intellectual interests and to pursue other interests.

The New School for Social Research was just the type of inventive idea that appealed to Ben, one that helped expand his social awareness. The college started as a type of adult school in New York with specialization in social sciences and languages. However, the school developed a distinguished faculty by serving as a refuge for displaced European intellectuals. In the early 1930s, the New School for Social Research President Alvin Johnson would assemble a discussion group of leaders that included William McChesney Martin, a chairman of the board of governors of the Federal Reserve and a president of the New York Stock Exchange and many other leading citizens. The group's purpose was to deliberate on the turmoil that had afflicted the United States in recent decades and dare to suggest ways to stabilize the economy and promote prosperity.

Few people in the country felt that they had a grip on economic issues, yet following World War I and during the Great Depression, the health of the global economy worried everyone. Furthermore, noted one insightful economist, "We know that depression is the enemy of democracy." It was in this intellectually stimulating group that Ben's interest in broader economic subjects was aroused and encouraged. As busy as he was with investing, writing and teaching, Ben made the time to present a lecture series at the New School.

Ben had pondered such matters before—especially during the post–World War I recession of 1921–1922. In the early 1920s, after the national economy took several roller-coaster rides, various public theories were contrived to cushion the fall of prices that inevitably followed a hyperactive economic period. The volatility of money is of fundamental importance to an investor, because if the market goes up but the value of the dollar declines, the investor makes no real gain. Ben began to theorize that recessions and depressions were triggered by the inability of consumers to purchase the increased production that results from an economic boom.

Ben soon learned that a similar thesis was put forth in J. A. Hobson's authoritative text, *The Economics of Unemployment*. Hobson's book had an important influence on John Maynard Keynes and Keynes's 1935 book, *The General Theory of Employment, Interest and Money*.

THE ENEMY INFLATION

The dollar still was pegged to gold during those years between the World Wars, and some observers felt that simply adjusting the gold basis of the dollar would do the job. As appealing as the gold standard is to many people, pegging the dollar to gold never had prevented inflation or economic gyrations. For example, between 1901 and 1910, wholesale prices advanced 27.5 percent. Between 1932 and 1937, prices climbed 90 percent in this country. Ben decided that gold no longer was an important enough commodity to serve its historic function as a proxy for money. Furthermore, with the burgeoning world population, there would not be enough gold to back every currency.

Ben figured that a better way would be to peg the dollar to a fixed group of 21 essential raw materials, in other words, a market basket of commodities that everyone needed and used. The basket of commodities would be exchangeable for a dollar at a fixed rate much like the gold point, which for years was $35 an ounce.

Soon after Ben came up with the idea, the inventor Thomas A. Edison proposed a similar plan, though nothing ever came of the inventor's suggestion. By the time Edison published his proposal, the economic recovery of the 1920s was in progress, prices settled down and people stopped fretting about the stability of prices. Ben, too, became absorbed by the rush of events and let his ideas rest.

But in the early 1930s, as deflation again racked the country, Ben again began to think about the theory. If there were adequate storehouses of basic necessities and if inflation could be kept in check, two of the world's most disruptive and painful problems could be circumvented: famine and war. What evolved from there was Ben's multiple-commodity-reserve— or buffer-stock—theory. It also was called the theory of the ever-normal granary. This concept was among four innovative ideas that Ben presented to Alvin Johnson's group in the form of a mimeographed memorandum.

The other ideas were a proposal for slum clearance and subsidized low-cost housing; a system of low-interest loans from the federal government to the unemployed; and most intriguing of all, a scheme for France to satisfy its World War I debts by sending to the United States 40 million bottles of wine per year. This suggestion would provide each U.S. citizen with a bottle of French wine.[10] In addition to adding gaiety to the dour mood of the country, Ben believed a wine-for-debt swap could create a cultural bond between the United States and France, two countries with a rather pedestrian relationship.

A STABLE CURRENCY

Two members of the New School group, William McChesney Martin and Joseph Mead, inaugurated an ambitious quarterly journal, *The Economic Forum*, and it was the idea for price stabilization that interested the new editors most. Ben contributed an essay to a 1933 issue entitled "Stabilized Reflation," which expanded on his commodity reserve plan. Ben's treatise was the first presentation of the idea in the United States, though, unknown to Ben, a professor of economics at the University of Rotterdam had come up with a similar strategy. Ben eventually became friends with the professor, Jan Goudriaan, as he would with other economists who had a concern for the issue.

A friend of Ben's forwarded a copy of the article to President Franklin D. Roosevelt, who was formulating his ambitious social engineering project, the New Deal. Ben's friend soon reported back that the concepts were under serious consideration in the nation's capital. Two years later, an economic adviser to the secretary of agriculture contacted Ben to discuss his ever-normal granary. It appeared that the plan might be useful in connection with the Commodity Credit Corporation, which had been created to support farm prices. Henry A. Wallace, who then was secretary of agriculture, liked Ben's idea. "From the standpoint of the national interest, the consuming interest and the agricultural interest," Wallace said, "the increased stability of supply and price that would come with the ever-normal granary is essential."[11]

Ben worked even more earnestly on the plan, compiling such a significant body of material that in 1937 he published his third book. McGraw-Hill, the publisher, had doubts about the sales potential for the new book, *Storage and Stability: A Modern Ever-Normal Granary*, but the publishing house was pleased to accommodate the senior writer of one of its best-sellers, *Security Analysis*. Bernard Baruch, who by then was an adviser to President Roosevelt, received galley proofs so that he could rush a copy to the president.

AN INFLUENCE ON KEYNES

Though this third book never sold in the quantities of its predecessors, *Storage and Stability* did arrest the imaginations of many eminent economists, including the leading architect of the post–World War II world economic structure, John Maynard Keynes. In one of Keynes's treatises on commodity policy, he made a footnote reference to *Storage and Stability*. In that paper, Keynes pointed out a difference in the way he personally calculated the cost of storing commodities versus Ben's method. It was a gentlemanly discussion, but later Ben and Keynes suffered a misunderstanding with a sharp edge to it.

On December 31, 1943, Keynes wrote to Ben from England:

> Dear Mr. Graham:
> The articles of yourself and Professor [Frank Dunstone] Graham made me feel that it was a great mistake for one, who, being occupied on official work, has no leisure except to write briefly on one particular point without the full background of his thought and is not free to publish the more detailed work he has actually been doing on the subject behind the scenes, to write for publication at all. For the result, as your article shows, is to lead to a wild misconception of one's opinions. And nothing is more futile than public controversy about what one has *not* said and does *not* mean.

Keynes wrote on, denying that he believed that any mechanism aimed at stabilizing prices is undesirable or that full employment can be maintained while money wages are rising faster than efficiency.

> On the use of buffer stocks as a means of stabilizing short-term commodity prices, you and I are ardent crusaders on the same side, so do not let a falsely conceived controversy arise between us.
> Yours Very Truly

The letter was initialed "K."[12]

In 1944, McGraw-Hill published Ben's second book on this subject, one that expanded his thinking and research in price stabilization to encompass the entire globe. The contract for *World Commodities and World Currencies* was again a simple, one-page letter and signature page, which gave Ben 40 percent of the list price for domestic sales and 20 percent of foreign sales.

In testimony before Senator James Fulbright's banking committee several years later, Ben summarized the premise of the book:

> I have been identified with a concept of stabilizing the economy by stabilizing the price level of raw materials taken as a whole and not in individual commodities. The objective has been to permit individual commodities to fluctuate but to establish a market basket of the important commodities. I have added to it the very important factor, quite radical, that those commodities would represent a sound backing for our money, because they represent the things that we need and use, and by so doing they would become commodity reserves and would be self-financing in the same way our gold reserves are self-financing. The consequence would be that by stabilizing pretty well the general level of raw materials prices you would add a very important degree of stability to the general economy.[13]

THE EVER-NORMAL GRANARY

Ben strove to forge a safety valve between something tangible—commodities such as wheat, corn, cotton, sugar and petroleum—and that global intangible, money. His "ever-normal granary" was a sophisticated bartering system. Anyone could take a basket of these commodities, or actually receipts for the combination of commodities that made up the unit, to the Treasury, which would then issue a dollar for each basket. The Treasury would simply hold on to the commodity units, leaving them in the storage facilities where they had always resided. In this way, there always would be a willing buyer for the commodities at a certain price. Commodity prices, therefore, always would enjoy some basic level of support and, additionally, reserves would build that could be used in time of drought, war or other crisis.

Conversely, a person could, if he or she wished, take a dollar to the Treasury and receive a commodity unit in return. When he or she did so, the dollar would be taken out of circulation, thus reducing the supply of money and curbing rising prices and hence limiting inflation.

The plan would place a general floor price on the commodities in the basket, under which prices would not fall, and a ceiling price over which prices would not rise. Because the exchange could be made only for the basket of commodities rather than for a single commodity (for example, oil, corn or cotton alone), the price of any individual commodity was left free to respond to market conditions. The price of oil might rise, for example, but if the price of corn had fallen, the value of the entire commodity unit would stay the same.

The long-term impact of the ever-normal granary, Ben believed, would be a secure and expanding world financial structure in which both large and small nations could participate. It would have the added advantage of protecting consumers and governments from the domination of cartels and taxpayers from the extravagant spending of government bureaucrats.

"The plan is automatic, impersonal, nonpolitical and self-controlling, involving no use of an index number, no curtailment of production or regimentation of any store, no modification of banking or market procedures, no vesting of discretionary powers in anyone for managing the currency or regulating prices or production or consumption," wrote the Committee for Economic Stability in its white paper on the subject. That committee was made up of a cadre of Graham's Wall Street regulars such as Irving Kahn, Walter Schloss and Jerry Newman, plus several dozen academic and government executives. On the whole, the committee seemed to be the offspring of Johnson's discussion group at the New School for Social Research.

BRETTON WOODS

Under the sponsorship of the Committee for Economic Stability, Ben forwarded a paper describing his concept to the 1944

Bretton Woods Conference. At this historic New Hampshire international conclave, formally dubbed the United Nations Financial and Monetary Conference, the International Monetary Fund and the International Bank for Reconstruction and Development were created, establishing the groundwork for post–World War II recovery.

Though Ben's plan was not adopted, he did not give up. His related booklet, *National Productivity: Its Relationship to Unemployment in Prosperity,* was reprinted in the May, 1947, issue of the *American Economic Review.* The reserves concept was presented again at an International Monetary Fund Conference in Mexico City in 1952 and Ben explained his theories in testimony before the U.S. Senate Banking Committee in 1955. The idea of using commodities as a backing for currency arises anew from time to time, and even now, its proponents believe it could relieve some of the inequities that continue to vex world economies.

It is difficult to measure the impact that Ben's ideas had on Keynes and others whose influence is undisputed, but it is clear that his recommendations were heard as respectfully by scholars and policy makers as they were by the investment community.

In the midst of all the sober debate on economic stability, Ben still found time to lampoon some of the foibles of finance, especially the accounting practices that are intended to delude security analysts and investors. In 1936, Ben satirized one of his perennial targets, the venerable U.S. Steel Corporation. At the same time, he burned in effigy the new accounting practices that were sweeping the corporate world in general.

NEEDLING U.S. STEEL

U.S. Steel's chairman had just announced a "sweeping modernization scheme," Ben wrote mischievously. "Contrary to expectations, no changes will be made in the company's manufacturing or selling policies. Instead, the bookkeeping system is to be entirely revamped. By adopting and further improving a number of modern accounting and financial devices, the corporation's earning power will be amazingly transformed. Even under the subnormal conditions of 1935, it is estimated that the new bookkeeping methods would have yielded a reported profit of $50 per share on the common stock." Ben cleverly explained how a loser could be turned into a winner simply by switching accounting categories as swiftly as peas under walnut shells. The satirized U.S. Steel was not worried about being edged out by competitors who adopted the same tactics, Ben explained. "Should necessity arise, moreover, we believe we shall be able to maintain our deserved superiority by introducing still more advanced bookkeeping methods, which are even now under development in our Experimental Accounting Laboratory."

The parody was not published at the time, but it did appear years later in the *Financial Analysts Journal* and Ben gave a copy to Warren Buffett, who printed it as an appendix to his chairman's letters to Berkshire Hathaway shareholders. The satire, sorry to say, has as much relevance in the 1990s as it did in the 1930s.[14]

CITIZEN GRAHAM

Ben's concern for global issues expanded his reputation far beyond the cloisters of Wall Street. The entire decade of the 1940s was a flurry of speeches, conferences and voluntary government service. He served as associate director of the Treasury Department's New York State War Finance Committee and as chairman of the government's War Contracts Price Adjustment Board during World War II. His appointments carried only a token salary. He was a so-called dollar-a-year man for the government.

Many of Ben's speeches were delivered to academic and scientific groups. In 1941, he addressed a joint dinner meeting of the regular and business sections of the American Statistical Association at the University Club in Hartford, Connecticut. The dinner cost $1.10 and Ben spoke on his favorite passion—"A Program for Stabilizing the Purchasing Power of the Dollar."

His subject was equally serious when he addressed the 1946 Summer Institute for Social Progress in Wellesley, Massachusetts. He spoke there on "Our Economic Future, Its Direction and Control." Ben became so popular that in the early 1940s, the National Concert and Artists Corporation asked to represent him on the lecture circuit.

Walter Schloss remembers hearing him in a debate for the first and only time, though the subject was not so high-minded as most of Ben's speeches.

"In 1941, I went to a dinner meeting at the Downtown Athletic Club, where Ben debated Floyd Odlum, chairman of Atlas Corporation," Schloss said. A flamboyant Coloradan who made and lost money in many different industries, Odlum hobnobbed with Howard Hughes and was married to aviatrix Jacqueline Cochran.

"Odlum decided the way to make money was to buy companies in trouble and revamp them. Graham debated him, saying that it was safer to buy a variety of stocks."

Odlum had his own ideas though, and, according to Schloss, later invested all of his money in uranium companies. "They went down, and he had all his eggs in one basket," Schloss said. "It's the only time I heard Ben debate."

COSMOPOLITAN NUPTIALS

Even though Ben now was widely recognized and his wisdom valued, his personal life continued to dismay his family.

Marjorie remembers meeting Carol Wade, Ben's new girlfriend, for the first time. "She was only about nine years older than me."

"I was a teenager, and my father invited me out to a nightclub," she said, remembering how pleased she was that her father wanted to spend an evening with her. "I was excited and got all dressed up. I was somewhat overweight and self-conscious and didn't get dressed up much at that age. We went in, and there he introduced me to Carol. She was a model, thin and beautiful by Hollywood standards. I was crushed. I hated her."

Carol was 26 years old and Ben was 44 when they were married at the Sherry Netherland Hotel in May of 1938. The elegant Italian-Renaissance Sherry Netherland, which is on Fifth Avenue next to The Pierre and across the street from The Plaza, was a handsome setting for a wedding. The ceremony was performed by a minister who described himself as "leader of the Society for Ethical Culture." Ben's brother Leon served as best man.

Mickey Newman was a teenager when Ben and Carol married. "I was at his second wedding," Mickey recalls. "At the time, divorce was not as normal a course of events as it is today. I was shocked and interested. This new young wife of his—of course, today wouldn't have aroused anyone's interest as it did then."

Ben had a reputation for fondness for willowy blonds, but in fact, Carol was the only blond he married. His other two wives were brunettes, as was his final paramour, whom he did not wed.

"The second marriage didn't last long," Marjorie said.

Within a year of their wedding, Ben and Carol were divorced. Friends and family attributed the breakup to the age difference and Ben's inability to keep up with the pace of his young Canadian bride. But the actual difficulty was not known. In general, says Marjorie, "His wives felt he was cold and unemotional. He thought this was the way to be. He was influenced by the early philosophers and was inclined toward the stoic."

A family member once accused Ben of being humane, but not human. Ben admitted that beginning in his youth and for most of his adulthood, he had felt that most women were demanding, bossy, unappreciative and—worst of all—aggravating in their quest for emotional intimacy. Unfortunately, he added, this tendency to protect his inner self had kept him from having truly close friends, either female or male.

STREET CRIME

Ben's stoicism, unfortunately, constantly was tested. His mother, by now nearing her 70th year, was in excellent health, living independently in New York and taking good care of herself. Old-fashioned, indomitable and elegant, she went about her business with vigor. An avid bridge player, Dora met with her friends several nights a week for a game. She also was building family ties.

In 1944, Marjorie Graham, who since had gone to college and married Irving Janis, returned to New York City with her newborn daughter Cathy to await her husband's return from military service. Marjorie remembered without much pleasure her childhood Sunday visits with her grandmother. They were formal and rather ritualized, and Dora often gave her grandchildren candy. The Graham children did not feel close to their father's mother.

"She was kind of a cold person," Marjorie recalled, "not the warm person my other grandmother was. She had this terrible habit of twisting our cheeks as a sign of affection, but it was horribly painful."

As adults, however, Marjorie and her grandmother began to get reacquainted. "She was just starting to tell me about herself," Marjorie explained. Then, one night, Dora was murdered.

On her way home from a bridge game, Dora was attacked by a mugger and struggled to hold on to her handbag. She was thrown to the ground and died when her fragile skull slammed to the sidewalk.

Ben grievously mourned the loss of his mother despite the fact that their personalities sometimes kept them at odds. "They were very close," Marjorie said, "in their own way."

Despite the tendency to obscure his feelings, Ben was cordial, nonjudgmental, and his friends and family saw his soft spots. "He was a very generous man," Marjorie explained, not the least bit avaricious. He wished people well, gave them a chance to prove themselves and lent or donated money without a second thought.

As indicated by his interest in economics and wartime government service, Ben's sense of civic responsibility was strong. From 1951 to 1953, Ben served as president of the Jewish Guild for the Blind in New York, a nondenominational charity to which he, Jerry Newman and his wife and Irving Kahn gave financial support for many years. Ben was a board member for 40 years, and even after moving to California, he maintained his interest in the Guild's work. Kahn became the Guild's treasurer, and in 1993, his son, Thomas Graham Kahn, replaced Irving on the board. In recent years, the Guild has been active in caring for young and adult AIDS victims of all races and religions, especially those who lose their sight because of the illness.

A THIRD TRY

Near the end of World War II, Ben took his third wife, this time his secretary, Estelle Messing. Estey was an astute young woman who saw humor in everything and enjoyed poking fun, especially at Ben. Ben and Estey lived in a building on Central Park South. Their neighbor was younger than Estey by more than a decade, but like Estey, she was married to an older man. Ben, then 51 and a grandfather, became a father for the sixth time. "I was born in 1945," explained Benjamin "Buzz" Graham, Jr. "I'm pretty sure they were married at the time."

By now, Ben was accumulating a rather large number of people to support, but the added expenses did not concern him. He told Walter Schloss, "It's easier for me to make money than it is for me to cut down on my spending."

Both women were expecting their first babies. Edythe Safron (who later became Mrs. Morton Kenner) and Estey shared a nanny for their young sons and kept an eye on one another's children when one was away. Edythe remembers how much Estey liked to give parties.

"Estey and Ben were having a dinner party for Professor Dodd and a few other people," Edythe recalls, "and Buzzy's nursemaid, who helped, took sick. There wasn't enough help at the last minute to serve dinner. I said, 'I'll get into a maid's uniform and do it.' I was about 23 or 24 at the time. I served the first and second course, and people were looking at me, including Professor Dodd. I gave him a wink, then he told everybody who I was and I joined them all for dinner. Dodd was rather a straight-laced kind of man."

Edythe Safron, a strikingly attractive young woman, got to know Ben well. "We laughed about him being an absent-minded professor," she said. "He would wear one black shoe and one brown shoe. Estey would give him a package to deliver and he would leave it on the subway."

Edythe Kenner also frankly discussed Ben's shameless sexual advances and how much that annoyed her. But, she says, she also enjoyed his personality and respected his intellect. "He loved women," she said, but he was nevertheless a kind and generous person. "He was not a pretentious man."

Though she rejected his propositions, Edythe sought Ben's guidance in investing a few dollars that she had managed to save from household expenses. Ben willingly told her what investments to make and offered to help each time she saved up more money. Under Ben's tutelage, Edythe built a respectable portfolio. As time went on, she, her children and her grandchildren became investors in Buffett's Berkshire Hathaway. Her grade-school grandson has become famous for asking piercing questions of Warren Buffett at the Berkshire Hathaway annual meetings. Obviously, not all of Ben's students met in his classroom or studied his books.

TO THE SUBURBS

Edythe Kenner continued to visit Estey after the Grahams moved to the suburbs. The Grahams bought a white clapboard New England-style home at Seven Harcourt Road in Scarsdale. The house was near the high school, across the playing field from the Boy Scout House. George Heyman, who became a neighbor in Scarsdale, often commuted with Ben on the train. Ben brought stacks of brokers' reports, which he scanned quickly, then tossed on the floor if they did not appear to be a stock that interested him. By the time they reached Scarsdale, Heyman said, "it looked like it had snowed around our seats."

Both Little Newton and Winnie, for a while, moved to Scarsdale to live with their father and stepmother. "After Ben and Hazel divorced," Marjorie Janis said, "Newton had a lot of difficulties. He went to live with Ben and Estey, who incidentally was a very nice person." Newton found it painful to relate to people and spent hours reclusively in the attic playing his cello. "They were not able to keep him. They sent him to boarding school."

Winnie, who was a preschooler when her parents separated, also had difficulty getting along with her domineering mother. "When Winnie was a teenager she was a free spirit. She had a good relationship with Estey, but she never got close to Dad. She never seemed to appreciate him, nor him her."

Buzz soon was old enough to go to Camp Winnebago on his own. His counselor wrote to Ben and Estey, assuring them that

Buzzy was a good little camper and was not, as they feared, spending too much time reading.

As if he did not have enough to do, Ben taught an evening class at Scarsdale Adults School and took up several new interests.

This was the era of dance sensations—Fred and Adele Astaire and everyone, including Ben, were caught up in ballroom dancing. Ben paid $25,000 for a lifetime membership in an Arthur Murray studio, where he religiously reported for dancing lessons. Not that it ever made much difference.

"One year, they threw a formal New Year's Eve party," remembered Ben's cousin-in-law Bernie Sarnat. "I talked with Estey afterward and she complained of how awkwardly Ben danced."

"He would dance counting aloud—one, two, three, four—he would mouth it," Rhoda Sarnat elucidated. Because he was consciously keeping time, Ben could not dance and carry on a conversation simultaneously. Still, he was faithful about his lessons, perhaps, observed a friend, because he cottoned to the dancing instructors.

Ben took an interest in another new sport. He built an addition on the house that jokingly was called Ben's "$10,000 Ping-Pong room." At the time, $10,000 was a lot of money to pay for a simple room addition. Despite his hectic schedule, the Grahams seemed happy together. In 1952, Ben sent Estey a large red-satin, boxed valentine, "A loving valentine for you dear," it read, "from your Ben."

CHAPTER 7

The Quiet Gardens of Safety and Value:
The Intelligent Investor

*"To achieve satisfactory investment results is easier than most
people realize: to achieve superior results is harder than it looks."*

—Benjamin Graham[1]

It was in 1942, eight years after *Security Analysis* was first published, that the New York Society of Security Analysts (NYSSA) first began discussing Ben's concept for a proficiency rating that would put qualified analysts on a par with accountants, attorneys and other professions. Ben first outlined the proposal and its advantages in the January, 1940, issue of *The Analysts Journal.* Because he had helped found NYSSA five years earlier with 18 other Wall Street buddies, Ben's opinion carried extraordinary weight. Driven by his passion for the subject, Ben ruffled the feathers of those who felt threatened by the prospect of being appraised by their peers.

Ben usually avoided rancor, but he felt so strongly about building the reputation of the profession that he was undeterred by opposition. As chairman of the New York Society's Committee on Standards, on May 8, 1942, he submitted a formal proposal to the organization for setting up a "board of qualifiers" to confer the title of "qualified security analyst" upon applicants who met certain standards, including character, education, practical experience and the passing of a stringent examination. He envisioned that a state board of regents or some other government body would someday supervise the test and confer certification.

TOWARD A RESPECTED PROFESSION

Such a system, Ben contended, would assure the public that a person calling himself or herself an analyst had the training, knowledge and competence to do the job. It would give the analyst prestige, improve his or her job prospects and possibly lead to increased salaries. Very soon, and by a margin of 90 to 6, the NYSSA voted "in principle" for the professional designation.

An opponent, Lucien Hooper, countered that regardless of the merits of such an idea, it had no support from the public, nor from employers, and that there was little enthusiasm within the analyst community itself. Furthermore, he argued, while so many younger men were away at war, it was unfair to set up standards that might exclude them.

Though the objectors were small in number, they were vocal and they had war-heightened patriotism behind them. They succeeded in postponing action for nearly two decades.

Ben continued to lobby for the idea. He wrote profusely and pushed for advancement of standards in *The Analysts Journal*, which in 1960, changed its name to the *Financial Analysts Journal*. His committee on standards published its reports there, but Ben also agitated for change independently. In the earlier years, Ben penned articles on many subjects for the journal anonymously under the pseudonym, "Cogitator." Later, he wrote under his own name.

A DRESSING DOWN

When the Financial Analysts Federation (which later became the Institute of Chartered Financial Analysts) held its first annual conference in 1947, Ben addressed the assembly and sang his familiar refrain—the group must have formal qualifications. Again in 1952, when the group split its annual meeting between Los Angeles and San Francisco, Ben made his customary plea during a speech entitled "Toward a Science of Security Analysis."

"With this week's elaborate and enthusiastic proceedings, one is tempted to say that security analysts and security analysis have finally come of age and are entering upon their full patrimony of dignity and power," he said. "But it is not my present purpose to compliment the Societies on their progress—impressive as it has been—but rather to summon you to deeper efforts and wider accomplishments."[2]

Ben restated his earlier arguments and in this 1952 speech additionally called for a regimen that eventually became commonplace and in certain cases, was mandated by law.

ACCOUNTABILITY

"The greatest weakness of our profession, I have long believed, is our failure to provide really comprehensive records of the results of investments initiated or carried on by us under various principles and techniques. We have asked for unlimited statistics from others covering the results of their operations, but we have been more than backward in compiling fair and adequate statistics relating to the results of our own work." Ben called for the collection and systematic analysis of information identical to the methods used in the sciences. He told the analysts quite frankly that they had problems with a poor public image. "It is unlikely that security analysis could develop professional stature in the absence of reasonably definite and plausible tests of the soundness of individual and group recommendations."[3]

AN EASIER BIBLE

Motivated by the need for consumer education and protection, Ben acted on his own to achieve some of these goals when, in 1949, he produced a version of his investment text designed for the individual investor. Such a reader was likely to be put off by the size and depth of *Security Analysis*.

The new book was published by a different publishing house, Harper & Row, and the contract was not so generous as the one for Ben's first book. The Harper & Row agreement called for the standard 10 percent of sales up to 5,000 copies,

12.5 percent to 7,500 and 15 percent thereafter. In this case, however, Ben would not be sharing royalties with a coauthor.

The Intelligent Investor was a hit. A book of less than half the size of *Security Analysis*, nevertheless it was written with the same clarity and integrity. In it, Ben clearly distinguished between investing and speculating. An investment, he explained, was based on incisive, quantitative analysis, while speculation depends on whim and guesswork. The book also focused less on bonds and railroad issues and more on stocks. Ben intended the book for the man on Main Street, but as with his earlier book, Wall Street professionals found it indispensable. Because it was so widely read, the book brought greater visibility, respect and prestige to the field of security analysis.

THE INVESTOR'S DEFENSE

The counsel in *The Intelligent Investor* is straightforward and simple to follow. In the section under per-share earnings, Ben points out all the insider tricks for making earnings look stronger, or to dump as many lost dollars as possible into an earnings period that is beyond resuscitation. By sweeping away losses that ordinarily would be amortized, subsequent earning periods will shine. The investor's defense is simple, he said—to average a company's earnings over a seven- to ten-year period to determine its true earning power. When the earnings average is combined with or compared to other measurable factors, a more accurate financial picture emerges.

Ben made liberal use of his favorite classroom techniques, choosing companies that appeared adjacent to one another in the newspaper stock tables, such as Eltra, Emerson Electric, Emery Air Freight and Emhart. The adjacent listings worked well as a group case study because their current price/earnings ratios varied much more than their operating performance or financial conditions.

Emery Air Freight seemed the most promising of the four according to Ben's calculations, and, indeed, the company was poised in a growing industry. The history of the stock prices of each of the "E" companies since the book was published proves Ben's point that at various times, share prices fluctuate between under value and over value and it is the investor's job to figure out whether a company is climbing a hill or descending to a valley before buying a stock.

FOR THE LONG HAUL

While Ben invariably advised individual investors to buy for the long term, he himself bought stocks with many different time objectives in mind. Arbitrage plays usually were short-term investments, for arbitrage situations ordinarily work themselves out within a matter of months. Yet, Ben believed that an individual investor, or any investor who lacked the time and temperament to track his or her securities on a regular basis, should invest with simpler and longer-term objectives.

YARDSTICK FOR PERFORMANCE

In using the E-companies example, Ben introduced the six essential business factors used to evaluate company performance: profitability, stability, growth, financial position, dividends and price history.

- Profitability can be measured in several ways, such as straight profits or profit per dollar of sales, but Ben preferred the ratio of operating income to sales as an indication of comparative weakness or strength.

- Stability is assessed by the trend of per-share earnings over a ten-year period, compared to the average of the most recent three years. No decline represents 100 percent stability.

- Growth of earnings per share can be compared to that of the DJIA as a whole.

- Financial position is determined by a company's debt ratio. A sound company should have no more than $1 of current liabilities for $2 of current assets, or stated another way, a debt of no more than 50 percent of its current assets.

- When considering dividends, what counts most is a history of dividend payment without interruption—the longer the payment the better. It is even better if dividends are paid at a fixed percentage of profits and show a steady pattern of growth.

- Price history is important. While a stock may periodically fall out of favor and lose share price for any number of reasons, it is encouraging when a company's share price keeps pace by regular appreciation over the long term.

A TIME WHEN IT PAID TO BREAK THE RULES

The Intelligent Investor is still a mainstay on the business-section shelves of well-stocked bookstores. It has evolved over the years, and some of the most interesting sections are added either at the front or the back of the text. In the postscript to *The Intelligent Investor's* fifth edition, Ben coyly recounts the parable of anonymous investment managers who took a chance on an also unnamed small company. The investors came close to backing out of the purchase because the company was unable to fully guarantee a minor technical point. Ironically, Graham wrote, this single investment earned more money for the partners than all others made "through 20 years of wide-ranging operations, involving much investigation, endless pondering and countless individual decisions."[4] To confound their theories even more, when the company's stock rose above the price where all their rules dictated a sale, they held on. The stock became worth more than 200 times what they had paid for it. What company could he be talking about other than GEICO, and what investors other than Graham-Newman Corporation? Ben constantly reminded his readers that there were many ways to make money in the stock market besides the ones he prescribed.

SUBTLE MISINTERPRETATIONS

Like so many other profound works, more people seem to pay lip service to *The Intelligent Investor* and Ben's other books than actually read them. As William Ruane is quick to point out, there are many misinterpretations of Ben's teachings. Graham himself once said that his books "have probably been read and disregarded by more people than any book on finance that I know of."[5] Some of the ignored or misunderstood points are subtle, but important.

In *Supermoney*, for example, Adam Smith notes that Graham originally divided investors into two categories—defensive and aggressive. "The defensive or passive investor was concerned with maintaining his principal and securing a return on it. The aggressive investor was to be rewarded for his attitude toward risk," Smith wrote.[6]

PRUDENT SPECULATION

While it is accurate that Ben distinguished between the aggressive (professional) and defensive (nonprofessional) investor, his message was much more subtle than that described by Smith. "It has been an old and sound principle that those who cannot afford to take risks should be content with a relatively low return on their invested funds," Ben wrote. "From this, there has developed the general notion that the rate of return which the investor should aim for is more or less proportionate to the degree of risk he is ready to run. Our view is different. The rate of return sought should be dependent, rather, on the amount of intelligent effort the investor is willing and able to bring to bear on his task."[7]

Many who quote Graham insist that he had no tolerance for speculation, which again, was not technically accurate. There are many intelligent ways of speculating, Ben told his readers, but there also are many ways in which speculation is not intelligent. It is best to know the difference between smart speculation and dumb speculation, or avoid speculation altogether. However, he added, just because an investor loses money on a speculation does not mean the decision was a bad one; after all, the very word *speculation* implies added risk and the acceptance of a certain number of missed calls. "A speculation is unwise only if it is made on insufficient study and by poor judgment," Ben told one of his students.[8]

Ben had seen other authors suffer his own fate of being only partially understood. In a 1951 speech before the New York State Bankers Association, Ben referred to an investment theory first put forth in one of his favorite books, *Common Stocks as Long-Term Investments,* by Edgar Lawrence Smith. "There is nothing wrong with that book except that too many people believed in it and didn't read it carefully," he noted.

WATCHFUL STEWARDSHIP

Ben went on to admonish his audience, "You bankers, I urge, should accept the theory of common stocks as a medium of investment; but accept it warily, not as a Gospel, but as a business proposition subject to continuous business tests."

The Intelligent Investor reached far and wide into the community of passionate investors.

A FLASH OF UNDERSTANDING

Warren Buffett, who read the book at 19, was among many thousands of investors who saw the light when they read *The Intelligent Investor.* "No one has ever become poor reading Graham," Buffett says. Buffett suggests investors pay special heed to Chapter 8, which tells them how to adopt the right attitude toward their investments, and Chapter 20, which distills all of Ben's prior teaching and writing on the concept of buying a common stock at such a price that the likelihood of losing money is small. Ben described this as a margin of safety.

MARGIN OF SAFETY

"Confronted with a challenge to distill the secret of sound investment into three words, we venture the motto 'Margin of Safety'," Ben wrote.

"Forty-two years after reading that," Buffett said in one of his annual reports, "I still think those are the right three words. The failure of investors to heed this simple message caused them staggering losses as the 1990s began."[9]

Anytime the stock market veers off in a dramatically different direction, Buffett suggests going back to *The Intelligent
Investor.* "You'll find something new every time you read it,"
he insists.

CONSISTENT RETURNS

The publishers of *The Intelligent Investor*, Harper & Row, will
not release total sales numbers on the book, but there are
published reports that in the first two decades after it came out,
more than 100,000 copies of the book were sold. An estimate
from royalty statements in recent years implies that while sales
have not been large, they have been consistent. For example,
through the 1970s, sales ranged from 3,500-plus to 7,000-plus
per year. This is an average of more than 4,600 annually. Over
the 44 years between 1949, when the book came out, until 1993,
that would mean more than 200,000 copies have been sold.
Because sales of the book were most likely higher in the early
years, total sales surely are much greater than this crude estimate. In 1992, the last full year for royalty reports, *The Intelligent Investor* sold 6,600 copies. Some books never sell that many
copies in their entire lifetime.

Benjamin "Buzz" Graham, Jr., who has owned the royalties
since his father's death in 1976, does not himself know how
many total copies of the book are in circulation. Book sales go
up, Buzz says, in a bear market but fall off in a bull market. For
years, Buzz received about $50,000 a year in royalties from all
of his father's books, more money than he was earning as a
rural physician.

Though the total publication number remains a mystery,
there is no question that Ben's books have been a terrific
blessing for the Graham family. The income has been reliable,
and because royalties are based on a percentage of the cover
price, which has risen steadily with inflation, book royalties
have multiplied as time passed.

In later years, Ben often said that he thought young people
starting out, or any investor for that matter, would profit more
from reading *The Intelligent Investor* than from reading *Security*

Analysis. He added that readers should pick from his advice those points that they feel will work for them, then stick with their plan. It was not part of his nature to insist that students, readers or colleagues be rigid adherents to his or other principles. In fact, he regularly questioned and challenged old ideas. For this reason, it was his intent to revise *The Intelligent Investor* every five to eight years.

THE WISE YOUNG LADY

Not all of Ben's attempts to educate investors appeared in learned journals or sober hardback books. In 1952, he composed a piece for *Mademoiselle* magazine—"When do you start investing?" In a rather condescending yet pragmatic way, he pointed out that "the native talent that women have for getting their money's worth when buying groceries can be very useful in finance. . . . If you are shopping for common stocks, choose them the way you would buy groceries, not the way you would buy perfume."

Women of today might be sorely offended by the piece, but at that time, only the nerviest woman would have shot off an indignant letter to the editor. These were the 1950s, after all, the Eisenhower years in the United States. The country was calmer and growing more prosperous, as were the partners of Graham-Newman. Ben's third book was a triumph, his business was strong and he pressed forward his favorite public causes, including that of professional standards for analysts. Eventually, he won that battle. In the early 1960s, a national society was formed from the numerous analysts societies in the 50 states, creating a sponsoring organization for the credentialing process. On January 30, 1962, the first examinations were given to certify financial analysts.

CERTIFICATION AT LAST

Paradoxically, Ben himself never took the Certified Financial Analyst examinations. By the time the tests were offered, he was retired and living in Beverly Hills. There seemed little point in carrying the professional designation. But today, there are more than 18,000 Certified Financial Analysts practicing around the country. They are constantly in demand and they receive among the highest salaries in the financial field. The Association for Investment Management and Research, as the former Financial Analysts Federation now is called, and the *Financial Analysts Journal* editors recognize that Ben was a resolute warrior in the battle for certification.[10]

ALEXANDER AND BENJAMIN

Through his writing for the *Financial Analysts Journal*, Ben became close friends with Helen Slade, who brilliantly guided the evolution of the journal. Both Ben and Helen loved cats. Helen's favorite cat was called Alexander. She purchased numerous stocks under Alexander's name, and after the cat died, Slade established an award in Alexander's name for the best article each year in the *Journal*.

Several years after Slade died, the award's name was changed to the Graham and Dodd Award.

"Ben never did make up his mind as to whether or not it was an honor to ascend to Alexander's place," wrote his friend Irving Kahn, though he recognized Slade's pioneer efforts in behalf of the *Financial Analysts Journal*.[11]

THE AFTERMARKET

There are many testaments to Benjamin Graham's gift to the world of finance. One of the most spontaneous of those can be found in the hills of Bel Air, California, not far from Graham's Beverly Hills home.

There, book collector and dealer Rod Klein putters around in his collection of Wall Street books, which he started as a hobby and now hopes to turn into a private library.

Almost as an offshoot of his personal interest, Klein has become an authority on Benjamin Graham and his writings. He is the man to contact to locate first or early editions of Ben's books. It has become a busy and lucrative avocation for Klein, who years ago took Ben's seminar at UCLA. Mint editions of *Security Analysis* can sell for more than a thousand dollars. Klein advertises for old copies and travels endless back roads, driving to used bookstores to see what can be found.

"I used to set the price [for Graham books]," Klein explains. "Now my customers bid the price up." Many of his clients work in the financial industry and want the collector's item to display on their office coffee table. They come from everywhere in the world. Klein often ships insured copies of Graham books to Europe and other continents. In 1993, he received a call from a man who had just won a lottery, and as a special treat for himself, he wanted a first edition of *Interpretation of Financial Statements* by Graham and McGolrick.

WORDS OF WISDOM FOR THE
INDIVIDUAL INVESTOR

Ben was a prophet in a very specialized but important realm of life. He preached commandments that any investor can use as stars when navigating the vast and mysterious seas of the investment world. An individual investor, who is not under pressure to shoot comets across the heavens but would like to earn a smart and substantial return, especially can benefit from Ben's guidance. In greatly simplified terms, here are the 14 points Graham most consistently delivered in his writing and speaking. Some of the counsel is technical, but much of it is aimed at adopting the right attitude:

1. Be an investor, not a speculator

"Let us define the speculator as one who seeks to profit from market movements, without primary regard to intrinsic values; the prudent stock investor is one who (a) buys only at prices amply supported by underlying value and (b) determinedly reduces his stock holdings when the market enters the speculative phase of a sustained advance."[12]

Speculation, Ben insisted, had its place in the securities markets, but a speculator must do more research and tracking of investments and be prepared for losses if they come.

2. Know the asking price

Multiply the company's share price by the number of company total shares (undiluted) outstanding. Ask yourself, if I bought the whole company would it be worth this much money?

3. Rake the market for bargains

Graham is best known for using his "net current asset value" (NCAV) rule to decide if the company was worth its market price.

To get the NCAV of a company, subtract all liabilities, including short-term debt and preferred stock, from current assets. By purchasing stocks below the NCAV, the investor buys a bargain because nothing at all is paid for the fixed assets of the company. The 1988 research of Professor Joseph D. Vu shows that buying stocks immediately after their price drop below the NCAV per share and selling two years afterward provides an excess return of more than 24 percent.

Yet even Ben recognized that NCAV stocks are increasingly difficult to find, and when one is located, this measure is only a starting point in the evaluation. "If the investor has occasion to be fearful of the future of such a company," he explained, "it is perfectly logical for him to obey his fears and pass on from that enterprise to some other security about which he is not so fearful."[13]

Modern disciples of Graham look for hidden value in additional ways, but still probe the question, "what is this company actually worth?" Buffett modifies the Graham formula by looking at the quality of the business itself. Other apostles use the amount of cash flow generated by the company, the reliability and quality of dividends and other factors.

4. Buy the formula

Ben devised another simple formula to tell if a stock is underpriced. The concept has been tested in many different markets and still works.

It takes into account the company's earnings per share (E), its expected earnings growth rate (R) and the current yield on AAA rated corporate bonds (Y).

The intrinsic value of a stock equals:

$$E(2R + 8.5) \times 4.4/Y$$

The number 8.5, Ben believed, was the appropriate price-to-earnings multiple for a company with static growth. P/E ratios have risen, but a conservative investor still will use a low multiplier. At the time this formula was printed, 4.4 percent was the average bond yield, or the Y factor.

5. Regard corporate figures with suspicion

It is a company's future earnings that will drive its share price higher, but estimates are based on current numbers, of which an investor must be wary. Even with more stringent rules, current earnings can be manipulated by creative accountancy. An investor is urged to pay special attention to reserves, accounting changes and footnotes when reading company documents. As for estimates of future earnings, anything from false expectations to unexpected world events can repaint the picture. Nevertheless, an investor has to do the best evaluation possible and then go with the results.

6. Don't stress out

Realize that you are unlikely to hit the precise "intrinsic value" of a stock or a stock market right on the mark. A margin of safety provides peace of mind. "Use an old Graham and Dodd guideline that you can't be that precise about a simple value," suggested Professor Roger Murray. "Give yourself a band of 20 percent above or below, and say, 'that is the range of fair value.'"[14]

7. Don't sweat the math

Ben, who loved mathematics, said so himself: "In 44 years of Wall Street experience and study, I have never seen dependable calculations made about common stock values, or related investment policies, that went beyond simple arithmetic or the most elementary algebra. Whenever calculus is brought in, or higher algebra, you could take it as a warning signal that the operator was trying to substitute theory for experience, and usually also to give speculation the deceptive guise of investment."[15]

8. Diversify, rule #1

"My basic rule," Graham said, "is that the investor should always have a minimum of 25 percent in bonds or bond equivalents, and another minimum of 25 percent in common stocks. He can divide the other 50 percent between the two, according to the varying stock and bond prices." This is ho-hum advice to anyone in a hurry to get rich, but it helps preserve capital. Remember, earnings cannot compound on money that has evaporated.[16]

Using this rule, an investor would sell stocks when stock prices are high and buy bonds. When the stock market declines, the investor would sell bonds and buy bargain stocks. At all times, however, he or she would hold the minimum 25 percent of the assets either in stocks or bonds—retaining particularly those that offer some contrarian advantage.

As a rule of thumb, an investor should back away from the stock market when the earnings per share on leading indices (such as the Dow Jones Industrial Average or the Standard & Poor's composite index) is less than the yield on high-quality bonds. When the reverse is true, lean toward bonds.

9. Diversify, rule #2

An investor should have a large number of securities in his or her portfolio, if necessary, with a relatively small number of shares of each stock. While investors such as Buffett may have fewer than a dozen or so carefully chosen companies, Graham usually held 75 or more stocks at any given time. Ben suggested that individual investors try to have at least 30 different holdings, even if it is necessary to buy odd lots. The least expensive way for an individual investor to buy odd lots is through a company's dividend reinvestment program (DRP).

10. When in doubt, stick to quality

Companies with good earnings, solid dividend histories, low debts and reasonable price/to/earnings ratios serve best. "Investors do not make mistakes, or bad mistakes, in buying good stocks at fair prices," Ben said. "They make their serious mistakes by buying poor stocks, particularly the ones that are pushed for various reasons. And sometimes—in fact, very frequently—they make mistakes by buying good stocks in the upper reaches of bull markets."[17]

11. Dividends as a clue

A long record of paying dividends, as long as 20 years, shows that a company has substance and is a limited risk. Chancy growth stocks seldom pay dividends. Furthermore, Ben contended that no dividends or a niggardly dividend policy harms investors in two ways. Not only are shareholders deprived of income from their investment, but when comparable companies are studied, the one with the lower dividend consistently sells for a lower share price. "I believe that Wall Street experience shows clearly that the best treatment for stockholders," Ben said, "is the payment to them of fair and reasonable dividends in relation to the company's earnings and in relation to the true value of the security, as measured by any ordinary tests based on earning power or assets."[18]

12. Defend your shareholder rights

"I want to say a word about disgruntled shareholders," Ben said. "In my humble opinion, not enough of them are disgruntled. And one of the great troubles with Wall Street is that it cannot distinguish between a mere troublemaker or "strike suitor" in corporate affairs and a stockholder with a legitimate complaint that deserves attention from his management and from his fellow stockholders." If you object to a dividend policy, executive compensation package or golden parachutes, organize a shareholder's offensive.[19]

13. Be Patient

". . . every investor should be prepared financially and psychologically for the possibility of poor short-term results. For example, in the 1973–1974 decline the investor would have lost money on paper, but if he'd held on and stuck with the approach, he would have recouped in 1975–1976 and gotten his 15 percent average return for the five-year period."[20]

14. Think for yourself

Don't follow the crowd. "There are two requirements for success in Wall Street," Ben once said. "One, you have to think correctly; and secondly, you have to think independently."[21]

Finally, continue to search for better ways to ensure safety and maximize growth. *Do not ever stop thinking.*

Benjamin Graham with his first group of disciples. Taken at Del Coronado (San Diego) in either May or June, 1968.

From left: Warren Buffett, Ray Tolles, Ben Graham, David "Sandy" Gottesman, Tom Knapp, Charles T. Munger, Jack Alexander, Henry Brandt, Walter Schloss, Marshall Weinberg, Ed Anderson, Buddy Fox and William Ruane. *Photo courtesy of Walter J. Schloss.*

Warren and Susie Buffet. Laguna, California, 1966.
Photo courtesy of Benjamin Graham, Jr., M.D.

Ben, Sr., with the second Newton and Ben, Jr.
Photo courtesy of Benjamin Graham, Jr., M.D.

Benjamin Graham taken in Seville, Spain, October, 1964.
Birds flocked around Ben the way his students and clients did!
Photo courtesy of Benjamin Graham, Jr., M.D.

Benjamin Graham portrait. A gift from Warren Buffet.
Photo courtesy of the Association for Investment Management Research.

Benjamin Graham (left) and William K. Jacobs. Jacobs was an
original director when GEICO went public. *Photo courtesy of GEICO.*

Ben and Estelle Graham. Sun Valley, Idaho, 1949.
Photo courtesy of Benjamin Graham, Jr., M.D.

Benjamin Graham addressing a Financial Analysts meeting,
January 19, 1965. *Photo courtesy of San Diego Historical Society.*

Benjamin Graham interviewing Geraldine Weiss on his 80th
birthday. May 30,1974. *Photo courtesy of the San Diego Historical Society.*

The Graham home in
Scarsdale, New York, 1948.
*Photo courtesy of
Benjamin Graham, Jr., M.D.*

Ben and Estelle with photo of Ben, Jr.
Taken in March, 1965, the year they
moved to California.
Photo courtesy of Benjamin Graham, Jr., M.D.

Ben and Estelle Graham with Benjamin, Jr. Mount Kisco, New
York, August, 1948. *Photo courtesy of Benjamin Graham, Jr., M.D.*

Wedding of Ben Graham and Estelle Messing. New York, early 1940s. *Photo courtesy of Benjamin Graham, Jr., M.D.*

Ben and Estelle Graham. Honolulu, Hawaii, October, 1953. *Photo courtesy of Benjamin Graham, Jr., M.D.*

CHAPTER 8

The GEICO Story

"Skill is helpful. Luck is essential."

—Howard "Mickey" Newman, 1993 interview with the author

B ecause of his cautiousness, Graham very nearly missed his most legendary investment feat, the purchase of a majority interest in the glamour growth stock of the 1960s, Government Employees Insurance Company, later known as GEICO.

The story began in 1948, as the luckless representatives of one of the owners of a small, private, mail-order insurance company trudged Wall Street, trying to find a buyer for a major chunk of the company. E. R. Jones and Washington attorney David Lloyd Kreeger sought in vain until they called on the Graham-Newman Corporation, hoping to convince Ben Graham that Government Employees Insurance Company fit his definition of a special situation. The small delegation was referred to Graham-Newman by Fred Greenman, a boyhood friend of Ben and Jerry and now their attorney. Greenman assured the partners that at 10 percent under book value, Government Employees Insurance was a good deal.

ATTRACTED BY THE FIGURES

Though GEICO was little more than a mom-and-pop operation, the numbers echoed a strong resonance. GEICO was earning premiums of $2 million to $3 million a year with earnings per share of $1.29 in 1946 and earnings per share of $5.89 in 1947.

"There was never any sales talk needed with Ben," insisted Lorimer A. Davidson, who also was involved in the discussions. Davidson was the company's operating head and later became chief executive officer. "He saw what Dave Kreeger and I saw—the great potential and bright promise of this company." Kreeger and Davidson became part of the investor group and in 1970, Kreeger followed Davidson as the company's CEO.

AN EXCELLENT IDEA

GEICO was founded in Fort Worth, Texas, in 1936 by a 50-year-old accountant, Leo Goodwin, Sr., his wife and their financial backers. The group believed that automobile insurance could be sold at a discount by eliminating much of the sales cost and reducing the underwriting risks. In the beginning, Leo and Lillian Goodwin worked 12 hours a day, 365 days a year for a combined salary of $250 per month. In the evenings, they did the books at home around the kitchen table. On weekends, Leo Goodwin drove to military bases to pitch the low-cost insurance to young service families. The insurance was sold by direct mail to consumers, thus sidestepping agents and their commissions.[1]

Insurance at GEICO cost 30 to 40 percent less than at competing companies. Goodwin originally reduced risk by offering policies to only government employees, a group of people who filed fewer claims than the public in general. Because there were more government workers in the Washington, D.C., area than any place else in the country, the company moved its operations there in 1937. Thanks largely to the dedication of Goodwin and his wife Lillian, the company enjoyed healthy growth in its early years.

PRESSURE TO SELL

Goodwin, however, owned only a 25 percent interest. A Fort Worth banker, Cleaves Rhea, was the majority owner with 55 percent. A deceased relative of Rhea's, A. D. Rhea, owned the other 20 percent of GEICO. It was the Rhea family who were anxious to sell.

Ben was sufficiently convinced of the company's value to enter negotiations to buy a controlling interest in the company. But as Walter Schloss recalled, Ben, who was then 54 years old and with more than three decades of experience under his belt, did suffer some reservations.

"Walter," Ben said to Schloss on the day that Graham-Newman made the decision to buy the pubescent insurance company, "if this purchase doesn't work out, we can always liquidate it and get our money back."

Ben's hesitation may have had less to do with the condition of the company than it did with the scope of the commitment. After all, the GEICO deal involved more of the fund's assets than any acquisition Ben and Jerry had made before.

A PHILOSOPHICAL PROBLEM

Furthermore, Ben had reservations about the industry in general. Earlier in the year, he explained to his students at the New York Institute of Finance that the insurance industry was a wonderful industry for everyone involved—management, underwriters, agents, customers—everyone that was, except the shareholder. His complaint about insurance companies was twofold. They did not earn high-enough returns on the money that policyholders left in their safekeeping until a claim is paid, and they did not pay sufficient dividends, a practice that both reduced total return and suppressed share price.

In fact, Ben admitted to his students that he was embroiled in a dispute with an insurer in which Graham-Newman was an investor. "The New Amsterdam Casualty Company has built up an asset value of about fifty dollars a share," Ben explained. "It has insisted upon paying a $1 dividend since 1943, although in this time average earnings have been on the order of $4 or more. The result is that the market has decided that $1 in dividends is not worth more than $36.50 at the top, and at the end of 1946, it was not worth more than $26. That is the situation which has existed for years past, and for all we know might exist for years to come."[2]

PUTTING QUALMS ASIDE

Somehow Ben managed to curb his suspicion of insurance industry practices in general. As a majority owner of GEICO, and through a position on the board of directors, he could prevent what he viewed as mistreatment of shareholders.

A half-interest—1,500 shares—in GEICO was purchased for $475 per share or a total of $712,500. The purchase price represented nearly 25 percent of Graham-Newman's total assets. At the last minute, the deal almost fell through because Ben and Jerry wanted the purchase price to be 100 percent covered by asset value. The asset account proved to be about $50,000 short. After some hesitation, the deal was consummated. For an investment manager who preached diversification and who often held several hundred different stocks, the GEICO deal was a bold departure from the past. Though his instincts led the way and they proved reliable, his comment to Schloss turned out to be unnecessary.

A REGULATORY BLUNDER

Ben did make an error, though it was not in evaluating the worth of the insurance company. And liquidating the company was not to be an option. Rather, as Ben and Jerry soon discovered, the mistake was in buying such a large stake in *any* insurance operation.

They learned, after the fact, that under the Investment Company Act of 1940, it was illegal for an investment company to own more than 10 percent of an insurance company. The Securities and Exchange Commission (SEC) demanded that Graham-Newman reverse the purchase and return GEICO to its founders. When Ben approached the Rheas, however, they refused to take the shares back.

A FORCED PUBLIC OFFERING

As an alternative, the SEC agreed to approve the sale of the shares of GEICO to Graham-Newman shareholders.

The partners tried to make the distribution as easy as possible for investors. The messy situation and its resolution were described to shareholders in a July 2, 1948, report. "We are advised that there will be an over-the-counter market for the Insurance Company shares. When and if transactions take place, the Directors of Graham-Newman Corporation will fix a fair market value of the shares presently distributed, which value may be used for tax purposes. We understand that the present distribution will be non-taxable to our Stockholders, provided that all the realized income of Graham-Newman Corporation for the present fiscal year is paid out in cash dividends."

As the managing partners, Graham and Newman were allowed to keep their own shares and to participate in the management of GEICO. Luck was on their side, and a major misstep in this case reversed itself. Very quickly, it became apparent that taking GEICO public was in the best interests of the company's investors.

A SUPERB MARKET RESPONSE

Indeed, in July of 1948, when the shares were distributed, the market value was $27 for 1.08 shares of GEICO. By the end of the year, Government Employee shares were trading at $30 per share and the price just kept getting better.

"It turned out later that we were worth—the whole company—over a billion dollars in the stock market," Ben said. "This was a very extraordinary thing."[3]

"It turned out to be the best luck Graham-Newman ever had," agreed Mickey Newman. "An over-the-counter market developed and Graham-Newman stockholders, in aggregate, held a very valuable piece of paper. It was just a fluke that it happened. If the SEC hadn't ruled the way it did, the market would have never developed."

A DOCK FOR WHEN YOUR SHIP COMES IN

Ben admitted that there was a certain amount of serendipity in the GEICO purchase, but insisted that other factors were present. ". . . behind the luck, or a crucial decision, there must usually exist a background of preparation and disciplined capacity. One needs to be sufficiently established and recognized so that these opportunities will knock at his particular door. One must have the means, the judgment and the courage to take advantage of them."[4]

Walter Schloss pointed out that the company's successful public offering was only the beginning of the pleasant surprises and rewards. In 1949, GEICO's profits progressed past the $1 million mark.

"When Graham-Newman bought it," Schloss said, "GEICO was ready to take off but they didn't know it. Nobody recognized that their gradual growth was about to accelerate. It was viewed as just a nice little company making money. After they bought it, of course, it suddenly took off and their timing turned out to be brilliant."[5]

A TRUSTED BOARD

The flight was powered, in large part, by an immediate reconstitution of the board of directors. Ben and Jerry took seats on the board and became active in the management of the company, as did two other of their representatives, William K. Jacobs, Sr., and Robert J. Marony. This was the same Marony whom Ben befriended in 1919 when he wrote an unfavorable report on the Milwaukee & St. Paul Railroad. The long-standing relationship between board members contributed to the fact that Ben and Jerry began to view GEICO almost as a family business—a natural and very robust progeny of Graham-Newman.

AN ADOLESCENT SPURT OF GROWTH

Growth became GEICO's magic password. In 1958, management expanded its customer universe to include nongovernment professional, managerial, technical and administrative workers. These decisions broadened the market from 15 percent to 50 percent of all car owners, but again, risk levels for this group were relatively minimal. Additionally, the company spun off Government Employees' Life Insurance and several other subsidiaries, for which Ben and Jerry became founders. The company's expansion was phenomenal. GEICO soon became the nation's fifth largest automobile insurer. By 1972, when the company was performing at a peak, the single original Graham-Newman share had grown in worth to $16,349. Ben estimated that the total investment had made a market gain of somewhere around $300 million.

TRUE TO HIS WORD

As a board member, Ben now was in a position to make sure that GEICO practiced policies that he had long advocated, including "a clearly enunciated policy with respect to the payment of cash and stock dividends." Under such a policy, Ben wrote in *The Intelligent Investor*, "stock dividends are paid periodically to capitalize all or a stated portion of the earnings reinvested in the business. Such a policy—covering 100 percent of the reinvested earnings—has been followed by Purex, Government Employees Insurance, and perhaps a few others."[6]

GENEROUSLY REWARDED

Though the acquisition seemed fraught with uncertainty and some aspects of the deal flew in the face of Graham's own teachings, the decision to buy half of Government Employees Insurance Company brought vastly more profits than any other one Ben had ever made. "An obvious [moral] is that there are several different ways to make and keep money in Wall Street," Ben noted.[7]

For 17 years, Graham and his colleagues served on the board and GEICO prospered. In 1965, when Ben was 71, he resigned from the GEICO board of directors. As a retirement gift, the GEICO board presented Ben with a bronze statue of Mercury created in 1888 by the sculptor Auguste Rodin. David Lloyd Kreeger, a noted art collector in his own right and by now GEICO chairman, explained that Mercury, the messenger of the gods in Greek mythology, represented "the most versatile man in the Golden Age of Greece."

THE GEICO SAGA

Certainly, Ben had his own sincere admirers, but the image of GEICO itself had assumed godlike proportions in the business community. "GEICO was close to a religion with many of its customers, who swore by its premium rates and its service. It was certainly a religion with its stockholders; they called it a 'Cinderella' stock," wrote journalist Carol J. Loomis.[8]

In 1971, Jerry Newman decided to follow Ben into retirement, closing a vital chapter in GEICO's history. Newman nominated Warren Buffett to take his place on the GEICO board and Ben wrote a letter to Chairman David Kreeger, seconding Newman's recommendation.

BUFFETT REBUFFED

"I am 100 percent for that idea," Ben wrote. "I have known Buffett intimately for many years, and I must say I have never met anyone else with his combination of high character and brilliant business qualities. His record as an investment fund manager is probably unequalled.

"In addition," Ben wrote, "I can recommend Warren as a good-humored, easy-to-get-along-with person, who could liven up your directors meetings. He would be sure to supply more than his share of worthwhile ideas for the benefit of the GEICO companies."

The board of directors were enthusiastic about Buffett's appointment, but problems arose with a conflict of interest because by then he held sizable investments in other insurance companies. The SEC had reservations about it and the idea was dropped. It is interesting to speculate on how GEICO's corporate history may have been different had Buffett been named to the board at that early stage. GEICO investors, management and employees, perhaps, might have been spared tremendous strife.

As most students of Wall Street realize, there was a Chapter 2 to the GEICO story following Graham and Newman's retirement from the board. When a company gains the visibility and respect that GEICO did, any trouble receives a painful level of public attention.

THE CRISIS YEARS

After Ben left the board, the company continued its rapid expansion. However, the industry was changing. At the same time that insurance carriers wrestled with the implications of no-fault insurance rules, inflation was driving many automobile insurers into the red. Management made serious miscalculations in claims and in underpricing its policies. In 1975, GEICO suffered its first unprofitable year in its 36-year history. The situation snowballed and by 1976 GEICO was on the brink of bankruptcy.

Tracking a dive in balance-sheet numbers, the GEICO share price went into the tank. In 1973, shares traded at about $60; by May of 1976, they were down to $5. Some of the Graham-Newman investors took a bath, though Buffett sold his stock very early in the game and most others in the Graham circle by then were rid of their shares. Walter Schloss had sold his GEICO stock to pay medical and other bills associated with his son's birth and then later sold the spun-off Government Employees Life Insurance stock to pay for his daughter's delivery costs.

". . . I did get two children, which I thought was a good buy," Schloss said. His son Edwin now works with Walter in his investment firm.[9]

GEICO's founder Leo Goodwin left his shares to his son, Leo, Jr., who was extremely hard hit by the collapse in GEICO's share price. The son had borrowed against the shares to go into other lines of business. When GEICO's price skidded, the bank sold the stock to recover what it could of its collateral. Leo, Jr., committed suicide.[10]

THE SHOCK

Professor David Dodd was among the losers, at least on paper and at least for a while. Dodd told Walter Schloss that he had broken his own rule of not letting tax liabilities affect a decision to sell. Dodd consulted with his friend Irving Kahn on whether to take a tax loss on the GEICO shares and, to his ultimate advantage, was advised to keep them. Interestingly, even when the company went into the slide, the shares were much more valuable than they had originally been. In 1976, for example, an equivalent share was valued at $2,407, nearly 90 times its value when it first traded.[11]

Though Ben was shocked at how much money the company lost in the mid-1970s and worried that GEICO had expanded too fast in difficult times, Ben told a reporter that he believed the company would recover. He may not have foreseen that his star student would pull the rabbit out of the hat.

A BARGAIN REDISCOVERED

Warren Buffett first began investing in GEICO while he was a student at Columbia. "In 1951, I had about 65 percent of my net worth in GEICO," he explained, a sum of about $10,000. Buffett enthusiastically peddled the stock as a rookie broker in Omaha, then cashed out of GEICO several years later when he had achieved a 50 percent profit. "Then 25 years later it came around again," Buffett said. "It got in trouble. It was just about the time Ben was dying."

In 1976—the year Ben passed away—Buffett bought nearly 1.3 million shares of GEICO at an average cost of $3.18 per share. Professor Dodd, in a 1976 letter to Buffett, commended his former student on the GEICO purchase. "Elsie and I are much heartened by your commitment, and by your future participation, we hope, in the GEICO enterprise."

Over the next five years, Buffett put $45.7 million of Berkshire's capital into the company. By the end of 1980, Berkshire controlled one-third of the common stock of GEICO. Buffett had amassed a total of 7.2 million shares at an average price of $1.31 per share. When the 1990 Berkshire Hathaway annual report was published, the company owned more than 48 percent of GEICO, a stock holding worth approximately $1.5 billion.[12]

THE RECOVERY

Though GEICO management at first had been slow to wake up to the impending disaster, it was quick to decree life-support measures. Under a new CEO and with the help of Salomon Brothers, GEICO returned to profitability, and operating profits snapped back by 1977.

"GEICO's problems at that time," explained Buffett in an annual report, "put it in a position analogous to that of American Express in 1964 following the salad-oil scandal. Both were one-of-a-kind companies temporarily reeling from the effects of a fiscal blow that did not destroy their exceptional underlying economics. The GEICO and American Express situations, extraordinary business franchises with a localized excisable cancer (needing, to be sure, a skilled surgeon), should be distinguished from the true 'turnaround' situation in which the managers expect—and need—to pull off a corporate Pygmalion."[13]

By 1981, the Leo and Lillian Goodwin's $200,000 seed capital had produced a company with $420 million in capital. At the end of 1992, GEICO had assets of $4.8 billion and shareholders' equity of $1.29 billion. GEICO's return on equity between 1989 and 1992 was 25 percent and its stock price increased approximately 40 percent. To top that off, GEICO's shares split 5 for 1 in 1992. Part of GEICO's appeal always had been its ability to accumulate a large float, or money generated by the insurance premiums that remain on the books until claims are paid. The float can be invested to generate even larger profits and to offset underwriting losses (losses on the insurance operation itself) when they occur. Unlike most of its competitors, GEICO seldom has underwriting losses. Buffett has lent his talent to the management of those considerable reserves to achieve a dramatic level of profitability.

In the 1990s, GEICO is again considered an astute buy. "Warren has a sensational investment," observed Mickey Newman. Even today, Buffett, who still is heavily into insurance investments, does not serve on the GEICO board, though several of his friends, including Bill Ruane, do.

A FAMILY LEGACY

Ben had sold most of his shares by the time GEICO ran into trouble, but not all of them. Some of his original shares rode the market down and then back up again. In 1993, Ben's grandson was financing his medical school education by selling some of his grandfather's original GEICO shares.

Graham could not have been more correct when he concluded the postscript to *The Intelligent Investor* with these words about GEICO and the stock market in general: ". . . interesting possibilities abound on the financial scene, and the intelligent and enterprising investor should be able to find both enjoyment and profit in this three-ring circus. Excitement is guaranteed."[14]

CHAPTER 9

The Kindred Soul of Young Warren Buffett

"Graham was the smartest man I ever knew."

—Warren E. Buffett

"Yes, Warren has done very well."

—Benjamin Graham[1]

Warren Buffett met Ben Graham the way most American investors did—he happened across a copy of *The Intelligent Investor* and read it. At the time, Buffett was 19 years old and a senior at the University of Nebraska. "I thought then that it was by far the best book about investing ever written," he said. "I still think it is."[2]

When Buffett enrolled at the Graduate School of Business at Columbia University in 1950 (after first being turned down by Harvard) with the intention of studying with Graham, he already was a serious, albeit small-time, investor. The son of a stockbroker who later became a congressman, Buffett first began reading investment books when he was eight years old. He was 11 when he bought his first stock. Before reaching his teens, Buffett was working at Harris, Upham & Company in Omaha, posting stock prices on a blackboard. By the time he enrolled in college, Buffett had built a tidy net worth of more than $9,000 from paper routes and from other youthful business enterprises.[3]

OFF TO COLUMBIA

Buffett already knew how to cut to the bottom line, and he quickly realized that choosing Ben's classes was one of the smartest investment decisions he had ever made. "Ben was imaginative. His mind was really interesting. He was very good at teaching," Buffett said.

EDUCATIONAL INTRIGUE

Graham built suspense into his classes by using anonymous companies, and often there would be a catch to the example, or a surprise lurking behind the illustration. In one class, he made a detailed comparison of Company A and Company B, which both turned out to be Boeing at different times in the aircraft manufacturer's history. "He was the Edgar Allen Poe of corporate study," Buffett laughed.

Underlying all the number-crunching was that familiar important message: Companies constantly change. A company's stock, therefore, may be a good buy at one time, then very quickly become overvalued. Or the reverse may occur. But it was not just an analytical approach to investments that intrigued Buffett. He also was captivated by Graham's personality.

A CERTAIN SAGACITY

"Ben looked something like Edward G. Robinson," Buffett noted, "and people had said this to him. He met Robinson one time and said, 'you know, people tell me I look like you.' Robinson replied, 'If I looked like you I'd be playing glamour roles.' Ben loved it."

Out of curiosity, Buffett went to the Columbia library to look up his professor's name in *Who's Who*.

"It said he was chairman of Government Employees Insurance Company," Buffett recalled. "So I went to the librarian and asked how to find out about insurance companies. He showed me the great big *A. M. Best* book. That's the first time I'd had any exposure to the insurance world."

After reading the report in *A. M. Best*, an insurance company rating guide, Buffett decided to prepare an analysis of GEICO as part of his class work.

AN EDUCATION IN INSURANCE

"So I went down to Washington where the company was located. It was on a weekend, since I was still in school. The place was locked, but I pounded on the door, and finally, a cleaning man came. I said, is there anyone here besides you that I can talk to? He said there's this fellow on the sixth floor. That was Lorimer A. Davidson. He spent about six hours educating me, and that's how I got interested in GEICO, through Ben's connection."

Davidson, who his friends affectionately called Davey and who later became chief executive officer of the company, apparently did a convincing job. Buffett immediately transferred three-fourths of his investment fund into GEICO. Ever since, insurance companies have had a special appeal for Buffett and they are at the heart of the Berkshire Hathaway portfolio of stocks.

A TREK TO NEW JERSEY

Buffett apparently was mesmerized by more than one of Graham's investments. Walter Schloss says he first met Buffett in 1951 at the annual meeting of Marshall Wells Company in Jersey City. Marshall Wells was a Minneapolis-based wholesale distributor, whose shares also were held by Graham-Newman. Buffett, who was still at Columbia, had bought some shares and he and a friend attended the meeting together.

"Whether he bought [Marshall Wells] because he saw it in the portfolio or because he liked it, I don't know," Schloss said. "But they all saw the list."

After the shareholders' meeting, Schloss's and Buffett's groups went out to lunch, and a camaraderie was established.[4]

ENDURING FRIENDSHIPS

Schloss was not the only new friend Buffett made while attending college in New York, and it was no wonder that young men interested in the stock market connected with one other. "Wall Street was not full of young people at the time," explained William Ruane. Ruane had graduated from Harvard in 1949 in a class of 652 from which only six of his classmates took jobs in the investment industry.

After his graduation from Harvard, Ruane went to New York to work at Kidder Peabody, then enrolled as an unmatriculated student in Ben's Columbia seminar. "He would allow people from Wall Street to sit in," Ruane said. "One of the great things in my life was meeting Warren Buffett there. He has had a tremendous influence on my life, both business and personal."

FLINT AGAINST FLINT

There was a special intellectual spark between Graham and Buffett that very likely made the 1951 seminars a little less egalitarian than some of those in earlier years. Ruane described his own role as mainly that of an observer. The discussion and debate between Graham and Buffett was so electric that only the most confident and daring students were willing to jump in. Graham gave Buffett an A+ in the class.

AN A, BUT NO JOB

When Buffett graduated with a master's degree from Columbia Business School, he asked for a job at Graham-Newman, offering to work for no salary if necessary. Jokingly, Buffett has said Ben "made his customary calculation of value to price and said no."[5]

More seriously, Buffett says Ben perhaps was too polite to tell him the real reason, but he did later indicate to Buffett that he preferred to give jobs to young Jewish men because at the time they had difficulty finding good positions on Wall Street. Ben promised, however, to keep an eye out for a position for Buffett with some other organization.

BACK TO NEBRASKA

At home in Omaha and working for his father's investment firm, Buffett, Falk and Company, Buffett could not stop thinking about Graham-Newman or about GEICO's stock.

"I tried to sell it around town without much luck, but I'd get so excited about it trying to sell it, I'd buy more shares," Buffett explained.

To his dismay, Buffett noticed that Newman & Graham were selling shares of GEICO.

"Gee whiz," he said, "I don't understand it. Graham is selling it and I'm buying it. One of us is wrong."[6]

In some ways, they both were right. "The following year, it doubled and I sold what I had," Buffett said. If he had stayed in the stock longer, however, his profits would have been even greater.

It was Ben's newest fund, Newman & Graham, that was selling the shares, but there was a motive. When the partnership was formed, some investors had contributed GEICO shares instead of cash, and the partnership was selling off the shares to gain greater liquidity. Except for this maneuver, Ben's funds retained the vast majority of their shares.

SHOWING HIS METTLE

Buffett did not let an apparent difference of opinion on GEICO quell his enthusiasm for Ben or Graham-Newman. He kept in touch with Graham, offering to do special studies and research for him, and, ultimately, hoping for a job. Buffett did an evaluation of the Baldwin Company and wrote to Ben recommending that Graham-Newman invest in the shares. Ben replied:

Dear Buffett:
Our delay in answering you on the Baldwin Company matter is due to the fact that we used it for a kind of test case to work out techniques for evaluation and decisions by our organization. We have finally come up with a conclusion, which is that we could take on between 1,000

and 1,500 shares if it is possible to get the price down to about $21 . . ."

Buffett wrote back, promising to locate a block of shares at the right price, and recommending yet another company, Greif Brothers Cooperage Company, which Buffett would not be able to buy for him, for it was listed on an exchange on which Buffett, Falk did not hold membership.

Buffett explained his reason for recommending new securities to Ben. "If I wanted to be starting quarterback on the Washington Redskins, I'd try to get them to watch me throw a few passes."[7]

Perhaps only someone as openly friendly and as persistent as Buffett could break Ben down on his hiring practices. In fact, in the correspondence between Ben and Buffett, the gradual warming of the relationship is visible. At first, Buffett wrote to "Mr. Graham" and Ben replied curtly to "Buffett." Gradually, they became Ben and Warren, and by the time Ben retired to California, they were exchanging messages about their wives, children and mutual friends.

But the relationship took time to build. "He couldn't have been nicer," Buffett explained. "But he had this kind of shell around him." Buffett once read a rough autobiography that Ben had started, in which he referred to himself in the third person. Ben described himself as someone with plenty of friends, but with no close relationships.

"Everybody liked him," Buffett went on. "Everybody admired him. Everybody enjoyed being around him, but nobody got close. That was a kind of challenge with women. Each one thought that she would be the one who really got close to him."

While many women were disappointed, Buffett said, "They got a lot closer than men did."

Ben obviously thought highly of Buffett, even if he did maintain a certain formality. In March of 1952, Ben wrote to Buffett, congratulating him on his pending marriage to Susan Thompson and saying that he had enjoyed meeting Buffett's parents. Ben wrote again in August of 1953, congratulating Buffett on the birth of his daughter Susan. Ben had heard of the newborn in a telephone conversation with Howard Buffett, the proud grandfather. Ben added that he had recommended Buffett to several Wall Street firms.

PERSISTENCE PAYS OFF

Finally, in 1954, Buffett's chance came. Graham wrote him a note saying that there was an opening at the company. Before Ben could change his mind, Buffett accepted and rushed to New York. He did not even ask about the salary.

"I knew Ben would pay me fairly," Buffett said. When he arrived, he learned his salary would be $12,000 a year, which at the time was generous enough to rent a nice apartment in the suburb of White Plains in Westchester County and to support a wife who was pregnant with their second child. Ben also helped Buffett land an evening job teaching investments at the Scarsdale adult school.

Buffett remembers his first day at work. Graham-Newman was by then in offices at 122 East 42nd Street. "Everyone at Graham-Newman wore gray cloth jackets," he said. "We all wore the same kind. I still remember what a thrill it was when I got my jacket."

NEWMAN & GRAHAM

In the years shortly before Buffett joined the firm, Graham-Newman had nearly doubled in size. Ben and Jerry's investors wanted to expand the fund, which by then had grown to a $5-million account. The investors insisted, however, that Ben and Jerry, who had not yet built a line of succession, take on understudies. In 1950, Ben hired Edward E. Laufer, who formerly had been with the Securities and Exchange Commission.

Jerry Newman decided to recruit someone he knew well. "I don't feel like guessing a stranger," Jerry told his 28-year-old son Mickey, "Why don't you come downtown."

Mickey had been working for textile converter Jerry Rossman in New York, who had a son who was likely to take over that business.

"I talked to Jerry Rossman," Mickey recalled. "He was disappointed. He said, 'I hate to lose you, but I think your place is with your father.' Rossman became an investor."

Rather than expanding by adding capital to the existing account, a new limited partnership, Newman & Graham, was formed. The minimum investment in the account was $50,000, which was a large sum at the time. Newman & Graham was launched with capitalization of $2.57 million. By 1954, the partnership had shot up to about $6 million.

"Ben and Jerry got an override of 20 percent of the profits that exceeded the book value of the fund," Mickey said. "That came as ordinary income and was taxable at a higher rate. Then Ben and Jerry got capital gains at the same rate as the investors."

THE BOYS IN THE BACK ROOM

Despite the additional account, Graham-Newman was still a small shop when Buffett arrived, both in terms of assets under management and in terms of staff. The company had only about $12 million in its two investment pools. In addition to a couple of secretaries, there was Buffett's pal from the Marshall Wells annual meeting, Walter Schloss. The two friends would leaf through Standard & Poor's, searching for stocks that could be bought for no more than two-thirds of their net working capital. Following that rule, Ben still believed, provided a comfortable margin of safety.

BASICS OF ARBITRAGE

Buffett also had the good fortune to learn about arbitrage, however odd the opportunities may have been. He told the tale of the cocoa-bean arbitrage in one of Berkshire Hathaway's annual reports. It seems Rockwood & Company, a Brooklyn chocolate products company, had switched to LIFO (last in, first out) inventory accounting back in 1941 when cocoa was selling for five cents per pound. A temporary shortage of cocoa in 1954 pushed the price to more than 60 cents and Rockwood wanted to unload its valuable inventory while the price was high. If, however, the cocoa was simply sold, the company would have a nearly 50-percent tax on the profits.

Hidden in the tax code was a provision that eliminated the tax due on LIFO profits if inventory was distributed to stockholders as part of a plan to reduce the scope of a corporation's business. Rockwood decided to close out its cocoa-butter operations, to which it attributed 13 million pounds of its cocoabean inventory. The company offered to redeem its shares in trade for beans, offering 80 pounds for each share of stock, which was the equivalent of $48 per share. At the beginning of the process, Rockwood shares were selling at $15.

"For several weeks, I busily bought shares, sold beans and made periodic stops at Schroeder Trust to exchange stock certificates for warehouse receipts," Buffett said. "The profits were good and my only expense was subway tokens."[8] Before the whole episode concluded, Rockwood, which was enduring large operating losses, was trading at $100.

ODD JOBS

Buffett had a host of other miscellaneous duties. R. Marshall Barnes, a Chicago investor, was shuffling through some of his old papers some 31 years later. By chance, Barnes discovered that he was among the few lucky ones to have Graham-Newman stock certificates that were signed by the new kid in the back room, Warren E. Buffett. By the mid-1980s, Buffett had forgotten that he did a short stint as treasurer.

Though the investment portfolios were performing well and Buffett was learning a lot, like Walter Schloss, he found certain of Ben's ideas to be frustrating.

EARNING MONEY THE OLD-FASHIONED WAY

Considering the lessons Ben had learned years ago at Newburger and Loeb and that were reinforced by the crash of 1929, it was no surprise that Ben's employees occasionally grumbled that he was overly conservative. Walter Schloss not long after he started at the company following World War II recommended a company called Haloid. The corporation held the rights to a revolutionary process called xerography and had been paying dividends throughout the 1930s. Ben, however, thought the stock, which later became Xerox, was too high at $21 per share.

"The only thing I should add," Schloss later said with a chuckle, "is that if Graham-Newman had bought Xerox at $21, I can almost guarantee that we would have sold it at $50. The fact that it went to $3,000 would have been beside the point." Ben believed in taking profits when a profit clearly existed and leaving the speculative excess to others.[9]

THE GRAHAM QUIRKS

Buffett also thought Ben's point of view could be self-limiting. "He didn't want us to go out and see companies," Buffett explained, "he thought it was sort of cheating."

Unless Graham-Newman used the same methods that the average investor was forced to use, Ben felt his concepts were not being validated. "We had to play by the same rules the fellow in Pocatello had to play by," Buffett said.

Schloss figured there was another reason. Ben did not like to talk to management because he was worried that he would be swayed by what they said. Ben may have worried that the "nice guy" in him would fail to be sufficiently circumspect, Schloss suspected.

Even Buffett admits that getting to know management has its drawbacks, but not because he is apt to be overly charmed by top executives. He says his biggest investing mistakes have been the failure to buy good business stocks because he did not relish the quality of management. "I'd have been better off trusting the business," he says.[10]

WHAT PRICE FOR GOOD MANAGEMENT?

Actually, Ben might have anticipated Buffett's experience. He once described his views on management, and they explain why he did not see much point in interviewing the leading executives of smaller companies, which was where he vested most of his funds.

"Management is one of the most important factors in the evaluation of a leading company," he said, "and it has a great effect upon the market price of secondary companies. It does not necessarily control the value of the secondary companies for the long pull because if management is comparatively poor, there are forces at work which tend to improve the management and thereby improve the value of the company."[11]

THE CRADLE OF FRIENDSHIP

In addition to gaining stock-picking experience, Buffett was learning about Ben Graham himself. On his own birthday, Graham would distribute gifts at the office and to his friends. He figured that he was the lucky one to be born, so he should be giving rather than receiving presents. Buffett remembers that on one birthday, Graham gave Diane Orenstein, one of the secretaries, some shares of GEICO. Ben was generous on other occasions as well.

"You know my son is named Howard Graham Buffett, named after my Dad and Ben," Buffett said. "When he was born in 1954, in the White Plains hospital, Ben gave me a motion-picture camera, a projector and all these things. I was a three-month employee! I've got some pictures from those days!"

A DANCE INVITATION

One evening, Susan Buffett complained that Warren did not dance, which was the wrong thing to say to Ben. Soon afterward, Ben, who was enamored with dancing, came by Buffett's desk at the office with a gift certificate to the Arthur Murray Dance Studio in White Plains, where Ben himself religiously reported for lessons.

"A short time later, he came by again and said the people at the studio said I hadn't been by for my lesson," Buffett laughed. "He encouraged me to go in." Buffett still does not dance.

In addition to Ben's "open-ended, no-scores-kept" generosity, Buffett was impressed by Graham's picture-sharp memory—virtual total recall.[12]

SNAPSHOT MEMORY

In 1955, Graham, along with John Kenneth Galbraith and other experts, was scheduled to testify before the U.S. Senate Committee on Banking and Currency, the Fulbright committee, and he needed some background material. "We were only a few blocks from the New York Public Library," he said, "He would say, 'There's some material in the *Commercial Financial Bulletin*, 1927, and you'll find it on a right hand page.' I would go over there, and I would find it."

Buffett was not taken by surprise when Ben and Jerry decided to fold the business less than two years after his arrival. Ben had warned him. When Ben and Jerry retired in 1956, Buffett returned to Omaha and went about the business of transforming himself into the greatest investor of the twentieth century.

One of his clients would be Graham himself, who occasionally had Buffett buy bonds or other securities for his account.

BUILDING ON THE BEST IDEAS

Buffett considers himself blessed to have been a student and understudy to Graham. He is not, however, a slavish follower. "Boy, if I had listened only to Ben," the 63-year-old Buffett says, "would I ever be a lot poorer."[13]

Buffett, nevertheless, displays some of the same inclinations as his mentor. Like Graham, Buffett does not use a calculator. Like Ben, Buffett is a talented writer, as shown by the wide readership of Berkshire Hathaway's folksy, witty and lengthy annual message from the chairman. Like his mentor, Buffett deplores deceit and shuns excessive leverage, though he is not afraid of it. "We're far from believing that there is no fate worse than debt," Buffett wrote in his 1987 report. "We are willing to borrow an amount that we believe—on a worst-case basis—will pose no threat to Berkshire's well-being."[14]

WEALTH IS A CONVENIENCE ONLY

Buffett is similar to Graham in another way. He is challenged by the earning of money but seems emotionally impervious to possessing money.

Despite his remarkable monetary achievements, Graham's interest had more to do with concepts than with cash.

"We were going to lunch at a little delicatessen near the office one day," Warren Buffett recalls. "Ben said to me, 'Money won't make any difference to you and me, Warren. We'll be the same. Our wives will just live better.'"

Though he deemed it a sacred duty to take care of his clients, to Graham himself money was nothing more than a way of keeping score. Instead, Graham was absorbed with the way the financial world was structured, the truth behind its mirrors, how it revealed its secrets and how investors could understand their own position and maximize their opportunities. The investor brought capital to the game and Graham believed the investor should be treated fairly in return. Buffett seems to perpetuate that philosophy.

Buffett is the lowest-paid executive among the top 200 largest companies in the country. "Warren wants to succeed," Louis Lowenstein, head of Columbia University's Center for Law and Economic Studies said, "but he's not greedy."[15]

MISTAKES DO HAPPEN

Both Graham and Buffett clearly show that being a brilliant investor does not mean never making a mistake. Buffett describes buying Berkshire Hathaway, a struggling shirt maker, as one of his earlier errors. Later, Buffett invested about $750 million in Salomon Brothers, Wall Street's premier investment banker. Shortly after Buffett expressed confidence in Salomon's management in his annual report, the distinguished company was stripped of its high reputation by a government securities scandal that not only brought down its leadership, but cast light on the company's lackluster performance. Buffett was compelled to step in as chairman for ten months to appease regulators and to protect Berkshire Hathaway's investment. Fortunately, Buffett usually is able to recover such fumbles. In the case of Salomon, the company more than regained its former profitability and status and Buffett ascended to a hero's rank in the investment banking industry.

PROSPERITY ALSO HAPPENS

Buffett, who controls 42 percent of Berkshire Hathaway shares, may well be the wealthiest man in the United States with a personal net worth of $8.3 billion. That would make Ben proud. But his old prof and former boss would be prouder to know that Buffett has achieved this stature while maintaining a reputation for being scrupulously ethical in his dealings.

Buffett is the first to acknowledge his debt to Graham, even in terms of the way his first investment partnership was structured. "I got the idea for my partnership form because I'd worked for Ben," Buffett said. "I was inspired by the example. I changed certain things, but it was not original with me. That has not been generally recognized."

THE BEST JOKES ARE AGELESS

His reports to Berkshire Hathaway shareholders are peppered with references to Graham, often as a way to reinforce a point or to bring in humor. In one shareholder report, Buffett repeated one of Ben's favorite gags about the oil prospector who died and went to heaven. St. Peter greeted him with the disconcerting news that although the prospector was qualified for residency, all the spots reserved for oil men were taken. There was no room for him. "After thinking a moment, the prospector asked if he might say just four words to the present occupants. That seemed harmless to St. Peter, so the prospector cupped his hands and yelled, 'Oil discovered in hell.'" The gate burst open and the oil men inside rushed toward the devil's gate. St. Peter was so impressed that he invited the prospector in. "No," replied the prospector. "I think I'll go along with the rest of the boys. There might be some truth to that rumor after all."[16]

WRITING THE NEW TESTAMENT

The modifications, revisions and additions Buffett has made to Graham's original concepts are well known. While Buffett eventually discarded Graham's specific numerical criteria, he is faithful to Graham's goal of buying stocks at a discount. Book value—even adjusted book value—he claims, does not accurately reflect the value of a company. He looks closely at market standings, earnings potential and management skills. He compares his role as a stock picker to that of a baseball player having an endless number of strikes. Such a batter can easily let good pitches fly by, certain that he will finally receive a pitch that suits him.

Some of the other departures from the Graham tradition are based on Buffett's own perceptive and unabashed approach to the world in general. For instance, Buffett buys companies he likes and understands. Though he does not actively manage the companies in which he invests, he does get to know and becomes involved with management. Some are reactions to changing investment circumstances. Others are refinements of Ben Graham's own attitude—take a look at what is out there and figure out the smartest way to deal with it. Among other things, he seeks companies with franchises in their markets and high returns on equity.

As a result, Buffett has made important investments in companies with little or no net worth. He has sunk money in American Express and in GEICO when nobody else could see the fundamental justification. Not only did he see the strength behind these companies when they were out of favor, he was willing to give considerable weight to that old intangible— goodwill. Buffett does rely on adjectives. He looks for *enduring, economic* goodwill, goodwill that brings something substantial to the business. For example, Berkshire Hathaway has considerable investment in the Coca-Cola Company. There can be little doubt that Coke's universally recognized red-and-white logo has worldwide, money-earning value.

"You can live a full and rewarding life," Buffett once wrote, "without ever thinking about Goodwill [capitalized in original copy] and its amortization. But students of investment and management should understand the nuances of the subject. My own thinking has changed drastically from 35 years ago when I was taught to favor tangible assets and to shun businesses whose value depended largely upon economic Goodwill. This bias caused me to make many important business mistakes of omission, although relatively few of commission.

"Keynes identified my problem. 'The difficulty lies not in the new ideas but in escaping from the old ones.' My escape was long delayed, in part because most of what I had been taught by the same teacher had been [and continues to be] so extraordinarily valuable. Ultimately, business experience, directed and vicarious, produced my present strong preference for businesses that possess large amounts of enduring Goodwill and that utilize a minimum of intangible assets."[17]

On the other hand, Buffett has harkened back to Ben's depression years experiences. In the early 1990s, Buffett explored ways to take advantage of the distressed New York City real estate market. Though he does not have Ben's fondness for Treasury securities, Buffett often invests in convertible preferred stocks in lieu of tax-exempt securities. Convertible preferreds, which can be cashed at face value or converted into a company's common stock, are regarded as safe and they pay a predictable, bond-like return.

William Ruane says that Buffett has brought Graham's concepts into the second half of the century. "If you take the two of them together [Graham and Buffett]," mused Ruane, "you have the whole package. One wrote what we call the Bible, and Warren wrote the New Testament."

A SECOND FATHER

On the wall in Buffett's office in Kiewit Plaza in downtown Omaha, there is a photograph of Ben and another of a group of former students, all now successful investors, who made the pilgrimage to California during the market decline of 1968 to seek Ben's solace and advice. After Ben's death, Buffett wrote to Ben's daughter Marjorie. In his letter, Buffett echoed a sentiment that he also expressed in the preface to *The Intelligent Investor:*

"Ben had more influence on me than any person except my father," Buffett wrote, "and he is still an important part of my life. I have tried to make sure that current and future generations realize just how important his thinking was."

Unlike others who worked at Graham-Newman, Buffett had invested none of his money in the firm. "It may surprise you," Buffett once wrote to Bernie and Rhoda Sarnat, "but I never owned a single share of Graham-Newman."

He obviously did not need to. Buffett was able to do quite well both on his own account and for his clients. If an investor had placed $10,000 in the Buffett Partnership in 1956, then reinvested when Berkshire Hathaway was created in 1969, that $10,000 would have been worth $35 million in 1992, after all taxes, expenses and fees had been deducted.[18]

The End of the Graham-Newman Era

"As the saying goes, a stock well bought is half sold.
I think Ben was an expert in that area."

—Walter Schloss[1]

W hat, exactly, was so special about Graham-Newman, a pint-sized investment company with a president that lacked the go-for-the-jugular style of others in his field? In an exchange with Senator James Fulbright during the U.S. Senate hearing in 1955, Ben explained exactly what he did for a living. In the process, he revealed what made Graham-Newman unique. The purpose of Fulbright's questioning was to determine if excessive speculation and insider trading had reached crisis proportions on Wall Street. Fulbright spent a lot of time laying the groundwork for his questions, obviously trying to satisfy his personal curiosity on certain points.

GRAHAM-NEWMAN ON THE PUBLIC RECORD—FRIDAY, MARCH 11, 1955

The Chairman: Is your company an open-end or closed-end company?

Mr. Graham: We are technically an open-end company and practically a closed-end company. Let me explain that.

The Chairman: I will be very happy for you to.

Mr. Graham: We are registered under the Investment Company Act of 1940 as an open-end company, which means that we are contractually obligated to repurchase shares at any time at the net asset value when presented to us. However, no such shares have been presented to us for a great many years. Our shares have sold consistently at well over their net asset value. Furthermore, we have not sold any shares of stock to the public at any time and have not increased our capitalization for many years, so we operate actually as a closed-end company, namely, with fixed capitalization.

NO SECRETS

The Chairman: What is the capital? Are these trade secrets or not?

Mr. Graham: Not at all. They would not be a secret in any case, Senator, but as it happens our figures are made public. They are filed with the Securities and Exchange Commission. We have 5,000 shares of stock with a present asset value on the order of $1,100 a share and with a market price rather considerably above that.

(Senator Fulbright, obviously unfamiliar with the workings of Wall Street and impressed by Ben's answer, probed further.)

The Chairman: To what do you attribute your great success in this business?

Mr. Graham: Well, Senator, that is assuming that we have made a great success.

The Chairman: Would you not consider it a success?

Mr. Graham: I will admit we think it is, but I did not want to be in the position of passing over your question as taking for granted that we have made a great success.

The Chairman: I will take responsibility for saying you obviously have made a success.

Mr. Graham: I think our success is due to our having established sound principles of purchase and sale of securities, and having followed them consistently through all kinds of markets.

The Chairman: I take it that ordinary members of the public cannot buy your shares. Is that right?

Mr. Graham: Well, they cannot buy them in unlimited amounts, but they can buy them over the counter in small amounts.

The Chairman: Are they quoted over the counter?

Mr. Graham: They are quoted over the counter; yes, sir.

The Chairman: At what, $1,100?

Mr. Graham: I would say probably around $1,250 or $1,300 a share now.

Mr. Chairman: Above the asset value?

Mr. Graham: That is correct, sir.
(After a brief diversion in the conversation, Fulbright confirmed what he had heard.)

The Chairman: If someone wishes to sell their shares, they still can demand what from you?

Mr. Graham: They can demand the net asset value.

The Chairman: Which, of course, they do not do because they can get more?

Mr. Graham: That is correct. We have not taken in any shares for many years.
(Probing deeper, Fulbright wanted to know both what Graham earned and how the investors were rewarded.)

A SUITABLE SALARY

The Chairman: Is it public knowledge what you charge?

Mr. Graham: Yes. We charge a great deal. We pay ourselves salaries on the order of $25,000 and $15,000, and we also have a profit-sharing plan under which after a $40-a-share dividend is earned and paid in any year, the management as a whole receives 20 percent of the additional amount earned and paid.

(And again, after a brief sidetrack. . .)

The Chairman: I hope it is clear that if you do not wish to say, if it is a matter you do not wish to discuss, particularly your own compensation, I am not trying to fish. That is just illustrative of what I assume is a typically successful man, and if you do not care to answer, I hope you will feel free to say so.

BY NO MEANS TYPICAL

Graham: I would just like to make two remarks about that. In the first place, I have no hesitation whatever in telling you things that the investors in my fund know, obviously; but, secondly, I think it is a misconception to consider that we are typical managers of a successful firm. Our arrangement is very unusual.

The Chairman: I want to clear up the misconception. That is exactly why you are here. Why is it not typical? I would like you to describe what is a typical situation.

Mr. Graham: The difference is first, that our compensation arrangement is much more liberal than that received by other investment funds. This 20 percent that we receive on excess earnings is a very large percentage.

The Chairman: But that depends on what you pay. You said $40 a share, which struck me as a rather liberal dividend.

Mr. Graham: That is just the base dividend. We paid $340 a share last year. (Ben explained later that Graham-Newman paid back to stockholders virtually all its earnings, so that the fund's value was very close to the original amount investors paid in. This differs from Berkshire Hathaway, which pays no dividends.)

The Chairman: That is still better than General Motors paid.

Mr. Graham: Yes. I just wanted to make two things clear, sir. One is that our compensation arrangement is much more liberal in its terms than the standard arrangement. Secondly, we believe, and I think our stockholders believe, that we earn our compensation because our results to them after deducting compensation have been good.

(While large funds charge a much smaller management fee as a percentage of capital, Ben explained, it is harder for a big fund to achieve high percentage gains because it must find a lot of investment opportunities, rather than stick to a few excellent ones.)

The Chairman: What percentage of the capital invested in your fund is represented by the compensation to management? Can you express it in terms that would be comparable? Would it be 1 percent?

Mr. Graham: Well, let us put it this way: Over a period of years, we have tended to earn about 20 percent on capital per year before compensation and about 3 percent of that has been paid to management as compensation, leaving 17 percent to the stockholders.

(Later in the hearings, Senator Fulbright explained why Ben had been asked to testify.)

A PRACTICAL OPERATOR

The Chairman: I saw you on television in an Ed Murrow show, but I did not understand that you were a professor. I thought they had brought you in as a practical operator to tell them how it was done. I misunderstood.

Mr. Graham: They made me a professor because I am a practical operator.[2]

As the testimony before the Fulbright committee implied, things were under control at the Graham-Newman Corporation and had been for some time. Ben began to feel that the pleasure was going out of the game.

"We had no real problems in running our business," Ben explained. "That's why I kind of lost interest. We were no longer challenged after 1950."[3]

THE MARKET IS HIGH, BUT HAS NOT CRESTED

Though Ben did not believe the market was in a danger zone at the time he testified before the Senate's Fulbright committee, he did suspect that before long the rising stock market would have to take a breather. ". . . leading industrial stocks are not basically overvalued," Ben told the Fulbright committee, "but they are definitely not cheap and they are in danger of going over into an unduly high level."[4]

WEARY OF WALL STREET

It was neither due to the vivid lessons of 1929 nor that he was too weary of investing to put his mind and energy to it that the "father of financial analysis" did not participate in the great bull market of the midcentury. That long market climb began around 1950 and lasted until the late 1960s. Ben backed away because he was bored. He simply was finished.

He had worked on Wall Street for 42 years and had managed money independently for 33 years. Though the Graham-Newman Corporation itself was only 20 years old, Ben and Jerry worked together and invested money for three decades.

PALM LATITUDES

Ben, now past 60, had an idea of what he would rather do. His brothers had moved to Los Angeles and Ben liked southern California, too. In 1951, he initiated a correspondence with Neil H. Jacoby, dean of the Graduate School of Business Administration at the University of California at Los Angeles regarding a teaching position there. The school, of course, would be delighted to have such a distinguished lecturer.

Ben and Jerry began to look for ways to wind down their business, but they were extremely cautious about who might run the company and maintain the reputation and service that they had built.

NO LINE OF SUCCESSION

None of Ben's children were interested in the investment world. Little Newton seemed temperamentally unsuited for the business and at any rate he had been drafted into the army. The daughters had chosen academic careers and were involved with their own families. Ben, Jr.—Buzzy—was still just a child.

The only members of Ben's family who went to work on Wall Street were his brother Victor's son Richard and many years later, Victor's grandson Peter. Both became bond dealers at Landenburg, Thalmann & Company.

Mickey Newman still was associated with the company when Ben and Jerry decided to retire, though he had recently recovered from a long illness and was working very hard on a special project, reorganization of the Philadelphia and Reading Company. Ben and Jerry approached Mickey and Warren Buffett about taking over the firm, with Buffett as a junior partner.

NO BEN, NO BUFFETT

"I didn't want to do it," Buffett said. "I went back there to work for Ben."

Buffett had noticed the many distractions of being in New York and was hankering for his hometown of Omaha. He had built his net worth of $140,000 in a short time, which seemed to him enough money to retire on, and now he was considering his various options.

Though both the younger Newman and Buffett have since proven themselves to be talented investors and keen businessmen, they are very different people. Mickey is much like his father, an astute and tough hands-on manager, but often brash in his approach. Buffett has operated much like Graham. He abhors hostile takeovers and maintains extraordinarily friendly relationships with his business associates. It is possible that Mickey Newman and Buffett would not have been able to work in harmony in the same way Graham and Jerry Newman did. The two men have limited contact today.

When that line of succession did not work out, Ben and Jerry approached Abraham & Company, where Ben had many good friends, including managing partner Arthur Schiff. They were offered the accounts. One of the senior partners objected to the acquisition of Graham-Newman, apparently because it would have required disclosing the Abraham's holdings as well. Ben and Jerry opted to terminate the operation.

FOLDING THE TENT

". . . we decided to liquidate Graham-Newman Corporation—to end it primarily because the succession of management had not been satisfactorily established," Ben said. "We felt we had nothing special to look forward to that interested us. We could have built up an enormous business had we wanted to, but we limited ourselves to a maximum of $15 million of capital—only a drop in the bucket these days. The question of whether we could earn the maximum percentage per year was what interested us. It was not the question of total sums, but annual rates of return that we were able to accomplish."[5]

The resolution of business proceeded in an orderly way. Securities that could be sold immediately at a profit were sold. Among the easily marketable securities held in the Graham-Newman portfolio at the time of its breakup were American Airlines, American Cyanamid, Olin Mathieson Chemical Corporation, American Telephone & Telegraph, Dictograph Products, Gruen Watch Company, Singer Manufacturing Company, Spiegel, Inc., and Hart, Schaffner & Marx. Also on the list was Grief Brothers Corporation. Apparently, Ben heeded Buffett's preemployment recommendation and found shares to buy somewhere. By February of 1957, liquidation payments of $760.62 per share were made on the 5,000 outstanding shares of the corporation, though that did not close out the accounts. Slower moving securities were turned over to the Manufacturers Trust Company for management and distribution.

One stock that was not sold outright was the Philadelphia & Reading Corporation, an earlier tax-loss shell that Mickey Newman was trying to mend. Investors were given ten shares of P&R for one share of Graham-Newman. They could sell the shares themselves if cash were preferred, or simply hold on. Ten P&R shares, at the time of distribution, had a market value of $220.625.

It was just before Christmas in 1960 when the last distribution from Graham-Newman finally was made. The settlement was delayed for four years because of a lawsuit against the New Haven Railroad that included, among a number of other defendants, the Graham-Newman Corporation. After Graham-Newman's liability of $10,000 was paid, stockholders received a final payment of $90.4962. The newer Newman-Graham Fund went through a similar destructuring process.

A NEW GENERATION PUTS DOWN ROOTS

The Graham-Newman staff, of course, had long since scattered. Once they were out on their own, all of the Graham-Newman Corporation former employees distinguished themselves in the investment field.

Mickey Newman was working on recovering the value of Graham-Newman's investment in P&R, a diversified company that among other holdings owned coal and railroad properties.

Ben had gone on the board of the company in 1950 when he first purchased the shares about 1950 from Baltimore & Ohio Railroad for $14 a share. The stock soon tumbled to $8. Anthracite coal was a shrinking industry, and the outlook was not good, for the value of the coal assets had been overestimated when the shares were purchased.

"Ben wanted to sell at a loss," Mickey said, "but we persuaded him not to because I could see some big pluses. I could see a huge potential tax loss due to abandonment of deep mines, and in addition, P&R coal had piled up small and unusual amounts of coal."

Mickey figured the odd-sized stock-piled coal, which only needed to be washed and separated, could be sold profitably at below-market rates.

"In 1955, I went on the board with Ben," Mickey said, "and by the end of the year, they elected me president." Sy Winter also served on the board representing Abraham & Company, which also had bought in around 1950 at Ben's suggestion. Newman managed to strengthen P&R's share price by acquiring successful private companies and in 1967, he sold the company to Northwest Industries.

AN AGE OF TRANSFORMATION

Walter Schloss had resigned from Graham-Newman the year before it closed. He had worked there as an analyst for nine and a half years. In 1955, he formed Walter J. Schloss Associates. Schloss left Graham-Newman, not because he knew it would be closing shop, but because he believed that to be successful, major life changes should be made by at least the age of 40. To finance his own business, Schloss sold his accumulated Graham-Newman shares at $1,300 each. "I was surprised a year later when they went out of business," Schloss said. By selling the year earlier, however, he got top dollar for his Graham-Newman shares. Once investors learned that Ben was going out of business, the shares lost some of their premium value and by then sold for only about $900. Schloss's step into the future got an extra boost, but like those of the other young men associated with Graham-Newman, his strike at independence required courage.

". . . armed only with a monthly stock guide," Warren Buffett said, "a sophisticated style acquired largely from association with me, a sublease on a portion of a closet at Tweedy, Browne and a group of partners whose names were straight from a roll call at Ellis Island, Walter strode forth to do battle with the S&P."[6]

Schloss stepped out cautiously at first because he was a little nervous. The year that Schloss launched his investment operations, a parade of experts had told the same Senate committee where Ben had testified that the stock market was high. The Dow was trading in the 400 range versus 381 in 1929.

"And here I was—I admired Graham tremendously and I was going into the business at just the time when he was saying the market was too high," Schloss marveled.

"It was just one of those things. You do what opportunity allows you to do. It turned out to be a fabulous decision. I didn't know it at the time."[7]

Tom Knapp, at Buffett's recommendation, replaced Schloss for the year before the dissolution. Knapp later became a principal at Tweedy, Browne and one of the men Buffett described as a "Superinvestor of Graham and Doddsville."

OFF AGAIN TO OMAHA

Twenty-five-year-old Warren Buffett, with two children and a notable net worth, at least temporarily rode into the sunset. "I had no master plan," he said. It took a little time before Buffett became recognized as both Graham's intellectual successor and before he fell heir to many of the Graham-Newman investors.

THE INVESTORS FOLLOW

The former Graham-Newman investors were searching for the same consistent pattern of earnings that Ben had been able to guarantee in his 30 years of money management.

When Graham-Newman Corporation held its final shareholders meeting on August 20, 1956, it was the end of a long, good run. A summary of the business showed that the returns in the late 1940s and 1950s were in line with the founder's expectations, pushing at 20 percent over the life of the venture. Analysis of the account displayed an exceptionally low sensitivity to average market risk. Before taking into consideration the distribution of GEICO shares, the annual rate of return for the company was 17.4 percent, with an average annual return to shareholders of 15.5 percent. If long-term returns from the distributed GEICO shares, plus returns from its GEICO Life are added in, the return becomes much higher. When GEICO stock was first publicly traded in 1948, its price (adjusted for subsequent stock splits and dividends) was 21 cents a share. Before GEICO suffered the crisis of the mid-1970s, shares peaked in 1972 at just over $61. The shares had a growth of more than 28,000 percent in 24 years. Those investors who rode out GEICO's crisis years have seen their investment continue to expand. As recently as 1992, the company shares made a five-for-one split and in 1994, the shares still traded in the $50- to $60-per-share range.

The Graham-Newman fund also was unusually stable. The fund showed a .39 beta coefficient (sensitivity to market fluctuations) and a 7.70 alpha coefficient. In other words, its volatility was low, as was its risk level.

Altogether and over the longer haul, Graham provided investors with a consistent annual return for its lifetime. Graham's only downyears were immediately following the crash of 1929.

Graham's alumni report similar results, and, as noted earlier, some have done even better. Buffett, so far, has achieved an annual return of about 29.5 percent. For the 33 years ending on December 31, 1988, Schloss earned a compound annual return of 21.6 percent per year on equity capital, compared to 9.8 percent per year for the Standard & Poor's 500.[8]

NO GLINT OF GREED

That Graham-Newman does not appear spectacular when compared to the performance of his apprentices is not surprising. They learned both from his victories and his forced retreats. But Ben's performance was more tempered by his philosophy than his proficiency. Ben did not push his investments to their absolute limits. Mickey Newman explained that Ben's ideology, reduced to its lowest common denominator, was to buy stocks when they are statistically and historically cheap, sell them when they are fairly priced.

"Let others get the speculative profit," Newman said. "You may not make the most money in the world, but you make good returns and you will not have significant losses."

While Buffett and other staff members, as well as some larger investors, knew that Ben and Jerry were planning to disband Graham-Newman, the more distant investors were taken by surprise.

THE SARNATS ARE SURPRISED

Rhoda Sarnat, Uncle Maurice Gerard's youngest daughter, was among the unprepared. Rhoda had gone to Chicago to attend college, married and stayed there. Her mother had been an investor in Graham-Newman, and in 1944, Mrs. Gerard received rights to be an original investor in the second fund. She passed along the Newman and Graham rights to Rhoda and her husband Bernard, who from then on used the fund as an important part of their investment portfolio.

"I had a full professorship and was head of a department at the University of Illinois," explained Bernie Sarnat. "But we always wanted to go to California. When we moved out here, our thought was that our investment in Newman-Graham would tide us over as we established a practice. But they retired at the same time."

The discontinuance of the company was not the Sarnats' only revelation. They arrived in Beverly Hills, where Bernie became a plastic surgeon, at virtually the same time the Grahams did.

GOOD-BYE PARTY

Before Graham left Columbia, Irving Kahn organized a department reception in his honor that was attended by colleagues and former students. It was announced that the teaching tradition Ben began in 1928 would be carried on by Roger F. Murray, a respected money manager and the man who first thought of the individual retirement account. Murray served as a director on the boards of some of the companies in which Graham invested. He is a champion of the Graham and Dodd "value" tradition, and after Ben died, he became an editor of the latest edition of *Security Analysis*.

Ben planned his move to Beverly Hills, California, where he would settle into life and continue his intellectual pursuits as an adjunct professor at the University of California at Los Angeles. The UCLA campus was only blocks from their new home. This would be an exciting change for Ben, Estey and Buzzy. But before they made the move, tragedy struck. As frequently was the case in Ben's life, death darkened what otherwise would have been a happy time.

SAD FAREWELL

Little Newton—who at best could be described as antisocial—had been drafted into the U.S. Army during the Korean War and was serving in Europe. He lived there with a mistress several years older than himself, Marie Louise. His mental state, however, seemed to be deteriorating and Ben became alarmed. He wrote letters to government officials and did what he could to get Newton discharged, believing that his chronically disturbed son should not be in the military service at all. Ben's fears were justified. The message came quite suddenly that Newton had committed suicide.

Neighbors George Heyman and his wife invited Ben and Estey to come for dinner the night that Ben got the word. They sat outside on the patio and talked about the tragedy. Even among friends he knew so well, Ben pulled an emotional shield around himself.

Heyman said it was difficult for him to know how Ben felt about his son's death. "Ben always detached himself from tragedy. He was not calloused. He just saw it like a boulder rolling down from a mountain. There was nothing you could do to get out of its way."

THE HORROR OF HELPLESSNESS

Marjorie Graham Janis, Ben's first daughter, especially was wounded by Newton's death. By then, she was settled into her life in New Haven, where her husband Irving was a professor and semantics expert at Yale. She was raising her own children and teaching at an inner-city school, where she specialized in helping disadvantaged children with learning difficulties. For a second time, Marjorie had lost a brother, and one that few members of the family understood.

But, she said, "My parents felt that [the suicide] was somehow inevitable—that they had nothing to do with it. He'd never been well adjusted. As parents, I suppose they had to defend themselves.

"He had a hard time with life," she said, but young Newton was talented. "He was a good musician." Marjorie felt that Newton never had a real family life, and in fact, despite Hazel and Ben's attempts to help, there was emotional distance between the young man and his parents. With a little more time, Marjorie felt, Newton may have been able to make it. "I was the big sister during this time. I wish he'd hung out with life."

FATEFUL FUNERAL ARRANGEMENTS

Ben hurried to Europe to settle Newton's affairs and collect his belongings. And while he was there, of course, Ben met his son's lover, Marie Louise.

CHAPTER 11

Graham As California Guru

"Pascal said that 'the heart has its reasons that the reason doesn't understand.' For 'heart' read 'Wall Street'"

—Benjamin Graham[1]

On June 1, 1956, Ben wrote to his young protegé in Omaha. By now, letters were addressed "Dear Warren." "Last week was a milestone for us because we moved into a house we had acquired in Beverly Hills. This seems to turn the love affair into a marriage. As soon as you have the next urge to come to California, succumb to it because we are anxious to show you our new domicile."

Ben continued to teach, now as a finance professor at the University of California at Los Angeles, and to do his research. Estey, who loved to entertain, blossomed. The adjustment to Los Angeles was made easier by Ben's and Estey's new neighborliness with Uncle Maurice's daughter Rhoda and her plastic surgeon husband, Bernie Sarnat.

FAMILY ON THE COAST

It was a visit by Rhoda's mother Mrs. Gerard that led to the renewed family ties. "I don't know that we would have connected with them otherwise. The minute she got there, she picked up the phone and called them. From then on, we became one family."

The Sarnats bought a house on North Maple Drive, across the street from Ben and Estey. Rhoda and Bernie took up residence at number 616 and the Grahams were at 611 North Maple. The Graham's housekeeper, Lucy, who moved with them from New York, became good friends with the Sarnat's housekeeper Emma. Bernard had no difficulty in establishing a medical practice so his nervousness over the closure of Graham-Newman was quickly put aside.

"There was never a day we didn't talk," Rhoda said.

"Buzz, Jr., and our son Gerard [Gerry] grew up together," said Bernie. "They are very close friends to this day."

Buzz was 11 when the Grahams moved to Beverly Hills, and for several years at least, he saw more of Ben than he had when they lived in New York. "I didn't know much about his work," Buzz recalled. "I got an idea of what he did after he died. I wasn't much interested. At Beverly Hills, he didn't go to work."

HOME LIFE

Ben tried, though he continued to be quite busy, to spend more time with his son. The Grahams traveled together, visiting friends and relatives in Deauville and Trouville in France. Buzz and Gerry Sarnat were in the same Boy Scout troop, and actor Glenn Ford was the scout master.

"For an outing, the fathers and sons were invited to Glenn Ford's for a barbecue," Bernie said. "The sons were supposed to cook for the fathers. Now Buzz, Jr., wasn't the most handy youngster, he was a little awkward, which was true of Ben, by the way. Ben, Jr., had a steak on the grill that he was supposed to share with his father. It dropped off and fell into the fire. Ben said, 'OK Buzz, let's go to town and have a steak dinner there.' That was the end of the outdoor outing."

Though Ben was not religious, he apparently felt that the children in the family should understand their heritage. When Buzz resisted going to Hebrew school, Ben conducted a Saturday school of his own. "My kids went over there and a few others did, too, to hear Bible stories," Rhoda remembered. "For a big treat, he took them to see Heston in *The Ten Commandments*."

ESTEY ENTERTAINS

Estey often invited the Sarnats to join them for dinner, even when the Grahams had other guests. Ben went along with the entertaining, but he never initiated it, and his endurance, as it always had been, was limited.

"Estey did all the socializing," Rhoda said. "She had beautiful dinner parties all the time and people were drawn to her. She did it easily, beautifully and warmly. Halfway through the evening, Ben would say, 'if you'll excuse me I'll go to bed.' There was just so much small talk he could tolerate."

Ben walked out on even the most mesmerizing conversationalists. Among the frequent dinner guests were the historians Will and Ariel Durant and best-selling author Irving Stone and his wife Jean. The movie producer Jack Skirball and his wife were good friends dating from Ben's school days. Warren and Susan Buffett, who happily responded to Ben's invitation, were occasionally among the visitors.

A YOUNG COUPLE FROM OMAHA

"I'd make all these excuses to go out and visit," Buffett explained. "Estey would invite us to their house. His wife was terrific."

"Ben was Buffett's mentor," Rhoda noted. "On one of those visits, Susie came in. She was so excited. She loved shoes, and she had bought two pairs at once. She had a sense of total extravagance, but it was worth it. She had really splurged!"

"When they first started coming, they stayed at a motel over a liquor store, the Sandy Koufax Motel in Santa Monica, to save money," Rhoda laughed. "Now, when Warren dies, Susie could be the richest woman in the world. It goes to show, you never know."

The hospitality in California lured the Buffetts back again and again, and for a while they had a home in Laguna Nigel. "Ben, as you know," Buffett wrote, "Susie and I can't understand why the state of California maintains a Chamber of Commerce while they have the Grahams and the Sarnats."

When he first started visiting in California, Buffett attempted to engage Ben in discussions about the stock market, but he soon realized it was futile.

SOMETIMES INDIFFERENT

"When [Ben] went out to Beverly Hills," Buffett said, "he more or less said good-bye. He would give a course at UCLA and people would drop by to see him, but he didn't care about securities any more."

Nobody was more aware of that than the Sarnats. "When I got my money from Graham-Newman," Bernie said, "I asked Ben, 'what shall I do with this money now?'"

Halfheartedly, Ben suggested buying American Telephone & Telegraph shares and several safe but dull closed-end funds.

"I was highly disappointed," Bernie said.

WARREN'S PATRON

Estey, who prided herself on her knowledge of the stock market, intervened. "Rhoda, Bernie," she advised, "Warren Buffett is probably Ben's most outstanding student and he's starting this thing up. I'm investing and you ought to, too."

"She was constantly being approached by people to invest," Rhoda said, "because if they could get her name on their list, it was a big plus. She said no to almost everybody. But this time, she had confidence in him."

Estey Graham indeed did invest in Buffett's early partnership, and eventually in Berkshire Hathaway. Buzz Graham still owns most of those shares, which have appreciated so much that he hesitates to sell them and settle the capital-gains taxes. Benjamin Graham, Jr., a physician with a strong social conscience, however, does not always approve of Buffett's investment policies. He wrote to Buffett to ask him to divest the fund of RJR Nabisco because he objected to the company's tobacco products. Buffett eventually sold the shares, though Buzz doubts that his letter had anything to do with it.

The Sarnats followed Estey's advice and now they go each year to Buffett's Berkshire Hathaway annual meeting.

Estey helped another old friend from New York, William H. Heyman, who started a partnership called Mercury Securities. It was Bill's father George who commuted with Ben to and from Scarsdale and it was the Heymans who comforted the Grahams on the night of Little Newton's death.

"Estey knew who was smart and who wasn't," Bill Heyman said. "Smart people tended to come see her."

GURU FROM THE COAST

Ben did turn his attention away from Wall Street when he moved to Beverly Hills, though not completely. Not long after he arrived, Ben delivered a rattling address to the prestigious Town Hall Meeting at the candy-pink Biltmore Hotel. Entitled "The Level of Common Stock Prices," his subject addressed a pressing theme of the day—how high will the stock market soar? A similar presentation received rave reviews in the pages of the *Beverly Hills Citizen.*

"The many facets of the problems facing the country and their solutions that Graham went into," wrote columnist Dave Heyler, "kept his small audience of financial editors rapt with attention and when the meeting closed at 2:30, we were amazed to realize we had had a seminar of over two hours.[2]

"This meeting was so interesting and so pertinent to so many people in our Westside area that I'm wondering if we couldn't have larger citizen group meetings and persuade [UCLA business school] Dean Jacoby and Graham to appear in front of more of us."

Several years later, Ben delivered a similar talk at UCLA, which was reprinted in the University's *California Management Review.* The article was typical of Ben's earlier work, detailed in its analysis and thorough in its research.

Even in retirement, however, Ben tended to dodge market predictions. Though he thoughtfully analyzed the possibilities and suggested likely trends, he expected the unexpected. "The Danish philosopher, Kirkegaard, made the statement that life can only be judged backwards, but it must be lived forward," Ben wrote in an article for *The Commercial and Financial Chronicle.* "That certainly is true with respect to our experiences in the stock market."[3]

SERVING IN AN ADVISORY CAPACITY

While not so busy as in the New York years, Ben did remain incredibly active. He spoke at a seminar for insurance company finance officers at the University of Texas in Austin. Ben served on several corporate boards and accepted an invitation to be financial consultant to Max Factor & Company.

Ben wrote prolifically, including a visionary piece for the Center of Study of Democratic Institutions on rising unemployment during a time when the economy generally was healthy. He proposed increased leisure time for workers, which would be offset by increasing levels of productivity due to technological advances. Detractors said the idea never would come to be, because workers would be loathe to give up overtime wages.

AN EYE ON THE ECONOMY

Ben wrote several articles for the *Financial Analysts Journal* during the years in Los Angeles, and one, on the international balance of payments, prompted another letter from Omaha. "I started [reading] with considerable doubt as to whether I would be able to wade through it since my understanding of international economics has always been minimal," wrote Buffett, "However, the usual 'Graham logic' was such that reaching conclusions was just like running down the 88 keys on a piano."

Even Washington had not forgotten one of its most interesting committee witnesses. In 1958, Ben again testified before the Ways and Means Committee, this time on the subject of dividend policy and the evolution of two classes of common stock. Ben was always uneasy about investors forsaking their ownership rights. In other testimony before congressional committees, Ben expressed himself frankly, speaking more as a citizen than as an investor. He shared his views on such controversial topics as margin rules and capital-gains taxes and on the mysteries of market pricing.

THE PERILS OF DEBT

It is wise, he told one committee, to have stiff rules regarding the buying of stocks on borrowed money. "I feel, in general, speculation on margin is expensive to the public, and is sound only when it is practiced by people who have a great deal of experience and a great deal of ability."[4]

KEEP CAPITAL-GAINS TAX

Unlike leading investors of today, Ben did not favor removing the capital-gains tax on securities gains, or even lowering it by a very large percentage. "On the whole, it would increase the attractiveness of speculation," Ben explained.[5]

MARKET MECHANICS

As to how stock market investors allow a company's shares to get undervalued, then invariably wake up and drive the price into the correct or even an overvalued range—"That is one of the great mysteries of our business, and it is a mystery to me as well as everybody else. We know from experience that eventually the market catches up with value. It realizes it in one way or another."[6]

Ben worked, but at a more leisurely pace, on projects that interested him. Buzz recalls that his father spent long hours in his studio, a cottage in the backyard.

AN INVENTIVE MIND

Among his projects was the invention of a new slide rule, this one based on similar triangles. After building numerous models, Ben finally worked out the problems and got a patent on the slide rule.

"Just about that time the electronic calculator came out and wiped the whole thing out," said Buzz, who later framed the patent and hung it on his own wall. "But it didn't bother him. He never cared much if things succeeded or didn't succeed. He was interested in the intellectual side of it."

KEEPING THE BOOKS CURRENT

Ben tinkered with inventions, but he also prepared a third edition of *The Intelligent Investor* in 1959.

Ben also revised *Security Analysis,* which came out in 1962. Two new authors, Sidney Cottle of the Stanford Research Institute, and Charles Tatham, a public utility expert with Bache & Company, joined Graham and Dodd in updating the book.

This fourth edition of *Security Analysis,* which hit the bookstores during a time when trendy publications such as *The Institutional Investor* implied that Graham and Dodd were straight from the Dark Ages, took some striking departures from the previous three.

Ben knew that markets were not the same as they had been. "We can look back nostalgically to the good old days when we paid only for the present and could get the future for nothing," he wrote in a journal article, "an 'all this and heaven too' combination."[7]

In the preface to the new *Security Analysis,* Ben and his three collaborators explained the changes. When the original edition came out during the depression, "a cautious view was almost compulsory. In fact, it took a certain amount of courage for us to assert that there was such a thing as sound investment in common stocks."[8]

Again in 1940 and 1951, market conditions made it easy to hold to the original principles. Beginning in 1955, the authors said, market conditions threw the old value standards into question. The authors were then on the horns of dilemma. If they clung to the past, they risked charges of "old-fogyism," but worse, could fail to recognize real changes in the market. If they embraced the giddy optimism of the day, they would encourage repetition of the errors of former bull markets. The middle ground would lead to nothing but muddled thinking. They chose to reformulate the concepts that seem to require it, and with the rest, let the chips fall where they may.

Among the modifications were recognizing that the stock market would value corporate earnings and dividends more liberally than in the pre-1950 years; allowing for more weight to be given to measuring current investment value in terms of future expectations; and expanding the part of the book that dealt with trends and growth stocks. A little crystal-ball gazing crept in.

"In that edition," said Ben's successor at Columbia, Roger Murray, "every once in a while Cottle and Graham would come to an impasse. Cottle wanted to do it this way, and Ben wanted to do it the other way. They were such gracious people that they couldn't ever get into a real argument. So what they would do is they'd call me up to arbitrate. What a miserable assignment! You can't win in that role. But anyway, I survived, and remained on good terms with both of them."[9]

The alterations in the fourth edition of *Security Analysis* were not necessarily pleasing to Graham and Dodd purists. While the changes may very well represent Ben's willingness to look at problems in new ways and to recognize change, some people suspected that because his interest in the stock market had diminished, he allowed himself to be unduly influenced by the new coauthors. "The last edition does not have the style of Graham at all," objected Walter Schloss.

KNOWING THE BIBLE, CHAPTER AND VERSE

Buffett apparently was in the same camp. William Ruane tells the story of when Warren Buffett was asked to testify on behalf of IBM in that company's long-fought antitrust battle. "Warren was on the stand for two days. It was wonderful to watch," Ruane said.

The prosecution's questions lead to an exchange on Buffett's adherence to the principles put forth by Graham and Dodd in *Security Analysis*. "Would you agree with everything in the book?" the prosecutor asked.

"Absolutely," Buffett replied.

"Tell me," the prosecutor continued. "Do you agree with this definition of depreciation?" He then read aloud.

"No, I don't. That's wrong," Buffett said.

"I want you to know that the statement's directly out of *Security Analysis*," the prosecutor declared.

"Tell me," Buffett replied. "What edition is that?"

There was a brief recess while the attorney fetched the book and determined that it was fourth edition.

"I thought so," said Buffett. "That's in Chapter [14] and that wasn't written by Ben Graham, but by Sidney Cottle. Cottle got it wrong."

Ben's most devoted disciples comb secondhand bookstores in search of a 1934, 1940 or 1951 edition. These books, they insist, reflect Ben's thinking at a time when his attention was more keenly focused on the analysis of securities and his collaborator was more rhythmically in step with his thoughts.

James Rea, who met Ben a few years later, insists that Ben himself was less pleased with the fourth edition of *Security Analysis.* As a result, when Rea and Graham taught a class together at UCLA in the mid-1970s, Ben chose *The Intelligent Investor* as the text.

In 1988, 12 years after Ben's death, the fifth edition of *Security Analysis* was published with the assistance of certified financial analyst and accounting expert Frank E. Block. Reviewers again longed for the old familiar voice of Graham and Dodd. "The new version of *Security Analysis* is drier than it needs to be. Messrs. Graham and Dodd had peppered their editions with real-life examples. In the 1962 edition, within a few pages, they cited actual figures for Foote Brothers Gear & Machine, United Whelan Corporation, Southern Nitrogen Company, Texas Gas Transmission Company and Spiegel, Inc.—in one case suggesting 'questionable reporting' practices. You could almost hear Mr. Graham's voice muttering his disapproval. In the new version, examples are more scarce and less controversial, the voice more distant and more academic."[10]

DEPTH AND CHARACTER

Nevertheless, the 1962 and the subsequent 1988 edition are of excellent quality. A 1993 MBA candidate at Columbia Business School, Andrew Fairbanks, said that he and his fellow students found the book more readable, both in language and examples, than any other text they had used. Indeed, those former students of Ben's who have shone the brightest have adapted, modified and tailored their practices over the years, and often in the direction suggested by the fourth and later editions of *Security Analysis*. Walter Schloss, for example, still believes assets are more reliable than earnings as a measure of financial fitness, but says that over time it has become increasingly difficult to find quality stocks that sell at deep discounts. Though they put their own spin on the original message, Schloss and his son do their best to keep the faith.

"Warren thinks that we operate a little like Noah's Ark," Schloss admitted. Buffett probably has been the most experimental of all the Graham alumni.

The last edition of *Security Analysis* that Ben actually worked on concluded with a topic that never was far from Ben's heart and mind even after he retired from active investing—the reputation of professional investors. The authors gave a rousing cheer for the growing professionalism in the field of security analysis and wished its practitioners well. ". . . for the outstanding man—who combines native ability, a flair for the subject, and a courageous, independent spirit—the sky is the limit."[11]

HONORED BY A PORTRAIT

In the midst of his writing and at Buffett's request, Ben patiently sat for a portrait that Buffett and several other former students commissioned and donated to the Financial Analysts Federation in 1963. When Buffet informed Ben of what he had in mind, Ben replied:

> Dear Warren . . . I was both flattered and touched by your letter of the 5th. Fancy, me getting my picture painted to hang in a place of honor! For a thing like that one must be mighty old!

The Dutch artist Jan Hoowig was selected by Susan Buffett and Estey. He prepared the 30-inch by 36-inch painting for a fee of $1,500.

THE FIRST HEART ATTACK

Ben liked to ski, but in the mid-1960s, he suffered a heart attack on the slopes of Mammoth Mountain, a California ski resort on the eastern face of the Sierra Nevada mountains. The next day, Buzz broke his leg, and he and his father were hospitalized together in Los Angeles. During their recovery, Estey, ever enthusiastic about her protegé's new fund, persuaded Buzz's orthopedist to invest in the Buffett Partnership. (Estey also encouraged family members to put their money with Buffet. In 1994, Ben's grandniece, Lorna Graham, was able to buy a New York co-op, thanks to the Berkshire Hathaway shares.)

Ben, never well coordinated but always energetic, nevertheless kept up with one of his hobbies from the East, ballroom dancing. In fact, he struck up a relationship with one of the dance teachers.

STILL LEARNING TO DANCE

"About this dancing instructor from Arthur Murray," Bernie said. "She had a problem he wanted me to consult with her on. A beauty she was not!"

Dr. Sarnat did not appreciate this particular referral because of his fondness for Estey. Professional ethics prevented him from talking about patients outside the medical environment in any case, but Bernie felt as if he hid a dirty secret. "I knew I *couldn't* tell Rhoda," he said.

The dance instructor was a passing fancy. Ben apparently had a different woman on his mind, a secret liaison that soon revealed itself. Buzz, now in his early teens, noticed that his father was spending less and less time at home, and that his mother was increasingly unhappy. More and more, his father traveled alone to Europe. Ben, it soon surfaced, had struck up a relationship with young Newton's lover, Marie Louise Amingues, or Malou, as she was called. Ben first saw the French woman when he went to collect young Newton's effects after his suicide.

THE FRENCH MISTRESS

Buffett received a letter from Ben in 1965 posted from 82 Boulevard Ornano in Paris. Ben said he would soon visit his daughter Elaine in Cambridge, England, but that he would return to Paris. "I have been trying out the life of a typical Parisian in a typical bourgeois [and workingman] quarter of Paris, and I am finding it very interesting," he wrote.

Early in the relationship, Ben commuted to and from Europe to see Malou, then she moved to an apartment in La Jolla. News of the scandalous alliance swept through the Grahams' bicoastal circle of friends. Speculation was rampant regarding the guilt/love origins of the affair.

A MODERN MARRIAGE

"Ben wanted to spend six months of the year in Beverly Hills with Estey," Mickey Newman recalled, "and six months in France with Malou. He couldn't understand why Estey wouldn't agree to it."

Buffett says that as strange as the arrangement may seem, Ben wanted to be fair. "Ben would stray periodically, and he wouldn't have minded if she had," Buffett said. "He had no double standard about it at all. He thought that absolutely, what was fair for him was fair for her. But she didn't want to."

ESTELLE'S ANGUISH

In the beginning, Estey put up with Ben's commuting between La Jolla and Beverly Hills because she thought the infatuation would cool, that the situation would be temporary. It was not. Estey reacted to the rift much the way Hazel did, but soon the similarity ended. Estey continued to protest and grieve.

Following the divorce, Hazel had moved on to a life of her own. She became very active in the Zionist movement and worked diligently as film chairwoman for the Jewish woman's organization, Hadassah. Using still and movie cameras, Hazel documented much of what happened in the worldwide Jewish community during and following World War II. Hazel Graham's photographs and reels are in a repository in Israel. She remarried twice. Later in their lives, Ben and Hazel became friends again, and Ben gave his first wife the money for the summerhouse she had always longed for. The cottage she bought on Martha's Vineyard now belongs to their daughter Elaine.

Mother "was a busy, very energetic lady up until she was about 80 years old," Elaine noted.

Estey, however, was inconsolable. Rhoda Sarnat, who considers Estey as the best friend she ever had, said that Estey was in psychoanalysis for years after the separation. Perhaps the rift was more painful because Ben had, in many ways, been dependent on Estey. She drove the car, carried the money and handled the household accounts. Because Ben was disinterested in such everyday aspects of life, Estey perpetuated her role as a supersecretary.

Estey "never went beyond high school, but she was a knowledgeable, well-read, educated woman," Rhoda said. "She was a very sensitive human being."

"Estey cried and cried, and I was the main shoulder for her to cry on," Rhoda said. Estey would come home from her analyst session, drag Rhoda into a secluded bedroom and rehash her feelings again and again.

THE SURVIVING SON

Though he was affected by the rift, Buzz always had been an independent youngster. In 1963, he went off to the University of California at Berkeley. Like many of his contemporaries, Buzz became active in the civil-rights movement. He left college, and in 1964 and 1965, he worked as an activist in the racially segregated Mississippi Delta.

His parents, Buzz said, "were not politically opposed to it, but they were concerned for my safety." It was not until the late 1960s that Buzz returned to the university, not to follow in his father's footsteps, but to study medicine.

LOVE AT LAST

Ben later explained that at age 60, when he met Malou, a miracle happened to him and finally he came to understand the essence of love—that it was not *a* life experience, it was *the* life experience.

Estey, who already knew what it was to love someone deeply, never found peace with her situation and would not agree to a divorce. When she died of lung cancer some years later, she still was unreconciled.

CHAPTER 12

Graham's Final Adventures

"In many ways [Ben Graham] was an undervalued situation."

—Walter Schloss[1]

After nearly a decade in Beverly Hills, Ben changed homes for the last time. Now, he and Malou would split the year between an apartment in La Jolla and her home—La Champousse—in Aix-en-Provence in France. Both in La Jolla, an affluent suburb of San Diego, and in Aix, in the hills above Marseilles, they enjoyed not a full view, but a glimpse of the sea. Malou's charming apartment in Aix also had a peaceful vista of Montagne Ste. Victoire, the mountain that Paul Cezanne painted obsessively. Cezanne and the astrologer Nostradamus both are buried in the beautiful and historic district of Aix.

RETREAT TO EUROPE

Neither of the California or Provence apartments were luxurious, though they were quietly gracious. "He never really was a man who wanted luxury," Ben's daughter Marjorie explained. "He wanted comfort and he had it."

Early in this era, in his 73rd year, Ben finished his last book, one that is far different from the others. His English translation of *The Truce* by Mario Benedetti was published in 1967 by

Harper & Row. Apparently, Malou's son introduced Ben to the romantic South American novel about personal discovery. Parallels between the story line and Ben's own life inspired the translation.

AN INTELLECTUAL WOMAN

Malou had grown up in the Basque region of France and spoke French, English and Spanish fluently, as did her son. Some 20 years younger than Ben, Malou was pleasant-looking but unremarkable in her appearance. According to those who knew her, she had been active in the French underground during World War II and had an impressive intellect. Their first La Jolla home was at an enclave of apartments at 600 Prospect Street.

A PROCESSION OF GUESTS

While Malou and Ben did not entertain in a particularly lavish way, they did receive a steady stream of pilgrims, including Buffett and his friends, who came to seek Ben's counsel on a recalcitrant stock market. Ben only attended Buffett's gathering that first year, 1968. Ben's wife Estelle Graham, who had been so kind to many of the participants, was invited to several meetings.

FINDING WRITING PARTNERS

Despite his weakening health, Ben continued to write. He completed a fourth edition of *The Intelligent Investor,* which was published in 1973 with a lot of support and help from his friends.

Adam Smith, author of the popular books, *The Money Game* and *Supermoney,* says that Ben wrote him a friendly note from France about this time, pointing out an error in a reference in Greek that Smith (a pseudonym used by George J. W. Goodman) used in *The Money Game.* The note was signed the way Ben frequently did, "Benj. Graham." On Ben's way home from France, he met Adam Smith at the Plaza Hotel in New York for breakfast, where Ben broached the idea of Smith collaborating on the new edition of *The Intelligent Investor.* According to Smith, Ben said that the only other person he would consider as a coauthor would be Warren Buffett.[2]

BUFFETT AND BEN BUMP HEADS

And turn to his former student he did. "Ben had some kind of illness," Buffett explained, and was in the hospital. "He asked me to come out, and he asked me to do the revisions. Harper was after him. So I had to say yes."

Buffett may have agreed even if Ben was not ill. The book had given him something of a divine revelation when Buffett first read it, and he wrote to Ben in 1970 saying that before then, he had "been investing with my glands instead of my head." (Quite likely true, for Buffett was only 19 years old when he first read *The Intelligent Investor.*)

Buffett penned a five-page letter outlining his ideas for the new edition, and it was clear in the letter that Buffett thought that both "defensive" and "enterprising" investors now were dealing with such an altered securities market that many of the book's earlier precepts required revision. The needs of both classes of investors were converging, he believed.

"It is difficult for me to revise the book utilizing anything close to the previous format when faced with this overriding conclusion," Buffett wrote.

BEN'S HEALTH IMPROVES

Ben apparently was feeling stronger when he wrote to Buffett on November 1, 1970. "We're off to Australia tomorrow, returning December 12. No doubt I'll get in some licks of work on the book on the SS *Statendom*—between gorge-ins that is. All my best to you and Susie—Ben."

In another exchange of notes about *The Intelligent Investor,* Buffett apparently expressed the belief that there was too much emphasis in the book on railroad securities that represented a much smaller percentage of listed corporate issues than when the first edition was written.

"I don't think I've favored railroads," countered Ben. "In fact, I've advised specifically against them, except for pervasive reasons."

Buffett now was devoting more thought to the new edition, but "as soon as I started doing it, I wasn't doing it his way. You could see one author against another. So that spurred him into doing it himself."

DIGGING OUT THE NUMBERS AGAIN

His work on the book brought Ben back into contact with the investment world. Charles Brandes, a California investment manager, was starting out in the field in the early 1970s. Ben often called in at Roberts, Scott & Company, which at the time had offices on Prospect Street in La Jolla, to study their copies of Standard & Poor's.

Brandes was broker of the day when Graham walked in and said he wanted to buy some stock. Graham had used National Presto Industries, a manufacturer of cookware and household appliances, as a classic example of an undervalued stock in the revision of the book. Despite his high opinion of the stock, he did not own any shares. Ben decided that he probably should, so he purchased 1,000 shares. When he first discovered the stock a year earlier, it was selling at $21.50, well below both its net current asset value and its book value. Ben bought Presto at $33, which he still considered a good price.

A WILLING MENTOR

"I decided to go back and read his books, and when I did, I realized, hey, this makes a lot of sense," Brandes said. "I called him up and he was willing to talk to me. We met several times. He asked me a lot of questions—but, of course, he already knew the answers. It was his teaching technique."

Brandes recalls that Graham and Malou lived an understated life, now at an Eads Avenue apartment. La Jolla, at the time, was a quiet and refined seaside village. Since then, it has become a traffic-jammed commotion of expensive restaurants, designer shops and lively nightlife.

Rereading Graham and Dodd, Brandes said, and talking to Ben gave him an investment philosophy at a time when he had no philosophy at all.

When Brandes established his own investment company several years later, Ben sent him a letter of congratulations.

Ben and Buffett's small differences aside, the two continued to consult on the last edition of *The Intelligent Investor.* The two talked on the telephone and traded drafts of chapters for comments. Obviously, Ben valued Buffett's judgment because he continued to write and telephone to keep Buffett posted on changes.

ENLIGHTENED BY RESEARCH

At the end of 1970, Ben assured Buffett that he was hard at work refreshing his familiarity with Wall Street and making new discoveries. "My latest is the extent of the deterioration of the financial position of most important companies since 1963 and since our last edition," he wrote.

In 1971, Ben wrote to Buffett again. The revisions were complete. "I gather that you modestly disdain coauthorship. However, I should be happy to follow the lead of *Security Analysis* [with respect to Charley Tatham] and add to the title page: 'with the collaboration of Warren Buffett,' some distinguished remarks about you. How about that?"

In the book's note of acknowledgment, Ben thanked Buffett for his help, but also thanked Irving Kahn's sons Alan and Thomas and a deceased friend and former student, Conrad Taff. The Kahns had reviewed and made current the charts and statistics in the book. The fourth edition of *The Intelligent Investor,* incidentally, remained dedicated to E. M. G., Estelle Messing Graham.

Buffett did not write the introduction to the original fourth edition, though in an edition printed after Ben's death, he contributed a preface. In it, Buffett explained that it does not take a "stratospheric IQ" to make money in the stock market, just strong principles and the character to stick with them. The book will provide the guidelines, Buffett says; the reader "must supply the emotional discipline."[3]

THE FAMILY GATHERS FOR BEN'S 80TH

During his years in La Jolla, Ben saw his children more frequently, especially Buzz, who brought along his own young tribe. The entire family, which included Ben's four living children plus ten grandchildren, gathered to celebrate Ben's 80th birthday. In honor of the occasion, Ben's brother Victor published a small volume of Ben's poetry. Most of his children did not think the poems were very good, but they were delighted at Ben's continued emotional growth and an increasing willingness to express his feelings.

Even Buzz, who had seen his mother suffer so deeply, and who had described his father as "difficult to engage emotionally," was pleased to see that his father at last had achieved an alliance that made him happy and gave him peace.

AT PEACE WITH HIS LIFE

Some visitors described Ben's relationship to Malou as primarily one of patient to nurse, and while that was partly true, it was not the entire story. If all he had needed was nursing, Ben and Estey could have afforded a care giver.

Elaine, who always felt her own relationship with her father was a diluted one, agreed. "I think this relationship [with Malou] was a very happy one," she said, "the best he had with any woman."

Marjorie, who always loved her father but struggled to fathom his proclivities, began to understand and appreciate him more.

"He was seen as 'eager' with the ladies," she said. "I think that is a very shallow view. He was very charming and I think women were important to him. I think he was able to relate better to women than to men. With Malou, there was the most giving and taking on both sides."

Just before his birthday, Ben told a friend that he hoped every day to do "something foolish, something creative and something generous." This comment was typical, Buffett observed. Ben's ideas were powerful, he noted, but their delivery was gentle.[4]

THE PATRIARCH

Ben's 80th year—1974—was almost as busy as some of his younger years. He gave numerous media interviews, including one for the local *San Diego Union*, another for the *New York Times* and gleefully, one for *The Institutional Investor*, a publication that previously had disdained the fundamentalist school of investing. In the difficult market mood of the 1970s, value investing was regaining stature. In *The Institutional Investor* article, Ben told of speaking a few months earlier at a money managers' conference held by Donaldson, Lufkin and Jenrette at the southern California resort Rancho La Costa. Ben was shocked at the attitude of the young managers, mainly, their notion that the appearance of doing well for their clients was as important as actual performance.

In September, Ben was the keynote speaker for the Institute of Chartered Financial Analysts. The seminar was to be titled "The Renaissance of Value," and he accepted with enthusiasm.

The analysts' meeting was scheduled at Ben's convenience, to coincide with his fall trip to France. As was his custom, Ben stopped on the East Coast to see his grandchildren in Connecticut and visit old friends in New York like Walter Schloss. "I saw him once a year at the St. Moritz Hotel," Schloss mused. "We would go up for drinks. We went to dinner once."

BEN SENDS ANOTHER WAKE UP CALL

When Ben spoke before the analysts, he shook them awake. "How long will such 'fire-sale stocks' continue to be given away," he asked. The Dow Jones Industrial Average, by then, had receded to near 600. Ben encouraged the analysts to buy as many bargain issues as possible while prices were uncharacteristically low. The post-crash conditions had returned and even in his advanced years, Ben saw clearly what was happening.

Excerpts from the presentation were reprinted in *Barron's*, were widely read and reprinted in the financial press. Just as he had done in the 1932 with his series of articles in *Forbes*, Ben inspired a disheartened investment community to go on a buying campaign that led to a revival of the stock market in general.

In "Renaissance of Value," Ben also spoke words of encouragement to the individual investor and inspiration to the professional investor. ". . . I am convinced," Ben said, "that an individual investor with sound principles, and soundly advised, can do distinctly better over the long pull than a large institution. Where the trust company may have to confine its operation to 300 concerns or less, the individual has up to 3,000 issues for his investigations and choice. Most true bargains are not available in large blocks; by this very fact, the institutions are well-nigh eliminated as competitors of the bargain hunter."[5]

STICK WITH WHAT YOU KNOW

For the professional, Ben advised, it is wisest to do the thing one knows best and succeeds at, whether it be charting, short-term trading or value investing.

"If you believe—as I have always believed—that the value approach is inherently sound," Ben continued, "workable, and profitable, then devote yourself to that principle. Stick to it, and don't be led astray by Wall Street's fashions, illusions and its constant chase after the fast dollar."[6]

BEWARE OF MANAGEMENT PROPOSALS

In the speech, Ben also offered a warning that few heeded. A decade later, they may have wished they had listened more carefully: "Several managements have recently asked stockholders to vote charter changes that would make such acquisitions more difficult to accomplish against their opposition—in other words, make it more difficult to deprive present officers of their jobs and more difficult for stockholders to obtain an attractive price for their shares. The stockholders, still sheep-like, generally approve such proposals. If this movement becomes widespread, it could harm investors' interests. I hope that financial analysts will form a sound judgment about what is involved here and do what they can to dissuade stockholders from cutting their own throats in such a foolish and reckless fashion."[7] Graham had put an accurate finger on the inherent danger in the golden-parachute and poison-pill defense that came to full fruition in the 1980s, leading to numerous class-action shareholder lawsuits.

At the end of the session, one member asked, "Mr. Graham, are you amused or disappointed that it takes a real bear market for analysts to be interested in your value approach toward investments?"

"Walpole said that the thinking man looks at the world and sees a comedy," Ben replied. "The feeling man looks at the world and sees a tragedy." In his serene later years, Ben was laughing. Nevertheless, his interest in Wall Street clearly had revived.[8]

NEW FOUND FRIEND

That winter in France, Ben became ill and was hospitalized with heart trouble. He suffered from a general weakness of the heart muscle, perhaps as a result of having had rheumatic fever as a child. "He received dental care in Europe and did not get the usual antibiotics," Marjorie explained. "He did recover, but he was sometimes very weak."

Ben gained enough strength to return home, and on his way, telephoned Californian James Buchanan Rea, who had written to Ben earlier in the year. Rea, who lived in Bel Air not far from Estey's Beverly Hills house, invested privately for individuals and had been told by a friend that he should contact Graham. The friend gave Rea a copy of Ben's article [in *Barron's*], "The Renaissance of Value," and noted how similar their approaches were. Through the publisher, Rea sent a computer printout of his own investment system.

When Ben was in the hospital in Europe, Rea's letter and printout were about all he had to read.

REA's ECLECTIC CAREER

Rea was born in Hawaii and is well-loved among California surfboarders as "Snodgrass," one of the oldest surfers still hitting the waves. An engaging guy, Rea plays jazz piano, flew Pan-American clippers in the Pacific, worked as a test pilot and has a doctoral degree from the Massachusetts Institute of Technology in aeronautical engineering.

After their telephone conversation, Ben invited Rea and his wife Fran to visit him and Malou in La Jolla. They did, and the two couples quickly became friends.

Ben's health, however, was failing rapidly. He had no pain, but he was very weak and sometimes had to use a wheelchair. At one point, he was gravely ill and all the children made pilgrimages to see him. Ben told Marjorie, "I've lived a long life, and I feel like turning to the wall,"

"Please don't do that," his daughter pleaded. "We still need you."

Malou fussed over Ben and made sure he took an afternoon rest, even when guests were present. "We visited them in La Jolla several months before he died," Bernie Sarnat said. "She was very good to him. There was a strong bond between him and Malou."

That year, Ben had been given the prestigious Molodovsky Award by the Financial Analysts Federation at their meeting in Chicago, and he did his best to carry on the research that the award was intended to fund. The cash grant that accompanied the award would be devoted to a research project attempting to develop rough filters or screens to make it easier to identify stocks that were undervalued and suitable for purchase. Like Columbus searching for a shorter route to the Spice Islands, Ben thought there should be some less-complicated way to build a safe and profitable investment portfolio.

THE SEARCH FOR SIMPLICITY

In a March 6, 1976, interview with Hartman L. Butler Jr., C.F.A., for a monograph the Financial Analysts Society was planning, Ben explained how his thinking had evolved.

". . . I have lost most of the interest I had in the details of security analysis which I devoted myself to so strenuously for so many years," Ben said. "I feel that they are relatively unimportant, which, in a sense, has put me opposed to developments in the whole profession. I think we can do it successfully with a few techniques and simple principles."[9]

Butler's interview was printed in the *Financial Analysts Journal* in an issue that had Buffett's portrait of Ben on the cover.

After breakfast each morning, Ben retired to his cluttered study, set a yellow kitchen timer for one hour and began to work. After lunch and dinner, he worked as long as his energy permitted.

PUTTING IDEAS TO THE TEST

The research involved a 50-year study of all the corporations in the Moody's Industrial Stock Group. Ben's study, which was assisted by Robert Fargo, a financial consultant and researcher in San Rafael, showed that the stocks that met his standards performed twice as well as the DJIA. Ben looked for, among other factors, an earnings yield twice that of the bond interest rate in most years. He also found that certain dividend and asset value criteria worked well.

"It was tremendously gratifying to be doing research on a period you knew very little about—say, 1938," said Fargo, "and discover the stocks that would turn out to be the real winners."[10]

Apparently, the idea that even an ordinary investor could buy a group of stocks that meet some relatively simple criteria and succeed in the market fanned the fire of Ben's rekindled interest in investing. On leisurely drives to Ben's favorite restaurant in Ensenada, Mexico—El Rey Sol—he and Jim Rea debated the criteria and wrangled out the details on how the concept could best be put to use.

They started with the ten stock-picking yardsticks that seemed most likely to ensure sound portfolio performance. Then, they tried to narrow those down to the few criteria that seemed to be the decisive ones.

"Imagine," Ben said, "there seems to be practically a foolproof way of getting good results out of common stock investments with a minimum of work. It seems too good to be true. But all I can tell you after 60 years of experience, it seems to stand up under any of the tests that I would make up."[11]

Ben intended to get other researchers to test the criteria to see if they would hold up.

GRAHAM SEARCH FOR A SIMPLE WAY TO SELECT STOCKS: TEN ATTRIBUTES OF AN UNDERVALUED STOCK*
(Few companies can meet all ten criteria.)

---

1. *An earnings-to-price yield (reverse of the P/E ratio) that is double the triple-A bond yield.* If the triple-A bond yield is 8 percent, the required earnings yield then will be 16 percent.

2. *A price-to-earning ratio that is four-tenths of the highest average P/E ratio achieved by the stock in the most recent five years.* (To get the average P/E ratio, an average stock price for a given year is divided by the earnings for that year.)

3. *A dividend yield of two-thirds the triple-A bond yield.* Stocks paying no dividends or those that have no current profits from which to pay dividends are excluded.

4. *A stock price of two-thirds the tangible book value per share.* This is calculated by adding up all the assets, excluding intangibles such as goodwill, patents, etc., subtracting all liabilities and dividing by the total number of shares.

5. *A stock price that is two-thirds of the "net current asset value" or the "net quick liquidation value."* The net quick liquidation value is current assets (those assets that are immediately convertible into cash, fixed assets omitted) less total debt. This, of course, was the foundation of Ben's original theory.

6. *Total debt that is less than tangible book value.*

7. *A current ratio of two or more.* The current ratio is current assets divided by current liabilities. This is an indication of the company's liquidity, or its ability to pay its debt from its income.

8. *Total debt at or less than the net quick liquidation value.* (Net quick is defined in Number 5.)

9. *Earnings that have doubled in the most recent ten years.*

10. *No more than two declines in earnings of 5 percent or more in the past ten years.*

*Criteria one through five measure risk; six and seven define financial soundness; eight through ten show a history of stable earnings.

ONE PROFESSOR'S CONFIRMATION

Henry Oppenheimer, professor of finance at the State University of New York, Binghamton, who has done extensive research on the Graham and Dodd principles, put Ben's ten criteria for an undervalued stock through rigorous tests. He studied the risk-adjusted return from 1974 through 1981, structuring his test in several ways to see how the criteria worked in different situations. When the test was applied only to the New York Stock Exchange, which is the exchange on which the largest companies are traded, results were acceptable but not impressive, especially in the years following Graham's death.

When Professor Oppenheimer's study included issues from the New York Stock Exchange and the American Stock Exchange to achieve a sizable universe with a mix of small and large companies, there were no years with negative results and the gains were excellent:

"By using Graham's criteria (1) and (6) to select securities from the combined NYSE-AMEX universe, an investor could have achieved a mean annual return of 38 percent! Use of criteria (3) and (6), [or] (1), (3) and (6) would have resulted in mean annual returns of 26 percent and 29 percent, respectively. Although the superior performance . . . declined after 1976, it did not disappear. Furthermore, the performance does not appear to be due either to systematic risk or to size effects."[12]

Rea attempted a small, informal confirmation study of his own. He was teaching an investment class at UCLA at the time, and the students in his class applied the precepts (retroactively) to the stock market between 1967 and 1976. They, too, found that stocks chosen with the criteria outperformed the Dow.

A FINAL VENTURE

Excited by these further findings, Ben and Rea decided to set up a fund to use these criteria for investment purposes. The timing was not ideal, but it was not the worst of times either. Two years had passed since Ben's article "Renaissance of Value" appeared, and the market had risen briskly. Ben told financial writer Dan Dorfman that though he considered the market now to be trading at a fairly high level, "there are still a lot of attractive stocks selling at seven times earnings and under."[13]

THE NEW GUIDELINES

Graham insisted that the fund be called the Rea-Graham Fund—with Rea's name first—because he doubted that at age 82 and in precarious health, he would be around long to help with the management. Rea would manage the account using a condensed version of Ben's ten criteria for choosing undervalued shares. They would buy shares with:

- An earnings yield of not less than twice the average AAA bond rate for industrials;
- A dividend yield of not less than two-thirds the average AAA bond rate for industrials; and
- A price not greater than two-thirds the tangible book value.

Additionally, the company must meet a test for financial soundness. Only companies that met two out of three of the following points would qualify for purchase:

- A current ratio of at least two;
- A total debt less than a company's tangible net worth, or stated otherwise, a company that does not owe more than it is worth; and
- A total debt less than twice the company's net current asset value.

THE OLD VALUES

The fund also would follow other notions that Ben had adhered to for so long:

- It would be a balanced fund, with at least 25 percent of the assets in U.S. government securities and a higher level of government issues when few stocks could be found to meet the criteria.

- Like his other funds, the Rea-Graham fund would be highly diversified. It started with 170 different stocks.

- A stock would be sold when it had achieved a profit of 50 to 100 percent of cost, or in two years. If in two years the stock has not appreciated 50 percent, it would be sold, even if it was necessary to take a loss. By following the same principles, Ben felt that even an individual investor could achieve a consistent 15 percent return with a minimum level of risk.

The limited partnership for private investors was established on June 30, 1976. Ben and Rea each put up $50,000 and 20 other investors joined for a pool of $1 million under management.

BACK TO AIX

Ben stayed with the Reas in Bel Air while the final papers were drawn. He left his favorite gray cat, Minet, with Jim and Fran and departed for France.

Before leaving the country, Ben conducted a round of newspaper and magazine interviews to talk about his research and to coincide with the launch of the Rea-Graham Plan. In one he said, "On the whole I've had a very happy life, but perhaps I have not had enough enthusiasms, I never was enough of a gourmet, for example, or really appreciated nature or the aesthetic part of life. Perhaps I should regret not having made more mistakes."[14]

On September 8, 1976, Ben wrote from France to the Buffetts, who were at the time staying in Great Neck, New York. "My own health has been very poor," he said, "so Malou is serving as my nurse and 'secretary.' (Wonderful at both!) Don't know when or *if* we are coming back to California, Best Wishes Ben."

SCRABBLE IN FRENCH AND SPANISH

Jim Rea and his wife visited Ben and Malou in Aix-in-Provence 12 days later. The couples had dinner, then Ben and Malou played Scrabble, both in French and Spanish, and afterward the Reas said goodnight for the last time.

Ben died peacefully during the night of September 21, 1976. He was 82 years old. "When he died, I think he died well," Marjorie said. "His last years were his happiest. He became warmer. I admired him for giving up the whole game and battle of money making to live his life according to deeply established views and interests. The family really did afterward gather around him. We visited and spent time with him, but not just as a duty. We looked forward to it."

Jim Rea helped arrange Ben's cremation and the return of his remains to New York. "He was creative and brilliant to the end," Rea said.

FAREWELL AT COLUMBIA

A memorial service was held for Benjamin Graham at Columbia University, October 10, 1976, at 3:30 PM in the Faculty House, 400 West 117th Street at Morningside Drive. Ben's former partner Jerome Newman, who was executor of his estate, officiated at the memorial ceremony. About 120 old friends attended, including Columbia's relatively new President William McGill. He had met Ben in La Jolla when McGill was president of the fledgling University of California at San Diego. At the time, McGill had no idea that Ben was a renown investor. Also present were Professors David Dodd and James Bonbright, Ben's first wife Hazel (now Mrs. Greenwald), Irving Kahn and his sons Alan and Tom, Ben's brother Victor and his son Richard and Jim Rea. Additionally, a group of ten black parishioners from the Mount Zion Baptist church in Bridgeport, Connecticut, attended. Years earlier, Ben had quietly given the church $10,000 to rebuild after their original building burned.

AT REST WITH HIS SON

For his gravestone, Ben chose the closing lines from a poem he loved, Tennyson's "Ulysses": "To strive, to seek, to find, and not to yield!"

Sadly, when asked years later, none of Benjamin Graham's children knew for sure the location of their father's grave. His ashes, in fact, are in the same plot with his first son, young Isaac Newton. They are buried together at the Stephen Wise Free Synagogue Westchester Hills Cemetery at Hastings-On-Hudson, just north of New York City.

Later the same year, Hazel Graham died of cancer. The following year, their daughter Winifred Downesbury, just 42 years old, succumbed to the same disease. Four years after Ben died, Estelle Graham, like Ben's first wife, also died of cancer.

A FATHER's GIFT

Ben left an estate of approximately $3 million dollars. Most of that went to Estey, but Malou was given the apartment in La Jolla. For his heirs, as well as for his followers, Ben's greatest legacy has been his books, which steadfastly deliver royalties.

"I was very fortunate to be given the royalties to the books," explained Buzz. "They were set up in a trust for [the second] Newton, then when he died they were set up for me."

REA-GRAHAM GOES ON

As for the Rea-Graham Plan Fund, it has not dazzled. For the five years ended in 1993, it delivered a total return of only 4.7 percent and was ranked in the bottom 20 percent of all mutual funds. The full reasons for the fund's lackluster performance are not clear, except perhaps that in the 1990s the market has been on a rise and returns by the value-investing approach invariably cool at the top of a market. Some of Graham's former students claim that the fund failed to follow Graham's criteria closely.

In 1982, Rea converted the $28 million fund to a public mutual fund. In time, Rea says he liberalized the fund's guidelines to allow the sale of a stock after 100 percent appreciation or three years, whichever came first.

"I wasn't too taken with Rea," said Marjorie Graham Janis. "Sincere, but not impressive. Ben was very taken."

Many of Graham's old friends were suspect of Rea, a Californian and a newcomer to investments with a background stronger in aviation than in finance. Rea was not of Wall Street, and they figured that he had met Ben at a time when the master investor was aging, ill and perhaps vulnerable to persuasion. Few of Ben's former clients invested in the fund, and not long after Ben died, Jerry Newman, executor of his estate, sold Ben's own shares.

Rea said that the shares had to be cashed in so that Ben's estate could be divided up properly. "Newman wrote and said he was sorry," Rea said, "but it had to be done."

THE YEARS AFTERWARD

It is not unusual for financial experts to speak authoritatively of Graham without having all the facts. Indignation rippled through the older generation of professional investors when a 1992 guest on the Louis Rukeyser's television show, "Wall Street Week," contended that Graham may have written a nice book, but he had not been much of an investor.

Worth magazine was among the publications that struck back. That magazine quoted Professor Emeritus Roger F. Murray, who took over Ben's classes at Columbia University. Murray said he knew a number of professors at Columbia who invested in the Graham-Newman Corporation, "and they all became wealthy men." Murray admitted, however, that Graham himself "wasn't very interested in accumulating capital."[15]

MISREADING THE MASTER

There also have been claims, much debated, that in his later years, Ben lost faith in the creed of value investing. Apparently, this arises from a passage in *The Money Masters* by John Train.

"I am no longer an advocate of elaborate techniques of security analysis in order to find superior value opportunities," Train quoted Graham as saying. "This was a rewarding activity, say, 40 years ago . . . To [a] limited extent I'm on the side of the 'efficient market' school of thought now generally accepted by the professors."[16]

Efficient-market or random-walk theorists believe that all the information that can be available about a company is already afoot in the investment-analysis community, so that no analyst can have a real advantage over any other. An investor can do as well by randomly picking shares as he or she can by pouring over corporate reports.

In fact, these theorists say that Ben, who taught and popularized value investing, was in part responsible for the scarcity of misunderstood and undervalued securities in the market. With so many enlightened investors at work, good stocks often never get the chance to slip to the undervalued range. Most value investors, especially those who are racing ahead of the market averages every year, consider the efficient-market theory utter nonsense.

HOLDING TO HIS CONVICTIONS

"Investing in a market where people believe in efficiency" Buffett scoffed, "is like playing bridge with someone who's been told it doesn't do any good to look at the cards."[17]

In an interview just months before his death, Graham made his opinion quite clear. The interviewer asked Ben what he thought about academic research that supported the random-walk theory.

"Well, I'm sure [the professors] are all very hard-working and serious," Ben mused. "It's hard for me to find a good connection between what they do and practical investment results."

He added, "I don't see how you can say that the prices made in Wall Street are the right prices in any intelligent definition of what right prices would be."

And finally, Ben concluded that even when correct information is available, there is no guarantee that investors will reach the best conclusion as to a stock's worth. "To me [the efficient-

market theory] is not a very encouraging conclusion because if
I have noticed anything over these 60 years on Wall Street, it is
that people do not succeed in forecasting what's going to
happen to the stock market."[18]

That same year in the *Financial Analysts Journal*, Ben recon-
firmed his view on the subject.

"Common stocks have one important investment characteristic and one important speculative characteristic." he
wrote. "Their investment value and average market price tend
to increase irregularly but persistently over the decades, as
their net worth builds up through the reinvestment of undis-
tributed earnings. . . . However, most of the time common
stocks are subject to irrational and excessive price fluctuations
in both directions, as the consequence of the ingrained tendency of most people to speculate or gamble—i.e., to give way
to hope, fear and greed."[19]

On a more humorous note, he expressed his point of view
on the subject this way. "They used to say about the Bourbons
that they forgot nothing and they learned nothing, and I'll say
about Wall Street people, typically, is that they learn nothing,
and they forget everything."[20]

WILLINGNESS TO CONSIDER NEW IDEAS CONFUSES SOME

The confusion over what Ben thought about the efficient-
market theory perhaps evolves from the fact that his mind was
ever open and that he was willing to analyze and discuss any
possibility. The mystification is deepened in the 1970s when
Ben acknowledged change and evolving complexities in the
securities markets. These changes were influenced by new
major pools of investment capital—mutual funds and pension
pools. He reexamined and tested many concepts as he began
searching for a truer and simpler paradigm. In the end, he still
believed a smart investor could do better than the average
investor.

THE ACADEMIC EYE

A small but dedicated band of academic researchers continue to test Graham's theories. Invariably, their investigation shows good results.

Henry R. Oppenheimer, associate professor of finance at the State University of New York at Binghamton, has devoted much of his research to Ben's theories. Oppenheimer periodically rechecks the net asset value (NAV) basis for choosing undervalued shares in recent time frames. He claims that as recently as the 1970 to 1983 period, the test stands up. ". . . $10,000 invested in the NAV portfolio on December 31, 1970, would have grown $254,973 (with monthly compounding) by December 31, 1983. The comparable figures for the NYSE-AMEX and small-firm indexes are $37,296 and $101,992, respectively."[21]

Oppenheimer's findings are confirmed by Professor Joseph D. Vu of DePaul University. Vu claims that Ben's 1930 net current asset value rule still can be used profitably in contemporary markets. Vu drew his research data from the Value Line Investment Survey between 1977 and 1984.[22]

SPECIAL SITUATIONS

Irving Kahn, who with his sons manages more than $900 million in investment funds, says that he consistently has employed Ben's techniques in finding special investment situations. In 1993, his fund bought shares of Jamaica Savings Bank, which had been a New York State mutual bank owned by its depositors, but converted to a shareholder-owned institution. Initial shares were purchased for $10 for a company that already had $5 to $6 per share in surplus. For $10, an investor was getting a share with a book value of $15 or more. This created the margin of safety that Graham advocated, and the results were exactly as Graham's theories would have indicated. In 1993, the shares sold for two-and-a-half times what the Kahns had paid for them. Jamaica Savings Bank's shares could be bought at a discount because it was one of the early East Coast mutual bank IPOs. Later initial offerings of similar banks were not nearly so advantageous.

While Kahn says this type of special situation is not common, opportunities do arise for those who are alert to them. Kahn explained that this bargain situation arose because the bank's management had given itself generous stock bonuses and stock options. At the low stock price, the deal looked acceptable, but management expected that very shortly the share price would advance. Shareholders would be impressed that management was doing such a good job that the bank's share price was climbing nicely. For that reason, shareholders would not object to management's compensation package. There seemed to be no losers, for everyone got wealthier together.

BEN'S MANY FOLLOWERS

The editors of *Generic Stocks,* who also teach finance at Cornell University, in 1987 decided to check how well Ben's valuation model would have predicted the October, 1987, market debacle.

"Graham predicted the market was 17 percent overvalued the day before Black Monday," said Professor Avner Arbel, "and the actual drop in the Wilshire 5000 was 17.8 percent. His model predicted IBM's one-day plunge almost perfectly."[23]

In 1988, the year after the stock market had taken a shocking jolt but was climbing again, *Forbes* ran a column by Mark Hulbert entitled "Interpreting the Prophet." Hulbert made a survey of investment newsletters that espouse the Graham tradition to see how they were coping with the market.

Even a dozen years after Ben's death, Hulbert found many such tip sheets, though their catchy names sometimes belie their philosophy. Hulbert's list included Charles Allmon's *Growth Stock Outlook,* Al Frank's *The Prudent Speculator,* Gerald Perritt's *Blue Chip Values* and Steven Carvell and Avner Arbel's *Generic Stock News.* Other funds that follow the value-investing tradition are Neuberger & Berman's Partners, Guardian funds, Pennsylvania Mutual Fund, the Windsor Fund and Mutual Shares.

"Graham-style investment letters have been among the most successful of those I monitor in my *Hulbert Financial Digest,"* the author said.[24]

TRUE NORTH

Even though Ben made an occasional miscalculation on individual stocks, his lifetime portfolio performance was excellent. Even though the scars left by the Great Depression and his deep sense of responsibility to investors caused Ben to tilt to the conservative side, his clients never lost money that they entrusted to him. Even though he walked away from one of the most important bull markets of our times, Benjamin Graham's tenets hold water. His emphasis on analytic information serves his followers well. Ben is still true north, the point of safe navigation, on the compass of the most skilled investors.

While most of the world appreciates Benjamin Graham for his contribution to the financial well-being of anyone who cares to seek the wisdom of his writings, there are many others who were enriched simply for having known a wise, generous and engaging person.

A WISE PERSON WITH MUCH TO GIVE

In addition to having a lightning-speed mind and a wide breadth of interests ranging from ice skating to opera, his colleague and disciple Irving Kahn described Ben's personality this way:

"A needy colleague would always be helped—but always anonymously. He loved to make others laugh by means of his quick wit and large inventory of puns. Everyone that ever had dealings with Ben came away with certain strong reactions. These included the uplift that comes from someone who shares your enthusiasms and hopes, as well as the strong sense of a very fair mind, entirely objective, in distinguishing between what was fair rather than what was self-serving."[25]

UNIVERSE OF THE MIND

At his 80th birthday party, Ben had reflected on the meaning of his own life, and in doing so, demonstrated the complexity and depth of his own personality:

"I want to say that at least half of all the pleasures that I have enjoyed in life have come from the world of the mind, from things of beauty and culture in literature and in art. All this is offered to everybody, virtually free of charge, except for the interest to start and the relatively slight effort to appreciate the riches spread out before you . . . take that initial interest, if possible; make that continued effort. Once you have found it—the life of culture—never let it go."

HOMAGE FOR A COMRADE

Shortly after Ben's death, Walter Schloss wrote to Buffett about their mutual friend. He expressed again the enigma of Ben's personality. "Don't you think Ben was afraid of his emotions?" asked Schloss, himself a successful investor who seems able to trust his instincts, longings and loves. "He was so rational. Anyway, he was a great guy and we were lucky to have known him."

Irving Kahn concluded that only those who knew Benjamin Graham well over the years could fully fathom the whole man. Surely that is true. And a *whole* man—a full human being—a modern hero—was precisely what Ben Graham became over time. One by one, he played out the primary hero archetypes that mythologists and psychologists say each human being carries within. These heroic images give us our mission and confer meaning on our lives. Ben was the innocent, the orphan, the wanderer, the warrior, the martyr and, finally, he sought fulfillment as the magician.

ENDNOTES

Chapter 1   The Dean of Wall Street

1. Adam Smith, *Supermoney* (New York: Random House, 1972), 174.
2. L. J. Davis, "Buffett Takes Stock," *The New York Times Magazine* (April 1, 1990): 61.
3. Daniel Seligman, "Can You Beat the Stock Market?," *Fortune* (December 26, 1983): 85.
4. Benjamin Graham, "Renaissance of Value," *Barron's* (September 23, 1974).
5. "Benjamin Graham, Securities Expert" (obituary), *New York Times* (September 23, 1976).
6. Benjamin Graham, "The New Speculation in Common Stock," *The Analysts Journal* (June, 1958): 17.
7. Irving Kahn and Robert D. Milne, *Benjamin Graham: The Father of Financial Analysis* (Charlottesville, Va.: The Financial Analysts Research Foundation, 1977), 2.
8. Benjamin Graham, "Are We Too Confident About the Invulnerability of Stocks?" *The Commercial and Financial Chronicle* (February 1, 1962): 1.

Chapter 2   Graham's Early Years on Wall Street

1. Benjamin Graham, *The Intelligent Investor*, 4th rev. ed. (New York: Harper & Row, 1973), ix.
2. "The Stock Market is Like a Pendulum," *Forbes* (June 15, 1975): 36.

3. Benjamin Graham, "Current Problems in Security Analysis," Transcripts of Lectures, September, 1946–February, 1947, New York Institute of Finance, 46.

4. Ibid., 37.

5. Irving Kahn and Robert D. Milne, *Benjamin Graham: The Father of Financial Analysis* (Charlottesville, Va.: The Financial Analysts Research Foundation, 1977), 3.

6. Patricia A. Dreyfus, "Investment Analysis in Two Easy Lessons," *Money* (July, 1976).

7. Kahn and Milne; *Benjamin Graham*, 3.

8. Ibid., 4-5.

9. Benjamin Graham, "The New Speculation in Common Stocks," *The Analysts Journal* (June, 1958): 18.

10. Benjamin Graham, "Current Problems in Security Analysis," Transcripts from Lectures, New York Institute of Finance, September, 1946–February, 1947, 146.

11. *This Fabulous Century*, Vol. II, 1910–1920 (New York: Time-Life Books, 1969), 23.

12. Ibid., 238.

13. Kahn and Milne, *Benjamin Graham*, 8.

14. Ibid., 8.

15. Benjamin Graham, *The Intelligent Investor: A Book of Practical Counsel*, vii.

16. Kahn and Milne, *Benjamin Graham*, 9.

17. Benjamin Graham, "The New Speculation in Common Stocks," 20.

Chapter 3   Pushing a Poker Hand for All It's Worth

1. Interview with author, New York, October 8, 1993.

2. Extract from Hearings before the Committee on Banking and Currency, U.S. Senate, 84th Congress, U.S. Government Printing Office, March 11, 1955, 526.

3. Irving Kahn and Robert D. Milne, *Benjamin Graham: The Father of Financial Analysis* (Charlottesville, Va.: The Financial Analysts Research Foundation, 1977), 12.

4. Benjamin Graham, "The New Speculation in Common Stocks," *The Analysts Journal* (June, 1958): 19.

5. Kahn and Milne, *Benjamin Graham*, 12–13.

6. Walter & Edwin Schloss Associates, LPs, *Outstanding Investor Digest*, Vol. IV, No. 2 (March 6, 1989): 13.

7. Extract from Hearings before the Committee on Banking and Currency, U.S. Senate, 84th Congress, U.S. Government Printing Office, March 11, 1955, 545.

8. Benjamin Graham and Charles McGolrick, *The Interpretation of Financial Statements* (New York: Harper & Brothers Publishers, 1937), 20.

9. Kahn and Milne, *Benjamin Graham*, 19.

10. "Remembering Uncle Ben," *Forbes* (October 15, 1975): 144.

11. Kahn and Milne, *Benjamin Graham*, 20.

Chapter 4 The Crash—1929 and the Great Depression

1. Irving Kahn and Robert D. Milne, *Benjamin Graham: The Father of Financial Analysis* (Charlottesville, Va.: The Financial Analysts Research Foundation, 1977), 22.

2. *This Fabulous Century: Sixty Years of American Life, 1920–1930* (New York: Time-Life Books, 1969), 96.

3. Kahn and Milne, *Benjamin Graham*, 16.

4. Ibid., 34.

5. Ibid., 18.

6. Berkshire Hathaway, Inc., Letters to Shareholders, 1987–1990, 39.

7. Benjamin Graham, "Inflated Treasuries and Deflated Stockholders," *Forbes* (June 1, 1932): 10.

8. Walter & Edwin Schloss Associates, LPs, *Outstanding Investor Digest*, Vol. IV, No. 2 (March 6, 1989): 5.

Chapter 5 The Gospel According to Ben: Security Analysis

1. Adam Smith, *Supermoney* (New York: Random House, 1972), 203.

2. Berkshire Hathaway, Inc., Letters to Shareholders, 1987–1990, 6.

3. Benjamin Graham and David L. Dodd, *Security Analysis: Principles and Technique* (New York: McGraw-Hill, 1940), 27.

4. Catherine Davidson, "Graham and Dodd's *Security Analysis:* The Fifth Edition," *Hermes* (Fall, 1987).

5. Graham and Dodd, *Security Analysis*, 659.

6. Ibid., 667.

7. Extract from Hearings before the Committee on Banking and Currency, U.S. Senate, 84th Congress, U.S. Government Printing Office, March 11, 1955, 545.

8. Benjamin Graham, David L. Dodd, Sidney Cottle and Charles Tatham, *Security Analysis*, 4th ed. (New York: McGraw-Hill, 1962), ix.

9. "Interview with Muriel Siebert," *Sylvia Porter's Personal Finance* (March, 1986).

10. Berkshire Hathaway, Inc., Letters, 41.

11. Thomas Easton, "The Biggest Question: Does the Market Have a Real Value?" *Baltimore Morning Sun* (July 29, 1990).

12. Berkshire Hathaway, Inc., Letters, 40.

13. L. J. Davis, "Buffett Takes Stock," *The New York Times Magazine* (April 1, 1990): 62.

14. Benjamin Graham and Charles McGolrick, *The Interpretation of Financial Statements* (New York: Harper & Brothers Publishers, 1955), 71.

15. Irving Kahn and Robert D. Milne, *Benjamin Graham: The Father of Financial Analysis* (Charlottesville, Va.: The Financial Analysts Research Association, 1977), 25.

16. Extract from Hearings before the Committee on Banking and Currency, U.S. Senate, 84th Congress, U.S. Government Printing Office, March 11, 1955, 527.

Chapter 6   Graham's Economic Influence: A Cure for War and World Hunger

1. Neal Ascherson, *The Struggles for Poland* (New York: Random House, 1987).

2. Walter & Edwin Schloss Associates, LPs, *Outstanding Investor Digest*, Vol. IV, No. 2 (March 6, 1989): 8.

3. Schloss Associates, *Outstanding Investor Digest*, Vol. IV, No. 3 (June 23, 1989): 13.

4. Benjamin Graham, "Current Problems in Security Analysis," Transcripts of Lectures, September, 1946–February, 1947, New York Institute of Finance, 19.

5. Ibid., 26–27.

6. Schloss Associates, *Outstanding Investor Digest*, Vol. IV, No. 3 (June 23, 1989): 13.

7. Schloss Associates, *Outstanding Investor Digest*, Vol. IV, No. 2 (March 6, 1989): 6.

8. Ibid., 7.

9. Extracts from Hearings before the Committee on Banking and Currency, U.S. Senate, 84th Congress, U.S. Government Printing Office, March 11, 1955.

10. Irving Kahn and Robert D. Milne, *Benjamin Graham: Father of Financial Analysis* (Charlottesville, Va.: The Financial Analysts Research Foundation, 1977), 24.

11. "Summarization of the Multiple Commodity Reserve Plan," Committee for Economic Stability, March, 1941, New York.

12. *The Collected Writings of John Maynard Keynes*, Vol. XXVI. Edited by Donald Moggridge (London: Macmillan, 1989), 36–37.

13. Extract from Hearings before the Committee on Banking and Currency, U.S. Senate, 84th Congress, U.S. Government Printing Office, March 11, 1955, 543.

14. Berkshire Hathaway, Inc., Letters to Shareholders, 1987–1990, 89.

Chapter 7   The Quiet Gardens of Safety and Value: The Intelligent Investor

1. Benjamin Graham, *The Intelligent Investor* (New York: Harper & Row, 1973), 287.

2. Proceedings, Fifth Annual Convention, National Federation of Analysts Societies, Financial Analysts Journal, August, 1952, 8.

3. Ibid., 9.

4. Graham, *The Intelligent Investor*, 288.

5. Milton Moskowitz, "The Intelligent Investor at 80," *The New York Times* (May 5, 1974).

6. Adam Smith, *Supermoney* (New York: Random House, 1972), 195.

7. Graham, *The Intelligent Investor*, 40.

8. Benjamin Graham, "Current Problems in Security Analysis," Transcripts of Lectures, September 1, 1946–February, 1947, 146.

9. Berkshire Hathaway, Inc., Letter to Shareholders, 1987–1990, 81.

10. Irving Kahn and Robert D. Milne, *Benjamin Graham: The Father of Financial Analysis* (Charlottesville, Va.: The Financial Analysts Research Foundation, 1977), 27.

11. Nancy Regan, *The Institute of Chartered Financial Analysts: A Twenty-five Year History* (Charlottesville, Va.: The Institute of Chartered Financial Analysts, 1987) 1–11.

12. Extract from Hearings before the Committee on Banking and Currency, U.S. Senate, 84th Congress, U.S. Government Printing Office, March 11, 1955, 546.

13. Graham, "Current Problems," 48.

14. Catherine Davidson, "Graham and Dodd's *Security Analysis:* The Fifth Edition," *Hermes* (Fall, 1987): 30.

15. Benjamin Graham, "The New Speculation in Common Stocks," Benjamin Graham, *The Analysts Journal* (June, 1958): 17–21.

16. Frank Lalli, "The Money Men," *Forbes* (January 1, 1972): 89.

17. Graham, "Current Problems," 96.

18. Ibid., 128.

19. Ibid., 102.

20. "The Simplest Way to Select Bargain Stocks," Special Report, *Medical Economics* (September 20, 1976).

21. Kahn and Milne, *Benjamin Graham*, 41.

Chapter 8   The GEICO Story

1. John J. Byrne, *Government Employees Insurance Company, The First Forty Years* (New York: The Newcomen Society of North America, 1981).

2. Benjamin Graham, "Current Problems in Security Analysis," Transcripts from Lectures, the New York Institute of Finance, September 1946–February 1947, 117.

3. Irving Kahn and Robert D. Milne, *Benjamin Graham: The Father of Financial Analysis* (Charlottesville, Va.: The Financial Analysts Research Foundation, 1977), 33.

4. Milton Moskowitz, "The Intelligent Investor at 80," *The New York Times* (May 5, 1974).

5. "Walter & Edwin Schloss Associates, LPs, *Outstanding Investor Digest,* Vol. IV, No. 2 (March 6, 1989): 4.

6. Benjamin Graham, *The Intelligent Investor,* 4th rev. ed. (New York: Harper & Row Publishers, 1977), 275.

7. Ibid., 289.

8. Carol J. Loomis, "An Accident Report on GEICO," *Fortune* (June 1976): 127.

9. Schloss Associates, *Outstanding Investor Digest*, 9.

10. Ibid., 9.

11. Kahn and Milne, *Benjamin Graham*, 27.

12. Andrew Kilpatrick, *Warren Buffett: The Good Guy of Wall Street* (New York: Donald I. Fine, Inc., 1992), 83.

13. Berkshire Hathaway, Inc., Letters to Shareholders 1977–1986, 32.

14. Graham, *The Intelligent Investor*, 289.

Chapter 9 The Kindred Soul of Young Warren Buffett

1. The first quote is from an interview with Warren Buffett on May 25, 1993. The second quote is from a conversation between Benjamin Graham and Charles Brandes in the early 1970s in La Jolla, California.

2. Benjamin Graham, *The Intelligent Investor* (New York: Harper & Row, 1973), vii.

3. Andrew Kilpatrick, *Warren Buffett: The Good Guy of Wall Street* (New York: Donald I. Fine, Inc., 1992), 37.

4. Walter & Edwin Schloss Associates, LPs, *Outstanding Investor Digest*, Vol. IV, No. 2, (March 6, 1989): 10.

5. Carol J. Loomis, "The Inside Story of Warren Buffett," *Fortune*, Vol. 117 (April 11, 1988): 30.

6. Schloss Associates, *Outstanding Investor Digest*, 10.

7. Kilpatrick, *Warren Buffett*, 41.

8. Berkshire Hathaway, Letters, 26.

9. Schloss Associates, *Outstanding Investor Digest*, 10.

10. Loomis, "The Inside Story of Warren Buffett," 28.

11. Extracts from Hearings before the Committee on Banking and Currency, U.S. Senate, 84th Congress, U.S. Government Printing Office, March 11, 1955, 520.

12. Warren Buffett, "Benjamin Graham," *Financial Analysts Journal* (November/December, 1976).

13. Berkshire Hathaway, Letters, 36.

14. Ibid., 20.

15. L. J. Davis, "Buffett Takes Stock," *The New York Times Magazine* (April 1, 1990): 17.

16. Berkshire Hathaway, Letters, 5.

17. Ibid., 68.

18. *Dick Davis Digest*, Vol. 11, No. 244 (July 20, 1992): 1.

Chapter 10 The End of the Graham-Newman Era

1. From the private writings of Walter J. Schloss, C.F.A.

2. Extract from Hearings before the Committee on Banking and Currency, U.S. Senate, 84th Congress, U.S. Government Printing Office, March 11, 1955, 524–531.

3. Irving Kahn and Robert D. Milne, *Benjamin Graham: The Father of Financial Analysis* (Charlottesville, Va.: The Financial Analysts Research Foundation, 1977), 35.

4. Extract from Hearings, 518.

5. Extract from Hearings, 40.

6. Personal correspondence of Warren E. Buffett, February 3, 1976, reprinted in Walter & Edwin Schloss Associates, Lps, *Outstanding Investor Digest*, Vol. IV, No. 2 (March 6, 1989): 3.

7. Walter & Edwin Schloss Associates, LPs, *Outstanding Investor Digest*, Vol. IV, No. 3, (June 23, 1989): 18.

8. "Cheap is Good Enough," Walter & Edwin Schloss Associates, LPs, *Outstanding Investor Digest*, Vol. IV, No. 3 (June 23, 1989), 13.

Chapter 11   Graham As California Guru

1. Benjamin Graham, *The Intelligent Investor* (New York: Harper & Row, 1973), 216.

2. Irving Kahn and Robert D. Milne, *Benjamin Graham: Father of Financial Analysis* (Charlottesville, Va.: The Financial Analysts Research Foundation, 1977), 41.

3. Benjamin Graham, "Will Market Grow to Sky?—Some Problems Ahead," *The Commercial and Financial Chronicle* (April 6, 1961): 1.

4. Extract from Hearings before the Committee on Banking and Currency, U.S. Senate, 84th Congress, U.S. Government Printing Office, March 11, 1955, 519.

5. Ibid., 532.

6. Ibid., 544.

7. Benjamin Graham, "The New Speculation in Common Stocks," *The Analysts Journal* (June, 1958): 20.

8. Benjamin Graham, David L. Dodd, Sidney Cottle and Charles Tatham, *Security Analysis*, 4th ed. (New York: McGraw-Hill, Inc., 1962), v.

9. Catherine Davidson, "Graham and Dodd's *Security Analysis:* The Fifth Edition," *Hermes* (Fall, 1987): 32.

10. John Dorfman, "Updating a Classic Guide to Market Investment," *The Wall Street Journal* (March 10, 1988).

11. Graham et al., *Security Analysis*, viii.

Chapter 12   Graham's Final Adventures

1. Letter to Author, July 8, 1993.

2. Adam Smith, *Supermoney* (New York: Random House, 1972), 175.

3. Benjamin Graham, *The Intelligent Investor* (New York: Harper & Row, 1973), vii.

4. Warren Buffett, "Benjamin Graham," *Financial Analysts Journal* (November/December, 1976).

5. Benjamin Graham, "Renaissance of Value," *Barron's* (September 23, 1974).

6. Ibid.

7. Ibid.

8. Irving Kahn and Robert D. Milne, *Benjamin Graham: Father of Financial Analysis* (Charlottesville, Va.: The Financial Analysts Research Foundation, 1977), 29.

9. Ibid., 36.

10. Paul Blustein, "Benjamin Graham's Last Will and Testament," *Forbes* (August 1, 1977): 44.

11. Kahn and Milne, *Benjamin Graham*, 37.

12. Henry Oppenheimer, "A Test of Ben Graham's Stock Selection Criteria," *Financial Analysts Journal* (September/October, 1984): 70, 71 and 72.

13. Dan Dorfman, "Which Way for Stock Prices?" *New York* (April 19, 1976): 10–12.

14. Patricia Dreyfus, "Investment Analysis in Two Easy Lessons," *Money* (July, 1976).

15. "Ben, We Hardly Knew Ye," *Worth* (June/July, 1992): 19.

16. John Train, *The Money Masters* (New York: Harper & Row, 1985), 85.

17. L. J. Davis, "Buffett Takes Stock," *The New York Times Magazine* (April 1, 1990): 62.

18. Kahn and Milne, *Benjamin Graham*, 39.

19. Hartman L. Butler, Jr., "A Conversation with Benjamin Graham," *Financial Analysts Journal* (September/October, 1976): 38–39.

20. Dave Heyler, "From the Desk of Dave Heyler," *Beverly Hills Citizen* (May 11, 1956).

21. Henry R. Oppenheimer, "Ben Graham's Net Current Asset Values: A Performance Update," *Financial Analysts Journal* (November/December, 1986), 40.

22. Joseph D. Vu, "An empirical analysis of Ben Graham's net current asset value rule," *The Financial Review*, Vol. 23 (May, 1988): 215.

23. "A Message from Ben Graham," *Forbes*, Vol. 140 (November 30, 1987): 258.

24. Mark Hulbert, "Wall Street Irregulars," *Forbes*, Vol. 142 (November 14, 1988): 366.

25. Kahn and Milne, *Benjamin Graham*, 31–32.

INDEX

A

Abraham, Otto, 85
Abraham and Company, 182, 183
Advice to individual investor, 139–44
Aggressive investor, 133
Ajax Tire and Rubber Company, 36
Alexander, Jack, 2
American Express, 155
American and Foreign Power Company, 60
American Statistical Association, 120
Amingues, Marie Louise, 187, 189, 202–3, 207–8, 212, 216, 222, 223
Analysts Journal, The, 128
Anderson, Ed, 2
Arbel, Avner, 228
Arbitrage, 4, 66, 111, 131, 164–65
Asking price, 139
Association for Investment Management and Research, 137

B

Babson, Roger, 63
"Baby Pompadour," 100
Bache & Company, 21–22
Bagehot, Walter, 16–17
Baldwin Company, 161–62
Baldwin Locomotive Works, 92, 109
Bandag, 31
"Bargains in Bonds," 31
Barnes, R. Marshall, 165
Baruch, Bernard, 23, 54, 55, 115
Baruch, Herman, 53
Benedetti, Mario, 207
Benjamin Graham Joint Account, 45, 64–66, 68–67, 74, 101–2
Berkshire Hathaway, Inc., 90, 159, 169–70
Black Tuesday (1929), 66
Block, Frank E., 97, 200
Bogle, John, 6
Bonbright, James, 76
Bonbright & Company, 33
Bonds, 142
Book value, 171